FOUNDATIONS *in*
Elementary Education ▷ *Music*

Related High/Scope K–3 Curriculum Materials

K–3 Curriculum Guides:
> *Language & Literacy*
> *Mathematics*
> *Science*
> *Learning Environment*

K–3 Curriculum Videotapes:
> *Active Learning*
> *Classroom Environment*
> *Language & Literacy*
> *Mathematics*

Supplementary K–3 Curriculum Materials:
> *Teaching Movement & Dance: A Sequential Approach to Rhythmic Movement,* Third Edition
> *Round the Circle: Key Experiences in Movement for Children*
> *Movement Plus Music: Activities for Children Ages 3 to 7,* Second Edition
> *Movement Plus Rhymes, Songs, & Singing Games*
> *Movement in Steady Beat*
> *Rhythmically Moving 1–9* (records, cassettes, CDs)
> *Changing Directions 1–5* (records, cassettes, CDs)
> *Learning Through Construction*
> *Learning Through Sewing and Pattern Design*

Related Publications of High/Scope Press:
> *A School Administrator's Guide to Early Childhood Programs*
> *High/Scope Buyer's Guide to Children's Software—1993*
> *Young Children & Computers*

Available from

HIGH/SCOPE PRESS
600 North River Street, Ypsilanti, Michigan 48198-2898
313/485-2000, Fax 313/485-0704

FOUNDATIONS

in Elementary Education

Music

Elizabeth B. Carlton
Phyllis S. Weikart

Series Consultant
Frank F. Blackwell

HIGH/SCOPE PRESS
YPSILANTI, MICHIGAN

Published by

HIGH/SCOPE PRESS

A division of
High/Scope Educational Research Foundation
600 North River Street
Ypsilanti, Michigan 48198-2898
313/485-2000, FAX 313/485-0704

Editor: Marge Senninger
Graphic Designers: Linda Eckel, Margaret FitzGerald
Photographers: Jim Barringer, Gregory Fox

Library of Congress Cataloging-in-Publication Data

Carlton, Elizabeth B.
        Foundations in elementary education—music/Elizabeth B. Carlton, Phyllis S Weikart.
            p. cm.
        Includes bibliographical references and index.
        ISBN 0-929816-60-9
            1. School music—Instruction and Study. 2. Kindergarten—Music.
3. Musico-callisthenics. 4. Movement education—Study and teaching.
I. Weikart, Phyllis S., 1931–.   II. Title.
MT930.C2 1994
372.87'044—dc20   94-26875
                                                       CIP
                                                       MN

Chapter-opening quotes: From America's Culture Begins with Education. *Copyright © 1990.*
Published by Music Educators National Conference, Reston, VA. Used with permission.

The song on page 82, We'll Do the Best We Can Today: *From* Primary, Pre-Primary Songs and
Verses. *Copyright © 1978. Published by G. Nash Publications, Scottsdale, AZ. Used with permission.*

Printed in the United States of America

10 9 8 7 6 5 4 3 2 1

Contents

Acknowledgments

For kindness, patience, and support far above and beyond the ordinary, we express our grateful appreciation to the following people:

Our wise and loving husbands, Robert Carlton and David Weikart

Our children, Karen and David Wong, Kevin and Wendy Carlton, Cindy and Dale Embry, Jenny and Vince Danko, Cathy and Gretchen Weikart

Our parents, Ortie and Bernice Bradshaw, Randall and Esther Saxton

Our grandchildren, who provide our living laboratory: Wesley Carlton, Brian and Steven Embry, Zachary and Jacob Danko

Each and every child in the Movement and Music classes in the Catawba College Community Music School, Salisbury, NC

Jerry Bradshaw, for musical typesetting

Photographer Jim Barringer, *Salisbury Post*

Grace C. Nash, music educator, mentor, special friend

Chuck Wallgren, for steadfast support and enthusiasm

Endorsed Trainer contributors to Chapter 8 activities: Bev Boardman (Sarasota, FL), Helen Johnson (Dana, IN), and Judy Johnson (Chico, CA)

Loyal Endorsed Trainers, Certified Teachers, and friends of the "Education Through Movement: Building the Foundation" network

Our valued colleagues at Catawba College, the University of Michigan, and the High/Scope Educational Research Foundation

Our editor, Marge Senninger

Our creative designers, Linda Eckel and Margaret FitzGerald

We treasure the shared opportunities to walk and sing and learn with you on this significant journey.

Preface

The High/Scope Foundation's approach to education encourages children to actively initiate their own learning experiences. Thus this book on music education focuses on how teachers can guide children to acquire ownership of musical concepts through their personal construction of knowledge. We describe how teachers can create the conditions under which each child can actively learn and how they can support and challenge children who are engaged in productive learning activities. This focus on how the child develops ownership of musical concepts through personal construction of knowledge makes our book unique. We have written it for K–3 classroom teachers, music educators, and teachers-in-training who find the High/Scope active learning model compatible with their own philosophy.

We believe that children best learn about music by having their musical abilities stimulated each day and that movement can serve as the base for this learning. Music and movement are important to the development of the whole child and can be integrated within the academic curriculum throughout the day. The music key experiences described throughout this book serve as general guidelines that teachers can use to assess each child's developing musical intelligence.

Part 1 provides a general framework for implementing music in the K–3 classroom. Chapter 1 introduces some of the guiding principles that are developed throughout the book. Chapter 2 describes how to create an environment that encourages active learning. Chapter 3 discusses the environment for music development—how to consider the child's own body as the primary learning center and also how to make the classroom an effective music environment through scheduling, resources, and materials.

In Part 2, the music key experiences are introduced. Chapter 4 provides an overview of the types of music and movement experiences that are important to each child's development. Chapters 5 ("Exploring Music"), 6 ("Using the Elements of Music"), and 7 ("Creating and Performing Music") each focus on one of the three broad categories of music key experiences. Chapter 8 provides practical, active learning experiences that can be implemented throughout the day. Chapter 9 provides an outcome-based assessment for all the music accents. Finally, several appendixes provide a wealth of helpful resources: a Teaching Model for learning new songs, a list of supplementary sources of children's songs, a list of listening selections, a glossary of musical terms, and an alphabetical list of Chapter 8's activities.

Throughout this book, we frequently refer to the nine Rhythmically Moving (RM1–RM9) and five Changing Directions (CD1–CD5) recordings. These have been chosen for use because the selections are mainly instrumental, allowing young learners to work with the melodies. In addition, the melodies provide a rare, needed multicultural resource for the classroom teacher as well as *the music educator. The two sets of recordings, available as compact discs, records, or tapes from High/Scope Press, provide a library of high-quality musical examples that are not otherwise available to teachers.*

We hope that the movement and music ideas embodied in the active learning approach of this book will enable you to make a significant contribution to the life-long musical experiences of young children.

If you give a man a fish, you feed him for a day.
If you teach him how to fish, you feed him for life.
Author Unknown

ELIZABETH B. CARLTON
PHYLLIS S. WEIKART

If you can walk, you can dance.

If you can talk, you can sing.

African Proverb

Part 1 A Framework for K–3 Music

Chapter 1

Getting Started in Music

*A grounding in the arts will help our children to see; to bring
a uniquely human perspective to science and technology.
In short, it will help them as they grow smarter to also
grow wiser.*

Robert E. Allen
Chairman and Chief Executive Officer
AT&T Corporation

As the above statement clearly sets forth, music is essential to high-quality education and should be at the core of every K–3 classroom. How can educators best help young children to get started in music? To discover the many ways that classroom teachers can awaken and develop the basic musical intelligence that all humans possess, let's first look at some of music's basic properties.

Music—The Universal Language

Music is and has always been an integral part of human experience. The Greeks considered it to be a gift from the gods. Through the centuries, virtually every culture has found that music expresses what words alone cannot. Music is used daily to convey deep feelings, to express intrinsic and extrinsic meanings, to transmit cultural heritage, to lift the human spirit, and even to sell everything imaginable! Music communicates, heart to heart. Music is multicultural. Music is art. You do not have to know German to understand and feel the heroic message of Beethoven's Ninth Symphony. Neither do you have to sing Brahms' *Lullaby* perfectly to calm a sick baby. You do not have to read music notation to sing Gruber's *Silent Night* or to feel the rush of patriotism evident in Sousa's *Stars and Stripes Forever*. Music communicates any message across all language barriers. Even the movie *Close Encounters of the Third Kind* used musical tones and the Curwen-Kodaly **solfège** (see Glossary) hand signs to communicate. Music is needed by each of us because it brings value and meaning to our lives.

Music is also a science in that its sounds can be explained in terms of wavelength frequencies. Music's notational system is one of the world's most powerful and widely used symbolic systems. Music touches all major subject areas in the elementary school. It is central to comprehensive learning, organizing, attending, problem solving, and creativity.

Since music is essential to all aspects of life, how can you and your students become meaningfully involved in music? You can always begin where you are and progress from there. Sing the songs you already know, perhaps many of the ones you learned as a child. Use the **music key experiences**

Children can begin by singing the songs they already know, familiar songs from their early child-hood. Singing together builds memorable bridges of communication for singers and listeners alike.

(see *key experiences* in Glossary) that are introduced and developed throughout this book. View the music key experiences as friendly, personal coaches to guide your own musical development as you introduce musical concepts to your students. You will soon realize that all humans respond to music's many components. The discipline that music brings will enable, anchor, engage, and delight young students as they make vital connections to core knowledge—connections that can make a significant lifelong difference. Besides, music is irresistible to the K–3 child, especially when music is approached with movement as the base.

Combining Music and Movement

With movement as the base, an understanding of music occurs naturally, because movement supplies the kinesthetic link to learning. Children attain musical literacy not just through their voices but through all parts of their bodies as well as through their minds. Music and movement are strong, natural languages that children bring to all areas of learning. By bringing music and movement into the K–3 curriculum, teachers can provide children with a broad range of related learning experiences.

Bringing Music to the K–3 Classroom

Music is only now beginning to be recognized as "a form of intelligence, not merely a manifestation of it."[1] In his book *Frames of Mind,* psychologist Howard Gardner defines intelligence as "a distinguishable ability to solve problems, or to create products, that are valued within one or more cultural settings . . . thereby laying groundwork for the acquisition of new knowledge."[2] Gardner identifies **musical intelligence** as *one of seven basic intelligences* that all humans possess. Yet this basic musical intelligence that is inherent in all children will not be developed unless classroom teachers join with music specialists to realize the total impact that music makes on our day-to-day existence. "Since music is, for some learners, a powerful way of knowing, it can become, for teachers, a way of teaching. When important ideas, information, and ways of thinking can be approached through the strategies and structures provided by music, learning can be reinforced."[3]

Research in music education indicates that a child's musical aptitude is fully established by the age of 6;[4] therefore, K–3 classroom teachers have an opportunity to play a vital role in the future of music education. The classroom teacher knows the strengths and weaknesses of each child and can use musical activities throughout the day, whenever they are most appropriate. Classroom teachers are grounded in child development and learning theory, and many can and do use this excellent background to teach music concepts effectively. Without the guidance of the classroom teacher, many young children would have no opportunity to develop their individual musical abilities, because not every school can afford to enlist a music specialist. To help in guiding and assessing children's musical development, the music key experiences have been developed specifically for classroom teachers who use the active learning model.

Children use all parts of their bodies in attaining musical literacy. Here a group of young children are growing in many important ways while performing the action song Bluebird, Bluebird.

Introduction to the Music Key Experiences

The High/Scope educational approach is based on the belief that children learn best through an active process of doing and experiencing rather than through a passive process of absorbing information presented by the teacher. As children engage in this active process, the teacher brings a focus to each child's efforts, based on that child's emerging abilities. In addition, the High/Scope educational approach is based on the Piagetian principle that children develop and learn in stages, not at specific age levels (see Chapter 2 for a longer discussion of Piaget's levels of learning). With these principles in mind, High/Scope has formulated **key experiences** for each of the major K–3 curriculum areas. The key experiences for each area constitute a detailed developmental sequence of children's learning experiences.

Teachers can use the music key experiences presented in this book as guides to help them assess children's developmental levels, provide for appropriate activities, and recognize and encourage important musical processes as they occur in the classroom. The key experiences should be thought of as approximate guidelines, not as a prescribed step-by-step progression. They provide a blueprint for music learning that is much like the blueprint an architect uses to build a home. In this analogy, the classroom teacher can be thought of as the general contractor who guides construction of the child's lifelong musical "home."

The **music key experiences** represent basic music concepts that must be acted on by each learner to construct a meaningful music knowledge-base. The music key experiences use movement as the basis of furthering children's understanding of various concepts. Consistent with this approach, Phyllis S. Weikart's program, "Education Through Movement: Building the Foundation," is referred to throughout this text in describing how teachers can use movement to enhance children's learning; therefore double benefits are derived—for children and teachers.[5]

The music key experiences serve as the framework for activating and developing each child's musical intelligence. They bring integrity to music learning and illustrate the necessity for bringing music in its many forms into classroom activities throughout the day. The teacher is responsible for presenting the musical concepts within the proper time frame; for using quality materials (musical selections) that will transcend growing, changing musical tastes (styles); and for providing the distinct decorative accents (enthusiasm) to make learning memorable. The teacher does not have to do it all. Parents, friends, music leaders in the community, and music specialists are all ready resources. All of the necessary materials are provided within this text for ease in implementation, so let's begin the building process.

Beginning the Building Process

As teachers become comfortable using music in the classroom, certain questions arise. How do children learn to sing and play instruments and progress toward musical literacy? When do they create or improvise? Why does music fill the void that so often results when learning is compartmentalized into subject areas? These questions lead teachers to discover the natural process all children use in constructing their personal music knowledge-base. This process occurs in the following sequence:

1. **Imitate.** Children initially need to listen to and copy words, melodies, or movement. Children begin by joining in group singing and eventually progress to singing song fragments on their own. Repetition until the knowledge is secure provides the safety net.

2. **Explore/extend.** The concept to be studied (such as high and low pitches) must be actively explored and extended by individuals through movement, language, and interaction with other learners. Since the kinesthetic mode of learning is so important during the K–3 years, a kinesthetic approach should be the *modus operandi* in the classroom.

Asking such questions as "What can you tell me about . . . ?" encourages children to reflect and to express their thoughts about an important concept that was explored earlier, during an active learning experience.

3. **Relate/create.** When enough exploration, extension, and repetition have taken place, facilitating, commenting, reflecting on music concepts, and sharing as partners in learning enable children to relate core concepts across subject areas. Once a concept is understood, creativity or improvisation can occur.

4. **Develop ownership.** A musically literate person is one who can sing, read, and write music and has ownership of knowledge about certain musical elements. Developing *ownership* in a subject area implies that an individual knows, uses, and incorporates that knowledge in meaningful ways to bring greater clarity to his or her total knowledge. *It is only as we each use the knowledge we possess that education has meaning.*

As the following examples point out, educators around the world have recognized the importance of music to the young child's overall intellectual development:

- The Key School, an inner-city public elementary school in Indianapolis, Indiana, has as one of its guiding principles the conviction that each child should have his or her musical intelligence stimulated each day. Every student participates on a regular basis in music activities and "bodily kinesthetics," in addition to other, theme-centered curricula.

Having many and varied experiences that encourage them to move to various tempos enables young learners to develop ownership of the concept of steady beat. A kinesthetic mode of learning is especially important in the K–3 years.

- In Australia, researchers have demonstrated statistically significant relationships between music instruction and positive performance in such areas as reading comprehension, spelling, mathematics, and learning ability;[6] listening ability;[7] primary mental abilities (verbal, perceptual, number, and spatial);[8] and motor proficiency.[9]

- The Waldorf schools in Europe and the United States use music as a powerful tool in integrating other curriculum components.

- The Chelsea schools in Boston have placed music at the core of their curricula, believing that "aesthetic development is critical to achieving other goals essential to education, among them, reducing dropout rates, increasing school attendance, improving self-esteem, emphasizing the importance of discipline, and producing culturally literate students."[10]

Music and the components of active learning are fundamental tools for every learner today. As with the other curriculum areas within the High/Scope educational approach, music learning is seen as an active process of doing and experiencing. Chapter 2 provides guidelines for creating an active learning environment for music—one in which effective, sensitive music-makers will develop their ability to joyously use, communicate, and share the "universal language."

ENDNOTES

[1] E. L. Boyer, *High School: A Report on Secondary Education in America* (New York: Harper & Row, 1983), p. 18.

[2] H. Gardner, *Frames of Mind* (New York: Basic Books, Inc., 1985), pp. x, 61.

[3] E. L. Boyer, *A Report*, p. 19.

[4] L. Davidson, "Preschool Children's Tonal Knowledge: Antecedents of Scale," *The Young Child and Music: Proceedings of the Music in Early Childhood Conference* (Provo, UT: Brigham Young University, June 28–30, 1984), p. 25.

[5] P. S. Weikart, *Teaching Movement and Dance,* 3rd ed. (Ypsilanti, MI: High/Scope Press, 1989).

[6] G. F. Herbert, "The Nature of Teacher Training in the Implementation of a Development Programme of Music for the Primary School," *Music in Teacher Education: National Conference Report* (Melbourne: A.M.E.L., 1979), pp. 44–49.

[7] J. T. Jetter, "An Evaluation of Musical Training in Auditory Perception for First-Grade Children," *Council for Research in Music Education,* No. 61 (1980), pp. 50–55.

[8] A. Gates, "Extra-Musical Benefits of Music Education: Preliminary Investigation," *Research Report to the Australia-Japan Foundation* (April 1980).

[9] A. Gates, "Extra-Musical Benefits."

[10] E. L. Boyer, *The Report,* pp. 24–25.

Chapter 2

Approaching Music Through Active Learning

The arts are an important part of this acculturation process. They help explain who we are and how we got here. They reach us and teach us in ways that can enlighten and inspire, often for a lifetime.

John H. Bryan
Chairman of the Board
and Chief Executive Officer
Sara Lee Corporation

High/Scope's active learning approach to education includes the belief, expressed so aptly by noted music educator Charles Fowler, that "every young person should be given access to the study of music, not to become a musician but to be better educated."[1] The words "every young person" imply that music education should be made available to *all*, not just to musically gifted and talented individuals. "To be better educated" means to acquire knowledge and critical thinking skills across *every area* of one's life, as well as to develop the ability to see relevant relationships between new and existing knowledge. In addition to influencing all areas of curriculum, the skills we develop through our study of music may also influence our values, our social interactions, and our appreciation of America's diverse citizens.

The classroom teacher has a unique opportunity to enrich the lives of all children through music. Many children entering the K–3 classroom will have had previous music experiences at home, church, day care, or preschool; however, the range of their early experiences may vary greatly. The experiences may have been initiated by a teacher or parent, or by another child; experiences may have been adult-directed with expectations for "correct" child responses, or they may have consisted of children imitating other children. Some children may have had no opportunities to experience the joy that comes from participating in musical activities. Every child has the ability to be successful in music, however, no matter what his or her prior experiences.

Music education in the classroom should provide the student with a broad range of experiences, including singing, playing instruments, moving to music, listening, and creating. A balance between teacher-initiated and child-initiated experiences will occur when the High/Scope approach to music through active learning is employed.

As part of the active learning approach to education, the involvement of students in music education is viewed as a daily occurrence. Educating the whole child implies developing each child's musical intelligence along with the six other intelligences identified by psychologist Howard Gardner (see Chapter 1). Using music throughout the day *and* in a separate music period leads to a holistic balance among the academic, the psychomotor, and the arts. In addition, High/Scope's educational approach includes a unique **plan-do-review** process. In the plan-do-review process, children choose, carry out, and then evaluate their own learning activities by reflecting, together with their peers, on the results of those activities. Through plan-do-review, teachers are provided with valuable insights into children's interests and individual levels of development, and children attain a sense of responsibility, competence, and self-esteem. The active learning environment, key experiences, teaching model, and plan-do-review process are all essential aspects of the High/Scope developmental approach to learning.

The High/Scope Developmental Approach to Music Education

To offer appropriate and challenging music experiences, the classroom teacher must first assess each child's developmental status. High/Scope uses the Piagetian stages of development as guides to its K–3 Curriculum. According to Piagetian principles, children's learning develops through stages. Although children may pass through these stages at different chronological ages, each learner progresses through the stages in the same general sequence. Even within each stage, however, variation is expected. For example, each child's use and understanding of the various musical elements is unique because each learner brings his or her own prior experiences, sensitivities, and abilities to the development of musical literacy.

A broad range of musical experiences in the classroom incorporates folk dancing (top photo), listening and thinking before responding (middle photo), and learning together in a safe, interactive environment (bottom photo).

From a Piagetian perspective, learning takes place across four consecutive developmental levels: *preoperations* (intuitive thinking); *early concrete operations; late concrete operations;* and *formal operations* (abstract thinking). Since most children will not reach the fourth level (formal operations) until their preteen or early teen years, it will not be part of our discussion here. However, most K–3 children *will* pass through the first three developmental levels.

Level one, the **preoperational stage** has been described by Piaget as "intuitive." At this level of learning, children draw conclusions and plan their actions on the basis of immediate physical impressions. Generally, children in this stage cannot imagine the consequences of an action unless they have tried it themselves or have seen it tried. Thought processes characteristic of this stage are often evident in preschool and kindergarten learners. There are at least four types of cognitive-musical characteristics:

Children identify and compare high sounds on step bells and on an Orff instrument. Using concrete materials such as these helps them to understand abstract musical concepts.

1. *Intuitive*—Children's actions are based on immediate physical impressions, such as imitative-sound play for train, plane, truck, animal, and environmental sounds.

2. *Copy-cat*—Children begin to acquire knowledge through singing games that make use of repeated limited melodic phrases, simple rhythmic patterns, nonsense syllables, and movement. Repeating favorite singing games can be a "security blanket" for children when these games are child-initiated.

3. *Centering*—Children focus on only one aspect of a response to a song, to a musical listening lesson, or to the playing of unpitched percussion instruments. They tend to believe everyone thinks the same way they do, which is why an interactive environment is important.

4. *Imaginative*—Children often have trouble differentiating between fact and fantasy. They often exhibit a high level of creativity with language and musical improvisation.

First grade is considered a period of transition between the preoperational stage of learning and the stages that follow. Children will usually have mastered various aspects of level-one learning, and many will exhibit characteristics of thinking at the next developmental level. To simplify our discussion, we will combine level two, *early concrete operations,* and level three, *late concrete operations,* into a single category, the *concrete-operational stage.*

The **concrete-operational stage** is observable in most children in grades 2 and 3. At the beginning of this stage, children start to develop the ability to manipulate things mentally, as long as those things can also be manipulated physically at the same time. As children pass through this stage, their thought processes mature and their mental manipulations grow more varied and complex. Children thus proceed, through concrete experiences, to develop an understanding of the concepts that are at the core of the music key experiences. Teachers should remember that music is for the most part an aural, abstract experience; the **contour** (see Glossary) of a melody is not something concrete. Children at this stage of learning are concerned with rules and will take great

Examples of AB and ABA Forms

AB form:
    It's a Small World
    A = verse   B = chorus

ABA form (short form):
    Twinkle, Twinkle, Little Star
    A = first melodic phrase

        (Twinkle, Twinkle, little star, How I wonder what you are)

    B = second melodic phrase, which is different

        (Up above the world so high, Like a diamond in the sky)

    A = repeat of the first melodic phrase

interest in exploring the conventions of music notation and note values and in using instruments to play familiar melodies "by ear." Working with **AB and ABA forms** (see 2.1) also enables children at this stage to decode musical sections of songs or longer works. Integrating two specific concepts (see 2.2) enables them to play simple rhythms correctly and to perform the foot patterns of folk dances with competence.

Using these Piagetian principles as guides, educators can introduce music in developmentally appropriate ways into the K–3 classroom. Throughout this process, it is important to encourage young children to apply those skills that are already emerging. To help create a learning environment that is truly an active one, the High/Scope music curriculum uses movement as the base for learning.

Rationale for Using Movement as the Base for Learning

Proficiency in movement and in basic timing are readiness abilities that support a child's early success in school. Children who have had opportunities to move about freely in their environment, without constant adult directives, appear to naturally develop other, related abilities. These include the ability to process visually and aurally; to move comfortably with body awareness and spatial awareness; to move in coordinated ways; and to independently express the **steady beat** (see *beat* in Glossary) of a rhyme, song, or recorded musical selection. (Independent expression of steady beat is called **basic timing,** explained in Chapters 3 and 6; see also Glossary.) These move-

2.2

Integrating Two Specific Concepts

The concept of rhythm being layered onto the concept of steady beat is shown graphically below, with each box representing one steady beat.

X	X	X	X	X	X

Foot patterns being integrated with the concept of steady beat is shown below:

In	in	in		Out	out	out	

ment abilities can help children to develop personal organizational skills, academic skills, and skills in sports, music, and the arts.

A pilot research study conducted with first-graders in a Detroit, Michigan, suburb demonstrated the relationship between the ability to walk to the steady beat of music and other abilities in reading, vocabulary, and math.[2] The study suggested a possible relationship between beat and academic performance, demonstrating the need for more movement and music experiences to be included in the classroom. Other, informal studies reported by music educators who have been trained in Phyllis S. Weikart's program "Education Through Movement: Building the Foundation" have linked successful movement experiences with children's ability to sing on pitch as well as to perform in other successful ways in the music room, the classroom, and the gymnasium. In the music room, for example, music educators noted that movement presented in the early part of the music period resulted in better in-tune singing later in the period.

Clearly, movement is an essential base for acquiring musical literacy. Such music elements as form, phrase, high/low tones, pitch, and melody are abstract concepts that are better understood when movement is incorporated in their presentation. The child who learns these concepts in a passive manner

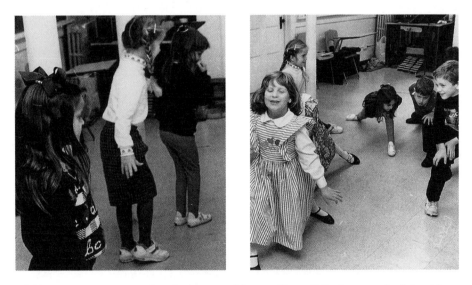

Children use movement to explore the concepts of short and long. Reflecting on and refining this activity leads to a broad understanding and ability to transfer and apply the concepts.

may understand them only in a narrow way (that is, be able to use them only in the way the concepts were initially presented). Ability to understand so that one can *transfer* or *extend* the concepts to new learning situations may be lacking.

Classroom teachers presenting musical concepts through movement exploration will find that children attain a broad understanding of those concepts, especially when thoughtful sharing of movement activities becomes a regular part of the daily schedule. Each musical element can be introduced through movement activities that permit students to act as leaders and to initiate ideas, thus enabling them to solve problems and demonstrate their understanding of the particular element.

The following **movement key experiences** provide the framework for the K–3 music program and are essential to children's development of musical literacy. "In the High/Scope Curriculum, teachers are encouraged to plan a classroom environment that is rich in materials for children's hands-on activities. The classroom environment and teaching approach are designed to stimulate the exploring, discovering, comparing, combining, constructing, and representing that are the external reflections of the child's inward construction of knowledge."[3] The movement key experiences reflect this basic approach to learning.

Movement Key Experience	Desired Outcome
Acting upon movement directions	Visual and auditory processing/responding
Describing movement	Thinking and language
Moving in nonlocomotor ways	Comfort with movement
	Awareness of body, space, and time
	Strength, balance, coordination
Moving in locomotor ways	Comfort with movement
	Awareness of body, space, and time
	Strength, balance, coordination
Moving in integrated ways	Comfort with movement
	Awareness of body, space, and time
	Strength, balance, coordination
Moving with objects	Comfort with movement
	Awareness of body, space, and time
	Strength, balance, coordination
Expressing creativity in movement	Student choice, creativity
Feeling and expressing steady beat	Basic timing
Moving in sequences to a common beat	Beat coordination[4]

The **movement key experiences** will be united with the **music key experiences,** presented in Part 2 of this text. Notice that *feeling and expressing steady beat* is both a music and a movement key experience, and in each case, it has the same desired outcome—achievement of **basic timing.**

Kindergarten and first-grade students should be involved in many movement experiences designed to increase their musical knowledge and ability. As students reach second and third grade, their motor development should have progressed to a point at which experiences that require more highly developed motor coordination will be possible. These experiences include more difficult movement sequences, such as hand jives (patterns of hand movements with a partner), playing patterns on instruments, rhythm layered on top of steady beat, and beginning folk dances. By the end of third grade the student should have the musical proficiencies to begin study of a musical instrument, to be involved in a choral group, and to be an intelligent music consumer.

When movement is used as the base for learning, the child's musical experiences will be meaningful. As the next section describes, the Education Through Movement Teaching Model developed by Phyllis S. Weikart can be used as a guide to begin incorporating movement and music into the K–3 classroom.

Importance and Use of the Teaching Model

Before presenting movement and music active learning experiences to young children, teachers should determine whether a specific activity is developmentally appropriate for the age group being taught. In a large-group setting, in particular, how easily children grasp various concepts often depends on how the teacher presents the activities. Phyllis S. Weikart's Teaching Model can be of great assistance in helping teachers present active learning experiences to children in any area of the K–3 curriculum.

The Teaching Model has three major components. In working with a new concept, the teacher should

- **Separate**—use only one method at a time to present a musical concept, e.g., using a demonstration (visual method), spoken directions (verbal method), or hands-on guidance (tactile method).
- **Simplify**—break the task into easier/shorter subtasks, so children are involved at their developmental level. These subtasks usually are simple precursor skills.
- **Facilitate**—encourage each child to *think,* not just respond, through language, problem solving, individual choices, and reflection.

Each of these three components is discussed in greater detail in the sections that follow.

To **separate** breaks from the traditional "show *and* tell" model by stressing use of only *one* modality at a time. For many teachers, this approach will be new, for we have been led to believe that engaging a group of learners via more than one modality at the same time will most effectively address individual differences within the group. This is not necessarily so. When used consistently, the **separate** strategy will strengthen any child's visual, aural (auditory), *and* tactile-kinesthetic responses as well as strengthen her or his abilities to attend to and understand information presented. The strategy has great value not only in movement and music experiences but also in other areas of the curriculum.

Because the visual mode of learning is particularly strong in young children, a teacher can **separate** by presenting a movement visually (demonstration) and expect that children will respond quite accurately. They will respond even more accurately if each movement is held ("static movement") to give time for them to respond and talk about the movement. Teaching children an action song is an example of when one might **separate** in this way. In the *Pizza Hut* activity (see Insert 2.3, on pp. 18–19), each motion is presented visually in a

(continued on page 20)

Pizza Hut*

Grade K–3

Key Experiences: *(See Chapter 4)*

⊶ **I. A. Moving to Music**
> 3. Using coordination skills in performing action songs

⊶ **II. A. Feeling and expressing steady beat**
> 4. Performing nonlocomotor movement to the steady beat

⊶ **II. C. Developing melody**
> 7. Identifying and singing phrases in the melody
> 8. Recognizing patterns and sequences in melodies

Students sing this action song, which enables them to use coordination skills, identify same and different phrases, and recognize melodic patterns and sequences while strengthening timing and singing abilities.

Materials:

Pizza Hut song on next page.

Activity to Experience:

The children copy the way the teacher makes a circle (a pizza shape) with both arms. (To make the circle, both arms are held in front of the body, with fingertips touching.)

Then they copy putting both arms overhead with palms touching, to make the shape of a hut.

Children sequence the two motions several times.

They label the first motion "Pizza" and the second motion "Hut," using learner SAY & DO.

The children copy a flapping motion of the upper arms twice against the body (like a chicken).

They practice flapping arms twice and then do the Pizza Hut movement once more. With this sequence of movements, they say "Kentucky Fried Chicken and a Pizza Hut."

Children supply the motions while the teacher sings the first half of the song.

Show children the new movement of raising both index fingers up in an arch and then putting them down again (to simulate the McDonald's arch). Do this movement twice while saying "Mc*Don*ald's, Mc*Don*ald's."

Repeat the words "Kentucky Fried Chicken and a Pizza Hut" while children supply these motions. Once the movements are secure with the text, the

*Adapted from P. S. Weikart, *Movement Plus Rhymes, Songs, & Singing Games* (High/Scope Press: 1988).

Pizza Hut

teacher sings the song while the children listen and perform the appropriate movements.

Children will naturally join in singing phrases as they are able to do so.

Facilitation and Reflection:

What kinds of things does this (pizza) shape remind you of?

What does this (hut) shape remind you of? What does this (arm-flapping) motion remind you of? (After labeling these motions "Pizza Hut" . . . "Kentucky Fried Chicken," continue this type of facilitation for the "McDonald's" motion.)

What do you notice about the melody for each of these motions?

What do you hear that is the same (or different) in the phrases of this song? (Phrase 2 is a repeat of Phrase 1. Phrase 4 is a repeat of Phrase 3. Phrase 3 is a *sequence* of Phrase 1. It has the same melody shape, and it begins on a higher pitch.)

Extensions:

Sing *Pizza Hut* as a two-part round.

Create other verses and motions for restaurants in your area.

static position, without verbal explanation, and the children copy. The song is not presented with the motions until the movement is secure.

Giving spoken directions without the accompanying visual actions strengthens the learner's ability to process and respond to language. When teachers "show *and* tell," an understanding of the spoken explanation may be delayed. Many of today's children have not developed effective listening skills. Using the **separate** approach—with spoken directions alone—strengthens this area of aural (auditory) processing in the same way that using demonstration alone strengthens visual processing.

Some children are aided by hands-on guidance. The leader moves the arms or legs of the learner into the desired position without simultaneous spoken explanation. This guidance is followed by an opportunity for the student to describe and then replicate the movement.

To **simplify** might include teaching only the words of a song by echo **phrases** (see *phrase* in Glossary) before adding the melody; dividing a two-part movement into single movements; presenting "static movement" sequences for an action song before the words and melody; or using the basic movements in a dance before teaching the more difficult, ethnic dance pattern. For example, in the action song *Pizza Hut,* the first two motions may be presented one at a time, with each motion held in a static position to make it easier for children to copy. Once children can perform two motions independently, words of the song are spoken with the motions. The next motions are presented in the same visual manner, followed by the words. The total sequence is then put together. Finally the teacher sings the song while the students perform the actions. The teacher has drawn upon knowledge of precursor skills to assist learners.

Students who have experienced the **simplify** approach in the early grades will be able to respond more musically. They will have strengthened their singing, listening, moving, and playing skills that secure the foundation for appropriate music experiences in grades 2 and 3. The **simplify** strategy enables children to develop their musical abilities with confidence.

To **facilitate** is to enable children to transfer and extend their knowledge to new learning situations, to develop ownership of a concept. The **facilitate** strategy is the most challenging to consistently apply, because it requires the teacher to *guide each learner's responses toward understanding.* This involves helping each child to construct his or her own knowledge and develop his or her own ability. In the *Pizza Hut* example, the music concept is *same and different phrases.* The teacher can **facilitate** by having the children

- *Describe* the movements in the sequence as they are presented and experienced.

- *Recall* the order of the movements.

- *Sing* the melody for the "Pizza Hut" section of the song.

- *Sing* the melody for the "McDonald's" section.

- *Reflect* on the musical concept (use of same and different phrases).

- *Suggest* new words and actions.

Because *Pizza Hut* has been taught as more than just another action song, it now has obvious value and reinforces an important music concept—same and different phrases. Discoveries for the learner that come from combining active learning experiences with the **facilitate** strategy lead to ownership of concepts. When teachers **facilitate** to help children construct their own understanding of concepts, such engagement not only develops children's knowledge-base but also leads to their lifelong involvement in music.

Another aspect of f**acilitate,** the technique of **learner SAY & DO** (see Glossary), creates the bond between language and movement, enabling children to add basic movement patterns to music. Learner SAY & DO combines the cognitive with the motor and is a valuable process to use when practicing movement sequences or playing instruments.

The children's movement signifies "Hut" in the Pizza Hut *song. By pointing to the circular cutout, one child indicates that she is hearing the "same phrase" being repeated in the song.*

The Teaching Model, with its three components of **separate, simplify,** and **facilitate,** enables the teacher to participate as a partner, rather than to act as the director, in each new experience. This is extremely relevant to High/ Scope's active learning philosophy, where *shared responsibility for learning* is the ingredient for success.

Music—An Active Learning Link to the Academic Curriculum

When educators seriously consider the holistic ways in which young children learn, they will view music and movement as the "Super Glue" for all the academic, social, physical, and musical concepts that are so important to each child's development. Music and movement are truly at the *center* of the young child's learning from birth through approximately age eight.

Consider the various ways that music can enhance other areas of learning:

- Using music to develop quality movement responses and coordination sequences, directed or created

- Singing songs that tie into social studies, values, patriotism, history, language arts, math, the seasons, and science

- Listening to music to improve aural processing, discrimination, and imaginative responses

- Using music as part of an essential progression to reading, classifying, seriating, recalling, and analyzing

- Influencing moods, attitudes, choices, or aesthetic responses through musical experiences

- Learning to sing a new song, to play an instrument, or to improvise

- Linking music to the processes of problem solving and logical analysis

- Applying science and math knowledge to construct and create instruments or to study the technology of sound

Music helps children experience enjoyment in learning and forms the base for a comprehensive, high-quality education. Every K–3 classroom should offer movement and music experiences.

Classroom Involvement in Music

Incorporating the music key experiences on a regular basis in your classroom will provide each of your students with lifelong benefits as well as memorable musical adventures. Consider the following:

- A special bond develops in classrooms where students and teachers sing, dance, or play instruments together.

- Regular classroom singing experiences help children to build valuable language arts skills, develop leadership skills, and improve

A lasting bond develops when children request and sing favorite songs. Here, they sing Ghost of Tom.

health and posture; such experiences also improve student-teacher interaction and respect.

- Parents as special musical guests enrich the classroom environment by sharing various appropriate musical abilities.

- Discussions that lead to discoveries of the many ways music is heard and used during a day develop children's appreciation for the far-reaching influence of music.

Music is a gift you give yourself and your students. You cannot fail in this endeavor unless you fail to try. In Chapter 3, we present specific guidelines for developing an effective environment for music.

ENDNOTES

[1]C. Fowler, "Recognizing the Role of Art Intelligences," *Music Educators Journal* (September 1989), p. 27.

[2]P. S. Weikart, "Movement Curriculum Improves Children's Rhythmic Competence," *High/Scope ReSource,* Vol. 6, No. 1 (Winter 1987), p. 8–11.

[3]F. Blackwell and C. Hohmann, *High/Scope K–3 Curriculum Series—Science,* (Ypsilanti, MI: High/Scope Press, 1991), p. 12.

[4]For further information about the key experiences in movement and Phyllis S. Weikart's Teaching Model, refer to P. S. Weikart, *Teaching Movement & Dance: A Sequential Approach to Rhythmic Movement,* 3rd ed. (Ypsilanti, MI: High/Scope Press, 1989).

Chapter 3

The Environment for Musical Development

In the elementary grades, the arts are a valuable component in broadening a child's mind and talents. In secondary school, the arts provide a sense of history, connecting the past to the present. When a student reaches college, a liberal arts education teaches not just clear but creative, innovative thinking.

Willard C. Butcher
Former Chairman of the Board
The Chase Manhattan Corporation

The classroom is one important environment for musical development. But another, *natural* environment for musical development has been prepared in all children before birth. A newborn baby is already familiar with the steady beat of the heart, melodic voices, and musical pitches. Almost every toddler automatically perceives the range of emotions, from love through fear, that is evident in the voices of all the caregivers in his or her world. As the child matures, repetition and familiarity with nursery rhymes, lullabies, knee-bouncing games, singing games, rope-jumping chants, and songs should continue to become the important building blocks of musical development. All these activities occur either one-on-one or in group settings, with the *voice being the primary musical instrument.*

While modern-day sound technology is phenomenal, we cannot afford to allow tape recorders, compact-disc players, synthesizers, or television sets to replace the human contact needed to develop a love of music and music-making in our children.

It is important to remember that the music provided by the electronic devices that surround us had its beginnings in human efforts. People can and do make beautiful, meaningful music together, and it is evident that we can, and do, communicate effectively through music. It moves us beyond language barriers. *Music begins and develops within and through us.* Because young children naturally explore their environment and because their cognitive processing is evident through their sound representations, songs, and movement, *the young child's body can be viewed as the first and most important environment—the primary learning center.*

The Body as the Primary Learning Center

Educators who perceive the child's own body as the primary learning center are already aware that much of what young children naturally do occurs through music and movement experiences. Teachers will want to guide the development of these natural abilities by encouraging children to engage in active listening and to move, sing, and play simple instruments. High/Scope's leadership in the development and implementation of active learning has paved the way for others to build upon this valuable model. Several leaders in the field of education have written about the link between movement and active learning.

Thomas Armstrong, author, educational consultant, and columnist, believes that "many children need to learn **through their bodies** in order to make sense out of academic subjects."[1] Armstrong has stated, "Thinking begins in the body. However, as the child grows, thinking becomes clothed in the rich fabric of inner imagery."[2] Concepts can be better understood when the foundation for understanding them has been laid in the rich environment of integrated—not segregated—learning experiences. To reinforce this concept, Armstrong references Jerome Bruner's studies, explaining that any relevant learning experience cycles through three levels (see 3.1): *enactive* (through the body), *iconic* (through the image), and *symbolic* (through the concept).[3]

Grace C. Nash, nationally known pioneer music educator and author of numerous books on music and movement, gives us an important formula for today's educators: "Take a given number of children; add music and movement; multiply by active learning. The result equals Greater Human Potential."[4] Dr. Dee Coulter's research also bears study in this area.[5] Coulter, a nationally recognized neuroscience educator from Boulder, Colorado, is extremely articulate in stating the need for movement and music as basic learning components for all young children.

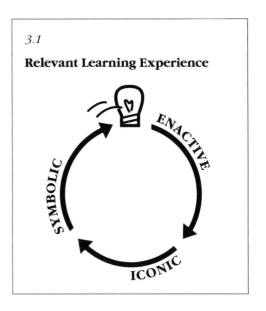

3.1

Relevant Learning Experience

Developing Steady Beat in the "Primary Learning Center"

Throughout the K–3 years, children need many and varied experiences that involve listening and responding to high-quality musical selections. These opportunities to respond naturally may evolve into flowing creative interpretation or into various beat-keeping actions, depending on the music used and the imagination of the children. Many gross-motor movement responses are needed in order for strength, balance, and coordination to be developed and refined at a level necessary for consistent beat-keeping.

Often, before preschoolers understand what steady beat is, their repetitive motor actions nevertheless show beat-keeping to their own *internal **tempo*** (see *tempo* in Glossary). In this case, individual timing, or tempo, is based automatically on the child's own internal pace. Consider, for example, the way a young child pounds with a hammer or pats Play-Doh. A teacher observing such actions can supply language (saying, for example, "pound, pound, pound, pound" as a child hammers away). Motor coordination depends on the refinement of basic **locomotor** and **nonlocomotor movements** (see Glossary) carried out through repetition, maturation, and cognition linked to the visual and aural discrimination pertinent to the task.

During music-listening experiences, young learners can be calmed by rocking motions synchronized to the *organizational **macrobeat*** (*macrobeat* is Dr. Edwin Gordon's term;[6] see 3.2). Children also can be helped to identify specific melodies, musical forms, and types of instruments while rocking to the macrobeat. This rocking motion is a nonverbal tie to the security felt *in utero*. Feeling and rocking to

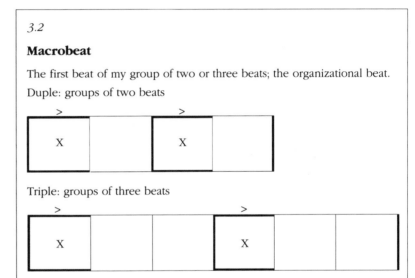

3.2

Macrobeat

The first beat of my group of two or three beats; the organizational beat.

Duple: groups of two beats

Triple: groups of three beats

Children play "Beat Train," in which the "engineer" determines the pathway for stepping the beat while the "cars" and "caboose" follow. Children take turns being "engineer."

this macrobeat also helps to strengthen children's attending and comprehending skills and to develop each child's "inner anchor," which is important for effective speech-flow, reading comprehension, and sequencing ability. The inner anchor helps to activate and develop the timing-cognition function, which strengthens a child's ability to concentrate, to comprehend, to organize thought, and to respond to directions. Children in grades 2 and 3 can continue to use this rocking/listening strategy to perceive musical rhythms played correctly, so they understand faster/slower and same/different rhythm patterns. Compare the child's need for this consistent rocking/listening strategy to the infant's need for a vast number of spoken repetitions before beginning to imitate speech.

Children who are asked to identify their own steady beat will almost always move their hands or feet to demonstrate the **microbeat** (*microbeat* is also Dr. Edwin Gordon's term;[7] see 3.3). Their initial concept of steady beat is derived from their own internal timing related to their heartbeat. The more active the child, the faster the beat. Children's understanding of faster and slower steady beat can come from feeling the variations in their own heartbeats, which become slow while resting and faster with running or jumping rope. Experiences matching another's steady beat, discussing how one beat differs from another, and labeling various beats ("like jogging" or "like walking") continue to develop the concept of faster or slower tempos. The students' concept of steady beat is reinforced and expanded whenever they are asked to listen to, feel, and demonstrate the beat found in names, (*Jen*nifer, Ka*trin*a), in companion words (*pea*nut *but*ter, *ted*dy *bear*), and rhymes, songs, and musical selections.

3.3

Microbeat

The steady walking beat; each beat of a group of two or three beats

>	
X	X

>		
X	X	X

Beat Awareness

As already mentioned, a person's awareness of steady beat begins with a sense of internal timing, and that steady beat is almost always expressed as the microbeat. Beat can be kept in many ways, such as by alternating hands or feet. Often, an infant first responds to the microbeat of recorded music and songs by bouncing in the crib; later, the infant might respond with foot movements. This is a natural response to steady beat for children and adults because of their many previous experiences marching or walking the microbeat. Children easily identify and respond to the microbeat because it fits their shorter limbs, their balance, and their coordination. First marching experiences should use music with tempos that are close to the child's heartbeat, which is about 120 to 130 beats per minute when the child is active (see 3.4). As proficiency develops, faster as well as slower tempos will extend children's attending to microbeat.

The Levels of Awareness of Steady Beat

The *first level of beat awareness* develops by beginning with one's own body and progressing through the following steps, using microbeat:

1. Visual or verbal demonstration of one's own steady beat
2. Visual or verbal matching of the steady beats of others
3. Listening/feeling/matching steady beats of names, words, companion words, and word phrases
4. Listening/feeling/matching steady beats of rhymes, songs, and recordings

3.4

Marching Songs for Children

John Philip Sousa's *Album of Familiar Marches* including
Stars & Stripes Forever
Washington Post
American Patrol

Yankee Doodle (RM2)

Cherkessiya (RM2)

Microbeat is often difficult to demonstrate consistently while children are singing or reciting a rhyme, because children's motor response, instead of matching the steady beat, can too easily synchronize with the rhythm of the words. When the spoken or singing response matches the rhythm of the words or melody, rhythm is demonstrated. This response to rhythm and the consequent performance of rote rhythm patterns alone is not precise unless the learners possess **basic timing** (see Glossary; see also p. 38, "Developing Rhythm in the 'Primary Learning Center'"). While responding to *microbeat* is the first level of understanding steady beat, the awareness, use, and understanding of *macrobeat* are essential to each learner's understanding of the total concept of beat.

Teachers can help guide the child's discovery of **macrobeat** (the rocking beat, or the first, emphasized beat of any *group* of two or three microbeats). Almost all Western music is grouped into microbeats of two or three or combinations thereof, and the macrobeat organizes microbeats. Saying a rhyme while children rock and pat the macrobeat helps them comprehend. For children, practice speaking while feeling this macrobeat can often help to clean up "lazy" speech patterns and develop speech-flow. Listening to a melody while rocking the macrobeat can help students hear melodies with acuity, so phrases and sections of music are heard and organized with understanding.

The *second level of beat awareness* develops by starting from the body and progressing through the following steps, using the *macrobeat:*

Through movement and facial expressions, this 4-month-old infant responds happily to tape-recorded music.

1. Feeling, identifying, and demonstrating the rocking beat (with tactile endpoints) while *listening* to rhymes, songs, or recordings.
2. Feeling, identifying, and demonstrating by rocking/patting the macrobeat while speaking rhymes or word phrases, such as "*ov*er the hill," or "*un*der the rainbow" (see 3.5).
3. Feeling and demonstrating by rocking/patting the macrobeat while listening to a musical selection, learning a new melody or rhyme, or singing.
4. Playing a simple instrument as a macrobeat accompaniment to a rhyme or song.
5. Identifying, comparing, and organizing macrobeats or microbeats in any rhyme, song, or musical recording; for example, comparing the relationship of microbeats to macrobeats in the song *This Old Man,* as children (1) sing and rock the macrobeat, (2) sing and step the microbeat, and (3) sing and rock the macrobeat.

3.5

Macrobeat in a Rhyme

In the following rhyme, phrases representing the macrobeat are underlined.
    <u>Hick</u>ory dickory <u>dock,</u>
    The <u>mouse</u> ran up the <u>clock.</u>
    The <u>clock</u> struck one,
        the <u>mouse</u> ran down,
    <u>Hick</u>ory dickory <u>dock.</u>

Beat Competence

Beat competence is proficiency in demonstrating microbeat *and* macrobeat with either hands or feet while listening, moving, singing, or playing instruments. In their natural development of beat competence, children progress through four levels. Although the levels (which follow) represent goals for particular grades, each child progresses through the levels at his or her own rate, and according to his or her experiences interacting with and reflecting on the musical concepts.

Kindergarten level: Demonstrating the steady beat to one's own internal tempo; feeling, identifying, and demonstrating the *macrobeat* of rhymes, songs, or recordings in nonlocomotor movements and demonstrating the *microbeat* in locomotor movements

Grade-1 level: Demonstrating *microbeat* and *macrobeat* to one's own internal tempo; feeling, identifying, demonstrating, and leading the *macrobeat* and *microbeat* of rhymes, songs, or recordings in nonlocomotor motions and demonstrating the *microbeat* in locomotor movements

Grade-2 level: Demonstrating *microbeat* and *macrobeat* to one's own internal tempo; feeling, identifying, demonstrating, and leading the *microbeat or macrobeat in either nonlocomotor or locomotor movements* through a rhyme, song, or recording and in more complex ways, such as in various pathways, in rhymes, singing games, and simple folk dances, with levels of beat coordination, and in choreographed movement

Grade-3 level: Demonstrating and leading the *microbeat and macrobeat* in all of the above categories and also in simple rhythm patterns, such as those shown in Insert 3.6, when singing or playing instruments, when dancing, and when integrating movements.

Basic Timing

As mentioned earlier, *basic timing* is the goal of both the movement and the music key experience *feeling and expressing steady beat* (see 3.7 and 3.8; these concepts are explained more fully in Chapter 6). Basic timing is the ability to independently feel, express, and keep steady beat. Daily experiences throughout the

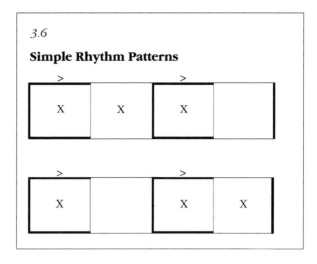

3.6

Simple Rhythm Patterns

3.7

Key Experience: Feeling and Expressing Steady Beat
Goal: Basic Timing

Basic Timing—Steps to Ownership
1. Finding one's own steady beat, visual and verbal
2. Matching another's steady beat tempo, visual and verbal
3. Expressing beat in words, companion words, word phrases
4. Keeping beat with rhymes, songs, and recordings
5. Extending timing to other areas

Basic Timing—Developmental Sequence
Single Dynamic Movements

Nonlocomotor Movement	Macrobeat → Microbeat → Either	
Locomotor Movement	Microbeat → Macrobeat → Either	

Grade	Timing
Kindergarten	Nonlocomotor movement in macrobeat Locomotor movement in microbeat
Grade 1	Nonlocomotor movement in macrobeat and microbeat Locomotor movement in microbeat
Grade 2	Nonlocomotor movement in macrobeat and microbeat Locomotor movement in microbeat and macrobeat
Grade 3	Extending timing to all learning areas, which includes singing and moving, performing accurate rhythm patterns, and integrating movement sequences from a solid foundation in steady beat

Macrobeat and *microbeat* are Dr. Edwin Gordon's terms.

Basic Timing: The Ripple Effect

Beat is like a pebble thrown into a pond of water. Ripples are composed of the many and varied experiences needed to attain basic timing, which affects all areas of lifelong learning.

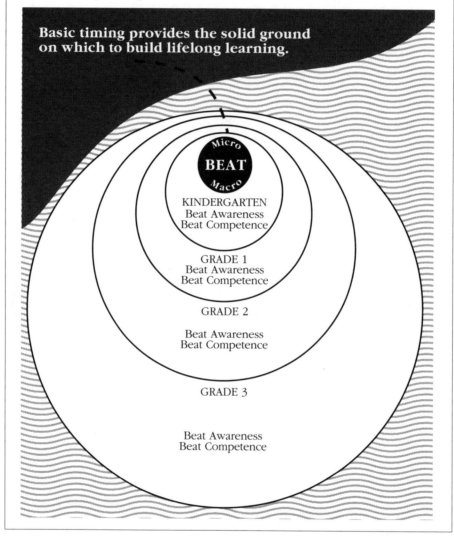

K–3 years give learners sufficient opportunity to develop each grade's level of competence. As each level of proficiency is reached in beat awareness and beat competence, one can trace the natural progression of *feeling and expressing steady beat* from demonstrating one's own internal tempo, to matching the timing of others. It then progresses through demonstrating the tempos of various media, and returns, with extended understanding, to all that has been internalized within the "primary learning center." The levels of beat awareness and beat competence target the organization, refinement, and flexibility needed to adapt and function in any tempo when expressing macrobeat and microbeat. Basic timing secures the foundation for success in every area essential to a child's construction of knowledge (see 3.9).

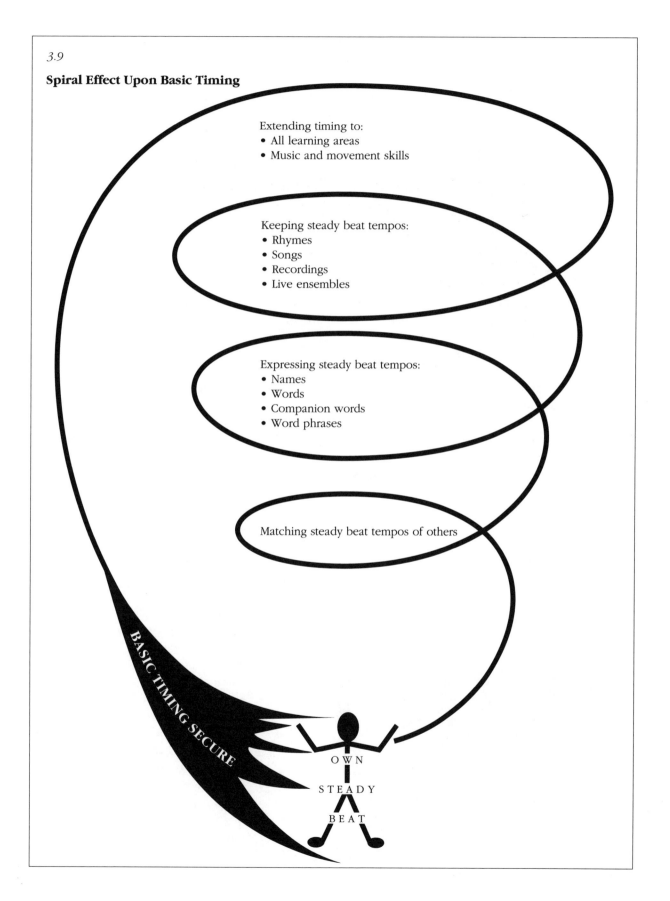

3.9

Spiral Effect Upon Basic Timing

Extending timing to:
• All learning areas
• Music and movement skills

Keeping steady beat tempos:
• Rhymes
• Songs
• Recordings
• Live ensembles

Expressing steady beat tempos:
• Names
• Words
• Companion words
• Word phrases

Matching steady beat tempos of others

BASIC TIMING SECURE

OWN

STEADY

BEAT

Feeling and movement responses are essential to the holistic development of the child. Without sufficient foundation or security in *movement*, how can children develop their cognitive and musical abilities to their fullest potential? Active learning experiences in movement and music during the concrete operational period also strengthen the child's social-emotional development. This domain, often overlooked in education, plays a large role in the timed, tuned, perceptive child's achievement of potential.

Developing Melody in the "Primary Learning Center"

Learning to use one's singing voice with increasing proficiency and delight is a major part of developing the body, or primary learning center. We all possess this "free" instrument, capable of expressing so much more than spoken language allows. For centuries, people have passed down their cultural folk songs from generation to generation as families and communities have united through song. With so much essential learning tied into these experiences, guiding children to develop rich "song banks" is a worthy goal for everyone who works with them. As our world grows smaller, our understanding of and communication with world neighbors can be greatly enhanced through singing meaningful songs from all countries. It is difficult to hate and sing at the same time. And singing together is so much healthier than merely listening to someone else sing. Singing activates the participatory response that all of us are born with.

The *first step* in developing the singing voice incorporates exploration of vocal sounds through active learning experiences in high-middle-low concepts, in singing versus speaking concepts, and in concepts related to matching specific tones. These areas are covered in the discussion of the key experience *exploring the singing voice* (see p. 74, Chapter 5).

The *second step* in developing the singing voice is to explore important kinesthetic, cognitive, and tonal relationships. When children use movement in a meaningful way to distinguish specific pitches, their aural discrimination among tones in any **major scale** can be refined. A major eight-tone scale, which is the tonal organization of specific pitches within many favorite songs, is organized according to the formula shown here (see 3.10; further dis-

---

3.10

Major Scale Construction

A major scale consists of eight tones—two groups of four pitches each. The intervals in each group of four pitches follow the formula *whole step–whole step–half step*. The two groups are joined by the interval formed by one *whole step*.

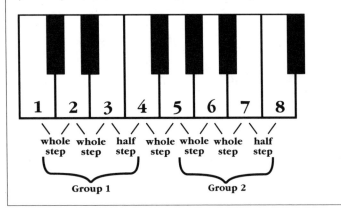

---

cussion of *major* and *minor scales* can be found in the Glossary and in Chapters 6 and 7). Children can link the organization of a major scale to movement through use of a **body scale.**

The Body Scale

The **body scale** (see 3.11) represents hand placements for the musical tones of a major scale. Introducing this kinesthetic link to pitch helps young singers sing specific tones with accuracy and forms the foundation for making pitch relationships. Our illustration of the body scale includes *scale degrees* and *solfège,* for teachers using either of these systems. However, such abstract systems are best understood by children only after they are familiar with the body scale and **tone games.**

Developing Melody Through Tone Games

In order for **melody** (see Glossary) to develop with accuracy, young learners need a tremendous amount of aural (ear) training, tonal discrimination, and singing. **Tone games,** which provide children with practice, interaction, challenge, and fun, prepare them to sing tunefully and to listen with discrimination. Tone games give children opportunities to link their musical, cognitive, and kinesthetic intelligences together for retentive, child-appropriate learning. Tone games might proceed like this:

Children first listen to all of the tones of the C-major scale, to hear the complete set of tones. (The D-major scale may be used as well. Many music educators believe this provides a better singing-range.) The teacher then presents a steady beat tone game visually (demonstrating, for example, shoulders, shoulders, waist) *or* aurally, using tones G and E (scale degrees 5 and 3), which children SING & SHAPE. They echo the pitches in the order heard. Sing all tone games on a neutral syllable, such as "bom," so children can focus clearly on the tones to be replicated by the voice. A beginning pattern for a tone game might

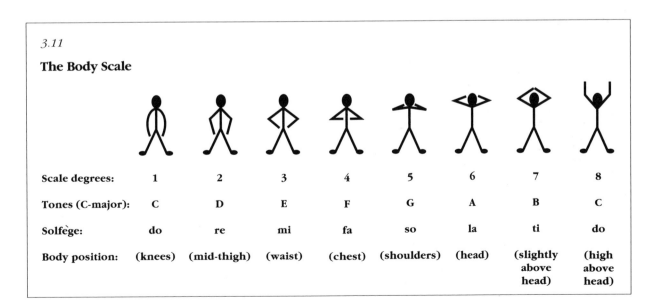

3.11

The Body Scale

Scale degrees:	1	2	3	4	5	6	7	8
Tones (C-major):	C	D	E	F	G	A	B	C
Solfège:	do	re	mi	fa	so	la	ti	do
Body position:	(knees)	(mid-thigh)	(waist)	(chest)	(shoulders)	(head)	(slightly above head)	(high above head)

be like the one shown in Insert 3.12. Including a "rest" gives children time to prepare their response and to begin in beat. Games of four beats are long enough for attending and short enough for safety. Other tonal patterns with four beats might be 5–3–5–3, 5–5–3–5, 5–3–3–5, or 5–5–5–3.

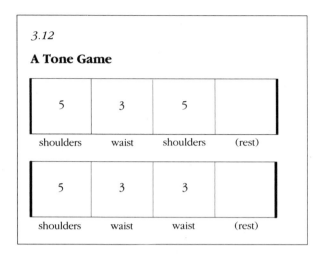

If the teacher or child leader SHAPES (places both hands on the body for each tone), the followers SING & SHAPE. If the teacher or child leader SINGS the tones, followers SING & SHAPE. Learner SING & SHAPE activates the cognitive-kinesthetic-tonal link, just as learner SAY & DO links the cognitive to the kinesthetic (see Chapter 2 for an explanation of Phyllis Weikart's Teaching Model). To keep the game going, individual children can lead, with each child choosing whether to lead with SING or SHAPE. The followers respond with learner SING & SHAPE in beat.

Games are best begun on G (scale degree 5), so the beginning pitch is always predictable, providing a safety net for the learners. Later, when the class is ready for more challenging tone games, begin with *any* pitches/hand placements familiar to the class. We suggest that no more than one new pitch and placement be added at a time. As warm-up to the game, review pitches and placements previously used. Refer to the following chart for the usual order of introducing new tones:

Order of Introducing New Tones (C-Major Scale)

Actual Pitch	*Scale Degree*	*Body Placement*
G	5	Shoulders
E	3	Waist
A	6	Top of head
C	1	Knees
C	8	Arms outstretched above head
D	2	Thighs
F	4	Chest
B	7	Arms slightly above head, hands touching

When tone games are used consistently in a safe environment, students will develop outstanding singing clarity in tonal problem solving, as well as "in-tune" singing, which lays a foundation for thinking within a **key system** (see

Students touch their shoulders to demonstrate the placement of scale degree 5 (top photo). Touching the waist demonstrates the placement of scale degree 3 (middle photo). Tone games begin with these two pitches and extend to include the remaining tones of the major scale (bottom photo).

Glossary). This thinking within a key prepares students to improvise on a melody, create a musical variation, or create a new composition. Developing this kinesthetic-tonal-cognitive link is crucial to perceptive musicianship.

Guidelines for Working With Tonal Concepts

The following guidelines represent a way to work with important tonal concepts for developing melody so learners develop ownership, proficiency, and joy in their understanding of single pitches, musical phrases (groups of related pitches), and melody.

- Make use of the body scale, as diagrammed, to reinforce tonal relationships. Begin with tone games using the first two pitches suggested (G and E). Have children visually copy the leader's static hand-placement on both shoulders for the first pitch. Add the pitch for that placement. Repeat with the second placement, followed by its pitch. Both hands should be used when establishing body placement.

- Guide beginning learners to concentrate on *body placement and pitch relationships presented on a neutral syllable,* such as "bom" or "la."

- At first, work in steady beat with these two pitches. Extend to other pitches when the class seems ready. Encourage children to be the leaders in small and large groups.

- Once learners know the positions on the body for the scale tones used, have them respond to your voice *or* movement (not to voice *and* movement at the same time). As the leader separates the voice and movement, learners respond with their voice *and* their corresponding movement (SING & SHAPE). The goal is for learners to respond accurately to the problem presented with correct placement and pitch.

- Guide their discovery to where these tonal patterns actually appear in songs, such as G-E-G in *This Old Man* and G-E-G-E in *Star Light, Star Bright* or *Bluebird, Bluebird.*

- When body placement and pitches are secure, scale degree numbers can be added. (See again "Order of Introducing New Tones.") Then in grade 1, scale degrees can reinforce the body scale, so that in grade 2 or 3, the Curwen-Kodaly solfège syllables and hand signs can be used by music educators who favor this music reading system.

Developing Rhythm in the "Primary Learning Center"

Rhythm is an element of music defined as *action of pitches or sounds within and among the beats.* For many young learners, rhythm is the musical characteristic that first captures their interest. Since children's response to rhythm is so natural, teachers will find it important to remember that in kindergarten and grade 1, rhymes and rhythms need to be spoken while steady beat is reinforced in the body. For young children, beat provides a constant pulse that lends clarity to spoken rhythms, so that later, in grades 2 and up, they can feel, identify, and precisely perform rhythms. A rhyming reminder of this concept is the following:

Keep beat in the body,
Speak rhythm in the mouth,
It's just as plain as
North and south.

Many young singers will naturally *move to the rhythms* of the words they are singing, which creates stimulus-response bonding. They are automatically responding to words and their syllables, or to the melodic rhythm, which may not necessarily correspond precisely to the rhythmic durations. Because no conscious thought is involved in this automatic response, no real understanding of rhythm layered upon the underlying beat is enacted or internalized.

The rhythm of the melody often causes words to be spoken in special ways; these words may be contrived from natural speech in such a way as to fit each particular melody. However, teaching melodic rhythm from the rhythm of the words puts the focus on words rather than on melodic durations or rhythmic relationships. Instead, rhythm should be associated with *durations* based on steady beat. (See Chapter 6, "Expressing Rhythm," for more information.)

When students possess basic timing within the "primary learning center," rhythms may be introduced and performed precisely. The basic relationships involved in reading and performing rhythms are shown in Insert 3.13. A box with one X represents the basic beat symbol. When the microbeat is represented by a box with one X to denote one sound (of a given duration), then that same box divided and with one X in each *half* represents two sounds covering that same duration. Two boxes, as also shown in Insert 3.13, represent one sound held for the duration of two microbeats.

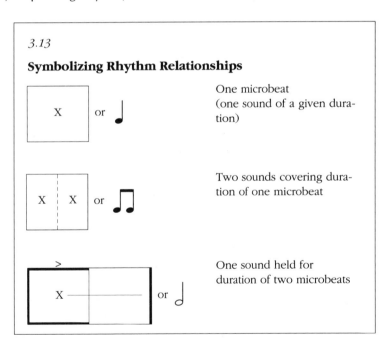

3.13

Symbolizing Rhythm Relationships

One microbeat (one sound of a given duration)

Two sounds covering duration of one microbeat

One sound held for duration of two microbeats

Guidelines for Building Rhythmic Security

The following guidelines for building rhythmic security may be useful:

- A **macrobeat** is the **weighted, organizational beat.** It is the first of a group of two or three microbeats, depending on the music. Movement response to macrobeat and microbeat *precedes* focus on rhythmic patterns.

• A **microbeat** is a **consistent pulsing beat** (steady walking beat). When macrobeat is the first of two beats, you have the feel of **duple.** When macrobeat is the first of three beats, you have the feel of **triple.**

• Echoing rhythm patterns initially using a single *neutral* syllable, such as "bah" or "choo," enables learners to focus on rhythmic duration, rather than on word rhythm. Rhythmic syllables can be added later, as discussed in Chapter 6, in connection with the key experience *expressing rhythm.*

• Movement is important for the understanding of rhythm (see 3.14). A rest is silent and *always* part of the rhythmic pattern.

• All **meter** (see Glossary) is determined by what you *feel, not what you see.* To later recognize meter, learners must have a feel for the microbeat organization, so they can eventually layer a spoken rhythmic syllable association (see 3.15). *Tempo does not affect meter.*

• When rhythm or word syllables are presented before learners are secure in steady beat, they may not develop *feel* of beat, and the timing foundation can be insecure. Word rhythms then serve only as an immediate solution or band-aid to the rhythmic problem and may result in developing only a narrow understanding for that particular selection (see 3.16) The link should be made to *feel.* Once children feel the macrobeat and can identify it through consistent rocking or patting to the music, they can begin to echo spoken rhythms and focus on divisions of beat. Begin by using a *neutral syllable* (ba), so focus stays on the rhythm *pattern* to be echoed. Beginning examples for echoing rhythm in duple and triple meter are shown in Inserts 3.17 and 3.18, pp. 42–43.

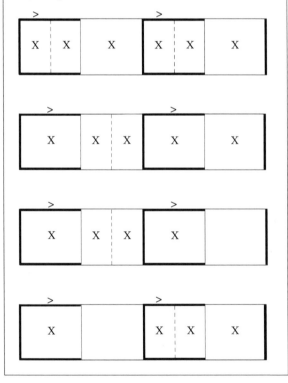

3.14

Movement and Rhythm

Pat the microbeat, and have students echo simple rhythm patterns such as these:

Use of Rhythm Syllables

Two systems of rhythm syllables presently used create a bridge to ♩ and ♫ rhythmic notation.

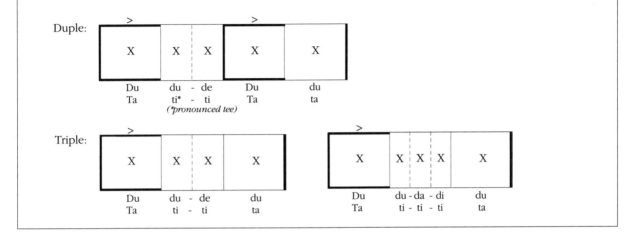

Developing the music concepts of **beat, melody,** and **rhythm** within the "primary learning center" through active learning experiences places movement at the very core of a young child's personal construction of knowledge and skills. When learners are guided to reflect on their movement experiences in meaningful ways, the resulting knowledge becomes very powerful indeed.

The Classroom as an Environment for Music Learning

Music learning can and should occur spontaneously throughout the daily schedule. The day can begin and end with an appropriate song led by a class volunteer. A classical selection can be inserted whenever the teacher or student feels the class will benefit by listening to it, or it can be used as quiet background music for reading or other independent study. But consistent learning through the music key experiences can best occur when planned segments of time for movement and music are written into

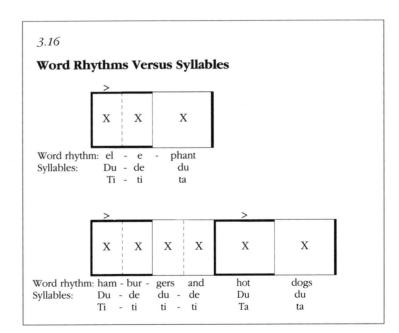

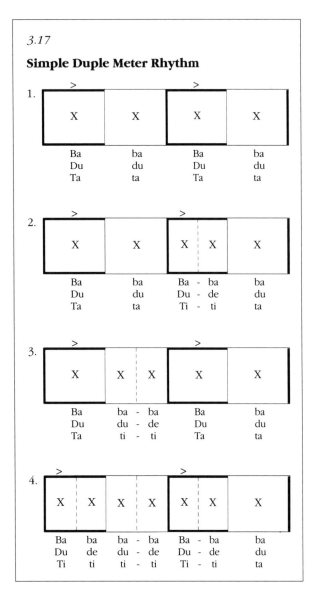

3.17

Simple Duple Meter Rhythm

1.

| X | X | X | X |

Ba	ba	Ba	ba
Du	du	Du	du
Ta	ta	Ta	ta

2.

| X | X | X X | X |

Ba	ba	Ba - ba	ba
Du	du	Du - de	du
Ta	ta	Ti - ti	ta

3.

| X | X X | X | X |

Ba	ba - ba	Ba	ba
Du	du - de	Du	du
Ta	ti - ti	Ta	ta

4.

| X X | X X | X X | X |

Ba	ba	ba - ba	Ba - ba	ba
Du	de	du - de	Du - de	du
Ti	ti	ti - ti	Ti - ti	ta

the daily schedule for the whole class (See the K–3 sample schedules, 3.19–3.23, p. 44).

Scheduling for Music

Teachers will find that time set aside each day for everyone to participate in movement and music activities and to sing together will do much to create a positive learning environment and will strengthen the singing and coordination of all. In kindergarten and first grade, it is essential that 30 minutes be set aside each day for movement and music activities with the total class. The music key experiences have been developed with this time block in mind. Supplementary music activities should be included where appropriate in language, math, science, social studies, computers, and art. Songs to begin and end the day, and songs or musical movement activities for transitions, are needed by everyone.

The grade 3 sample schedule for music shows a shared time block with science and social studies. Learners need *no less than two* weekly music periods, with the understanding that music activities are also woven into the academic areas when appropriate. In particular, part of the physical education time block should definitely include music and movement activities.

The 30-minute daily music period could be used for small music workshops occasionally when applicable, and certainly the daily plan-do-review period will be used by learners who choose to work on an individual music project.

High/Scope classrooms use flexible seating and room arrangements that facilitate three types of musical activities occurring within the daily schedule: whole-class activities, teacher-led or independent small workshops, and independent activities. Please study the sample room diagrams (see 3.24–3.26, pp. 45–46) for arrangements that are being employed in various classrooms currently. Computers may already be a part of the classroom environment; if so, the only new consideration will be where to locate the **music center (music activity area)**—for storage of music materials and for musical plan-do-review

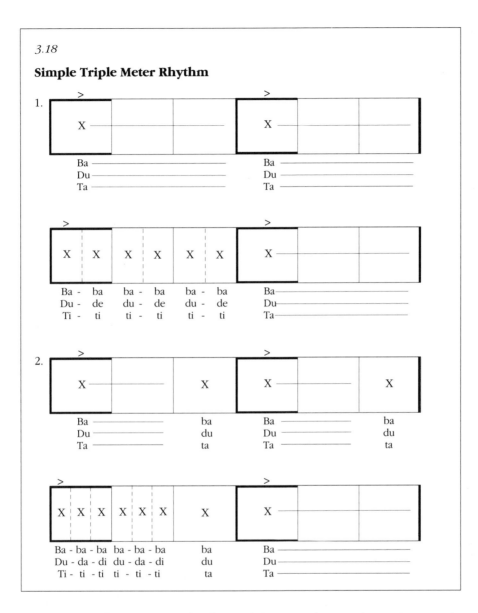

3.18

Simple Triple Meter Rhythm

projects. Units that can act as dividers and that provide room for storing materials on either side create a good sound buffer between the music area and other activity areas.

Materials and Equipment for the Music Activity Area

The following materials are essential to any K–3 music activity area:

- One or two tape recorders with headsets
- Prerecorded individual tape selections such as Phyllis S. Weikart's **Rhythmically Moving 1–9** series of recordings (see Chapter 5, p. 64)
- High-quality classical selections on cassette tapes
- Assorted good-quality rhythm instruments
- Autoharp and tuning cassette, or guitar, if teacher plays
- Simple autoharp song books

(continued on page 46)

3.19

Half-Day Kindergarten Sample Schedule

8:30 – 8:50	Opening/circle (include opening song)	10:30 – 11:00	Outside play/snack/physical education
8:50 – 9:30	Plan–do–review	11:00 – 11:30	Music/story
9:30 – 10:30	Language/math workshop	11:30	Song & Dismissal

3.20

Full-Day Kindergarten Sample Schedule

8:30 – 9:00	Opening/circle (include opening song)
9:00 – 9:45	Plan-do-review
9:45 – 10:45	Language/math workshop
10:45 – 11:15	Music & movement
11:15 – 11:45	Lunch
11:45 – 12:00	Prepare for outside
12:00 – 12:30	Outside play
12:30 – 1:00	Circle or theme activity
1:00 – 1:40	All read/write
1:40 – 2:00	Physical education
2:00 – 2:20	Story
2:20	Song & dismissal

3.21

First-Grade Sample Schedule

8:30 – 8:50	Opening (include song)
8:50 – 9:20	Music
9:20 – 10:30	Math workshop
10:30 – 10:45	Story time
10:45 – 11:10	Whole group reading
	* Music and movement transition needed
11:10 – 12:10	Language workshop
12:10 – 12:35	Lunch
12:35 – 1:05	Science/social studies
1:05 – 1:35	Physical education
1:35 – 2:50	Plan-do-review
2:50	Song & dismissal

3.22

Second-Grade Sample Schedule

8:10 – 8:30	Opening (include song)
8:30 – 9:00	Music
9:00 – 9:30	Science/social studies
9:30 – 10:15	Math workshop
	* Music & movement transition needed
10:15 – 11:05	All read
11:05 – 11:35	Physical education
11:35 – 11:55	Calendar and wash-up
11:55 – 12:25	Lunch
	* Music & movement transition needed
12:25 – 12:45	Story time
12:45 – 1:45	Language workshop
1:45 – 2:50	Plan-do-review
2:50	Song & dismissal

3.23

Third-Grade Sample Schedule

8:30 – 8:55	Opening (include song)
8:55 – 9:55	Math workshop
9:55 – 10:05	Music transition
10:05 – 10:40	Physical education
10:40 – 12:20	Language workshop
12:20 – 1:05	Lunch
1:05 – 1:45	Music/science/social studies
1:45 – 2:50	Plan-do-review
2:50	Song & dismissal

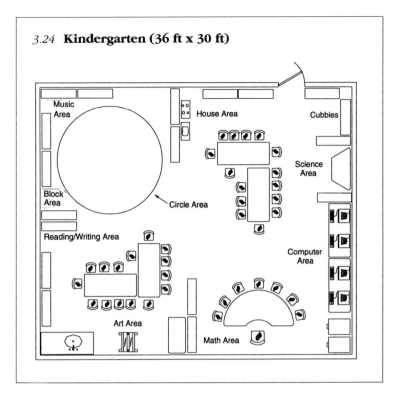

3.24 **Kindergarten (36 ft x 30 ft)**

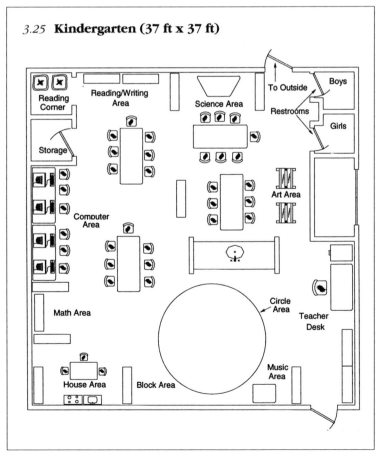

3.25 **Kindergarten (37 ft x 37 ft)**

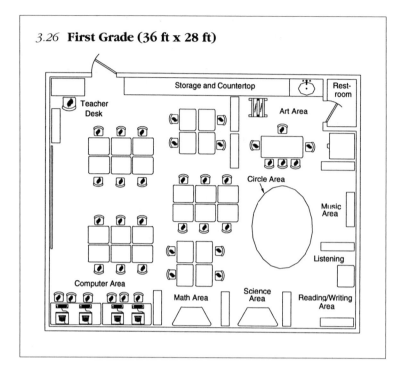

3.26 First Grade (36 ft x 28 ft)

- One electronic keyboard with headset (range of four octaves, regular-sized keys)
- Writing materials for individual projects, song lists, and graphs
- Manipulatives for work with musical concepts—various types that are already used in the classroom, or those mentioned in Chapter 7

Optional music materials include the following:
- Blank tapes for individuals to record original songs
- Compact disc player
- Compact discs, for example, *Rhythmically Moving 1–9* discs
- High-quality children's song collections on cassette tapes
- High-quality teacher-selected listening examples on cassette tapes
- One additional electronic keyboard with headset (range of four octaves, regular-sized keys)
- Resonator bells (three octaves)
- A few music books, mainly for teacher use
- High-quality computer software for music

It is advantageous to purchase top-quality instruments, which must be properly stored to increase their useful life.

Summary

In every "Music Methods for Classroom Teachers" course that we teach, this "positive-thinking" proverb sets the tone and presents the final challenge to our students.

One, two, whatever you do.
Start it right and carry it through

With such a positive attitude, which is *caught,* not *taught,* and with implementation of the active learning approach described in this book, teachers can help develop the musical intelligence inherent in each child. Part 2 of this book contains vital information about the three broad categories of music key experiences. Each key experience category is further explained, as is each specific key experience (Chapters 5, 6, 7) and each point of emphasis (accent) within each key experience. This is followed by classroom-tested active learning experiences (Chapter 8) and assessment (Chapter 9).

ENDNOTES

[1] T. Armstrong, *In Their Own Way* (Los Angeles: Jeremy P. Tarcher, Inc., 1987), p. 72.

[2] T. Armstrong, pp. 85–86.

[3] T. Armstrong, p. 86.

[4] G. C. Nash, *Creative Approaches to Child Development With Music, Language, and Movement* (Port Washington, NY: Alfred Publishing, 1974), p. 20.

[5] D. J. Coulter, *Why Children Need Music* (Longmont, CO: Kindling Touch Publishing), Tapes 1, 2, and 3.

[6] E. Gordon, *Learning Sequences in Music* (Chicago: GIA Publishing, 1984), Chapter 4.

[7] E. Gordon, *Learning Sequences,* Chapter 4.

Part 2 Key Experiences in Music

Chapter 4

Music Key Experiences: A Process-Oriented Approach to Learning

The energy that keeps a child's foot tapping, that paints purple leaves on a pink tree, that ranges freely in an open world of the imagination, will bring to our society a vitality that will energize any corner in which it finds itself.

Kenneth T. Derr
Chief Executive Officer
Chevron U.S.A.

T he key experiences in music are *an integral part of High/Scope's philosophy to educate the whole child.* As discussed in Part 1, the key experiences are designed to be a blueprint for educators to use in recognizing and encouraging important musical processes and activities in the K–3 classroom. The key experiences are developmentally sequenced and are designed to enable both student-initiated and teacher-initiated learning to occur. Key experiences are described in terms of **actions performed by learners,** for true learning at this age naturally requires activity. These essential experiences in learning support the development of specific, observable processes or outcomes that are relevant to a learner's understanding of the particular concept being studied. As a result, each learner has an opportunity to construct a knowledge-base under the guidance of and in partnership with a caring, supportive teacher.

The various key experiences may be introduced in whole-class activities, in small-group workshops, or in children's individual activities arising out of the plan-do-review process. Classroom teachers are the catalysts. As children explore and experiment with activities involved with the various music key experiences, they will develop individual competencies while constructing the essential knowledge-base needed for musical literacy and personal satisfaction. Learners will identify, compare, discriminate, internalize, reflect on, improvise, and show ownership of the concepts they encounter as they sing and listen to music. Through these processes, each child begins to construct his or her personal music knowledge. Eventually, the child's expanding abilities will provide the confidence needed to create, read, and write music, and to perform alone and with others. In addition, teachers will discover the importance of incorporating singing, playing instruments, and listening and moving to music into other areas such as mathematics, language arts, social studies, science, and physical education.

The music key experiences provide a framework for identifying the types of *active learning* opportunities each child needs in order to construct an understanding of and competence in the various musical elements. Chapter 8 describes in detail some specific, teacher-tested activities that are active learning opportunities and relates them to individual key experiences. Because children learn according to their individual stages of development, *daily musical experiences* are needed. Daily experiences help children learn to sing and play with increasing competence and to listen, create, and discover with delight. Throughout the daily musical experiences, teachers can use a variety of techniques to encourage communication—adopting a divergent questioning style, commenting on performances, and asking questions that children can answer with either their speaking or singing voices. Teachers need to provide an opportunity for children to discuss their music discoveries, both in small and in large groups. The music key experiences reinforce and extend the traditional musical experiences that were once easily available to children through family, church, and community life. Today, when children's access to these sources of musical experience may be more limited, the classroom teacher plays an especially vital role in providing relevant musical experiences.

Music and movement provide essential bridges to creativity, communication, and understanding.

The Importance of the Classroom Teacher

A knowledgeable and sensitive teacher can help children grow and develop through music. Supportive teachers enable learners to extend their abilities from singing and playing a simple accompaniment with a rhythm instrument to writing original melodies. The teacher's enthusiasm and love for music exhibited during music activities are paramount. Even without formal training, the classroom teacher can support children in important musical active learning, while parents or the music specialist can be invited to enrich specific areas of musical interest. Young children model the love and joy they see exhibited by adults who value and participate in relevant musical experiences. Children admire those who play a musical instrument well, and they should have opportunities to observe musicians as they play many different types of instruments. The objectives of the key experiences in music will be reached if children have frequent opportunities to listen to music, to sing, to play instruments, to create, and to *move* to music.

Combining Music and Movement

As discussed in Part 1, children need extensive opportunities to move to music. Movement activities activate the kinesthetic mode of learning, which is a naturally strong and important mode for the K–3 child. Movement also physically stimulates the child's vestibular system, which is vital in controlling balance and coordination, and it helps to develop the neural pathways, which are necessary for later cognitive processing. Active involvement through movement representation and through using hand percussion instruments (such as the wood block or finger cymbals) enables students to understand and make connections within and among the various music concepts (see 4.1).

Music and movement are everywhere in a child's world. A knowledgeable, supportive teacher can use movement to support the important cognitive and social abilities emerging during the K–3 years. A teacher who is aware of the normal motor-development cycle will engage children in developmentally appropriate, beat-coordinated activities and experiences that incorporate child choice and develop the "inner anchor" of beat. Contrived movement sequences or rhythmic responses that are not developmentally sound for this age-group will not build a firm foundation for strength, balance, coordination, and space awareness. Instead, children develop "splinter skills" in music and movement (see 4.2), which may inhibit their development of valuable cognitive and aesthetic insights. Movement activities can be designed to encourage and enhance High/Scope's active learning approach.

Using Key Experiences to Promote Active Learning

The music key experiences should not be thought of as something to be "taught" in a music period by a music specialist. Instead, activities embodying the music key experiences may begin and end the school day; provide smooth transitions from one subject to another; reinforce concepts in math, science, and language arts; help with dramatic interpretations of stories and other creative music

4.1

Representing Music With Movement

While Karen plays the wood block in a slow steady beat, the other children in the class listen. When ready, each child expresses his or her own representation of that sound through movement. Some jump; some pound their fists in the air; David moves like a robot. After several children describe how they have moved, Karen plays the wood block again. Class members move in the way that they choose to represent this sound.

Wendy plays the finger cymbals, and classmates listen, think, and move in the way each feels best represents this new sound. They describe the sustained "ching." Several demonstrate their movement ideas. They try out one another's ideas and each tell a partner how they plan to move.

The students move to the sounds of the wood block, then to the finger cymbals' sound. Kevin volunteers to be the director; then, Karen, Wendy, and Kevin hide behind the teacher's desk, as Kevin directs the players, to see if the game can become more challenging.

4.2

Splinter Skill Examples

1. When children play a repeated rhythmic pattern (such as the one shown below) taught by rote in grade 1 to accompany *Jingle Bells*, it may sound fine, but the players may not have made the cognitive rhythmic connection to be able to transfer this pattern to other songs.

>			>		
X	X	X	X	X	X

2. A preschooler may be taught to perform a repeated rhythm pattern (dancing a rhythmic sequence), but the foundation in beat may not be present to secure these rhythms.

interpretations; and develop a bond of trust between teachers and students. Music activities can be made available as one of the work-time options, and specific experiences relating to music concepts may be introduced during small-group workshops. Music also should have its own identified time within the day. Encourage students to become leaders in music activities, so they may learn to build on their developing musical abilities. Provide opportunities for children to perform at times other than special program times; learners can seize the moment to sing or play instruments as they create and perform for one another in various classroom settings.

During the daily music period, teachers will need to introduce and support activities in which children can initiate their own experiences involving the elements of music. Repeated experiences are as necessary in music as in all other areas of the curriculum. A child will not improve in listening, singing, moving to music, playing instruments, or leading a class song unless many comfortable, appropriate, and satisfying learning opportunities are provided and supported by teachers who value the immense influence music has on our lives.

The High/Scope key experiences in music are grouped into three broad categories: **(I) Exploring Music, (II) Using the elements of Music, and (III) Creating and Performing Music.**

Each category contains several key experiences, each representing a specific process or activity that is important to a child's overall musical development. Each key experience, in turn, contains a sequential list of four or more observable outcomes that children will show progress in during the K–3 years. We call these outcomes **accents** (denoted by the symbol >) to draw attention to their importance within each key experience. Since *accent* is a musically significant term (meaning "greater emphasis on a note or chord within a musical phrase"), its use in this music key experience context is particularly appropriate. The key experience accents are all interrelated. Just as individual music *interests* develop along a continuum that parallels other broad areas of learning, so will individual music *abilities* develop along a continuum. The pace of development will depend on each student's unique strengths and on the time and support he or she is given to encourage individuality in thinking and expression. Concluding this chapter is a list of the key experiences (marked **O⊷**) within each of the three broad categories. Listed under each key experience are its accents.

Meaningful movement experiences and manipulative aids have enabled students to confidently represent their understanding of line and space notes (left photo) as well as high and low notes (right photo).

The next three chapters present in detail the three general categories of music key experiences: Chapter 5 is "Exploring Music"; Chapter 6 is "Using the Elements of Music"; and Chapter 7 is "Creating and Performing Music." The key experiences within each category are discussed, along with specific elements, accents, and concepts. Chapter 8 provides numerous activities to support and help develop an understanding of the accents within each key experience. The activities in Chapter 8 are designed to help classroom teachers build a comprehensive music program based on each child's prior musical abilities. Chapter 9 includes a teacher-observation checklist for assessing student progress. These chapters, together with the book's appendixes, are all the tools necessary to translate your learners' musical blueprints into joyful, relevant musical experiences.

Music is powerful! Teachers, as musical architects, can provide more experiences in integrated learning through music than may at first be evident, because music affects all of us personally all of the time. From the wake-up music of the clock or radio, to the soothing music that lulls us to sleep at night, from the original tunes that we whistle, to the symphony concerts that dazzle us, music is powerful. It is at the core of a young child's being. Music is a natural language, begging to be activated. As the academic guide for your students this year, you now have in your hands a multifaceted, multicultural, irresistible aid to reaching every single learner's sensitivity to music. You will find relevant ways to incorporate music's many attributes into the school day and to encourage those who can to continue to pursue their natural interest through further study of special instruments, such as the piano or guitar.

> *All things shall perish from under the sky,*
> *Music alone shall live, never to die.*
> Text, German round

The Music Key Experiences

I. Exploring Music *(Chapter 5)*

A. *Moving to music*
> 1. Responding to different types of music
> 2. Using nonlocomotor and locomotor movements with music
> 3. Using coordination skills in performing action songs
> 4. Illustrating expressive and dynamic qualities of a musical selection
> 5. Moving to phrases of a musical selection

B. *Exploring and identifying sounds*
> 1. Making sounds with voices and instruments (musical and otherwise)
> 2. Working with percussion and melodic instrument sounds
> 3. Exploring sounds to fit with specific songs
> 4. Exploring lower/higher and same/different sounds

C. *Exploring instruments*
> 1. Trying out ways to play instruments
> 2. Discovering ways to play percussion, harmonic, and melodic instruments
> 3. Discovering pitch range and labeling the sound quality of instruments
> 4. Playing melodic phrases and known songs

D. *Exploring the singing voice*
> 1. Making pitched sounds
> 2. Exploring the singing and speaking voice
> 3. Exploring the broad range of the singing voice
> 4. Initiating singing alone and singing in tune with others

E. *Listening to and describing music*
> 1. Recognizing music versus sound
> 2. Talking about voices and instruments heard or the feelings expressed in the music
> 3. Identifying previously heard or sung musical selections
> 4. Discussing the type or style of the music

II. Using the Elements of Music *(Chapter 6)*

A. *Feeling and expressing steady beat*
> 1. Moving to one's own steady beat
> 2. Matching someone else's steady beat
> 3. Matching the steady beat of recorded music, songs, rhymes
> 4. Performing single nonlocomotor movements to the steady beat

> 5. Performing single locomotor movements to the steady beat
> 6. Playing instruments in steady beat
> 7. Combining nonlocomotor and locomotor movement to the steady beat

⊶ **B. *Identifying tone color***

> 1. Distinguishing different persons' singing and speaking voices
> 2. Hearing the differences in voices and percussion instruments
> 3. Distinguishing the different instrument sounds
> 4. Matching an instrument's sound with its picture
> 5. Identifying voices and instruments heard in a recording
> 6. Identifying special characteristics of tone color within the music

⊶ **C. *Developing melody***

> 1. Identifying higher and lower pitches
> 2. Identifying the direction of the melody (upward/downward)
> 3. Matching intervals and repeated pitches
> 4. Imitating three- and four-note melody patterns
> 5. Distinguishing *same* and *different* in short melody patterns
> 6. Responding to the shape of the melody
> 7. Identifying and singing phrases in the melody
> 8. Recognizing patterns and sequences in melodies
> 9. Singing and shaping phrases and songs

⊶ **D. *Labeling form***

> 1. Identifying the beginning and end of a song or rhyme
> 2. Identifying the verse and chorus of a song
> 3. Identifying same and different phrases
> 4. Identifying and responding to the different sections of recorded music
> 5. Labeling and using AB, ABA, and ABC forms
> 6. Labeling and using rondo form and simple theme and variations form

⊶ **E. *Recognizing the expressive qualities of tempo and dynamics***

> 1. Identifying *slow* and *fast* through movement and vocabulary
> 2. Identifying *loud* and *soft* through movement and vocabulary
> 3. Identifying *slow, medium,* and *fast* through movement and vocabulary
> 4. Identifying *loud, medium,* and *soft* through movement and vocabulary

> 5. Identifying *getting faster* and *getting slower*

> 6. Identifying *getting louder* and *getting softer*

> 7. Selecting suitable dynamics and tempo for a song or instrumental piece

F. *Feeling and Identifying Meter*

> 1. Identifying and moving with macrobeats and microbeats

> 2. Identifying same and different meter

> 3. Identifying and moving to duple meter

> 4. Identifying and moving to triple meter

> 5. Differentiating between duple and triple meter

G. *Expressing rhythm*

> 1. Listening for longer and shorter sounds

> 2. Moving to sounds of longer and shorter duration

> 3. Moving to rhythm patterns

> 4. Distinguishing same and different rhythm patterns

> 5. Recognizing and playing even and uneven rhythm patterns

> 6. Reading, writing, and performing rhythm patterns

> 7. Recognizing and using note and rest values (quarter, two-eighth, half, dotted half, and whole)

H. *Adding harmony*

> 1. Recognizing the difference between unison singing and singing accompanied by instrument(s)

> 2. Using chords to create harmony

> 3. Singing call-response and echo songs

> 4. Adding melodic chants

> 5. Singing rounds

> 6. Finding and using ways to add harmony to a song or instrumental selection

III. Creating and Performing Music *(Chapter 7)*

A. *Responding to various types of music*

> 1. Showing through movement the differences heard in music

> 2. Responding to *same/different* in songs children sing

> 3. Responding to *same/different* in instrumental music

> 4. Responding to different moods of a musical selection

> 5. Responding to a repertoire of different types of music

B. *Playing instruments alone and in groups*

> 1. Playing an instrument alone or in a group, using steady beat

> 2. Playing an instrument in steady beat while others sing

> 3. Playing an instrument in steady beat while singing alone

> 4. Playing an instrument in a rhythm pattern

> 5. Playing instruments together using rhythm patterns

> 6. Creating and planning instrument parts for a song or ensemble

○━ C. *Singing alone and in groups*

> 1. Singing simple songs alone and with others
> 2. Singing a short solo phrase during a call-response song or a single verse when the class sings chorus
> 3. Singing songs of increasing length and difficulty with others
> 4. Singing a solo with musical competence and confidence

○━ D. *Sharing music by performing*

> 1. Creating and singing a new verse to a known song
> 2. Creating and sharing an instrumental piece on percussion or melodic instruments
> 3. Playing a musical instrument while the group sings
> 4. Sharing songs created by students
> 5. Sharing an instrumental ensemble created by students

○━ E. *Moving creatively and choreographing movement sequences and dances*

> 1. Moving creatively alone or with a group
> 2. Creating movements and variations for a specific musical selection
> 3. Creating and using different movements for AB music
> 4. Creating patterns and moving creatively
> 5. Planning and using different movement and dance sequences for a specific song or recording

○━ F. *Creating and improvising songs and instrumental music*

> 1. Choosing instruments to play and accompany
> 2. Creating simple melodies vocally
> 3. Creating simple melodies on instruments
> 4. Improvising a variation on a melody, vocally and/or instrumentally
> 5. Creating an instrumental piece with two or more sections (AB)
> 6. Creating an original song with words

○━ G. *Reading music*

> 1. Reading one's own symbol system (icons) for rhythm *or* pitch
> 2. Reading melody or rhythm maps created by oneself or others
> 3. Reading short rhythmic and melodic phrases (conventional notation) and short songs
> 4. Reading conventional notation for simple songs

○━ H. *Writing music*

> 1. Showing a way to represent long/short sounds, high/low pitches, or repeated sounds (rhythm and/or melody maps)
> 2. Showing a way to represent part of a melody
> 3. Writing music using one's own symbol system (icons)
> 4. Using conventional notation to represent a phrase or short song

Chapter 5

Exploring Music

Ars longa, vita brevis: art is long, life is short . . . . Art alone endures; it is the highest form of human expression; and it is accessible to everyone. Even though most of us cannot perform as Beethoven, Leonardo, Sophocles, or Picasso did, we can appreciate and participate in their accomplishments.

David T. Kearns
Former Chairman and Chief Executive Officer
Xerox Corporation

Music is an art form created from sounds organized in relation to time. Because children are naturally curious and responsive to music, exploration of sounds, songs, and instruments should form a natural part of their learning. Carl Orff, German composer and music educator, observed that a young child uses his or her voice in conjunction with movement. He came to the conclusion that music, singing, and movement are inseparable components in the music education of the child. Teachers and parents have frequently noted that children playing alone often accompany their play with singing.

In fact, a child's musical exploration begins before birth. It is known that during the last trimester of pregnancy, the fetus responds to sounds through movement. Mothers-to-be often relate that the unborn baby is more active when music is sung or played. Once the child is born, this natural response to musical experiences continues. Infants who are held and rocked to music not only are calmed but also are developing the important early link between hearing and feeling. Singing between the mother, or any significant caregiver, and the child creates a powerful bond of security (see 5.1). Children sing before they speak, as they prepare their vocal cords for lifelong use (see 5.2). An early exposure to good music is important for the child's lifelong appreciation for and involvement in music. Lyle Davidson, in *The Young Child and Music,* stated, "Surprisingly, perhaps, the level that children reach by age 6 or 7 may represent a peak in normal musical development. That peak, for most people, may not be developed further."[1] The family that sings together, or that values the significance of music, exerts a very important influence on the child.

The changes that have occurred in society and within the family structure have had a direct impact on children's early music experiences. Today's parents and caregivers are sometimes too busy to recognize the importance of incorporating music experiences into a young child's life. Indeed, the stress of daily life impacts in more ways than we realize, for adults often find it difficult to sing after a stressful day at the office. In addition, music on radio and TV,

Singing: A Parent-Child Bond

When Wesley was a newborn, his father composed a lullaby for him. Throughout the lullaby, Wesley Hayden's name is sung. Wesley's parents established a nightly routine that concluded with the singing of Wesley's song as they rocked him to sleep. Now, no matter where they are at Wesley's bedtime, when Wesley hears his lullaby, he relaxes and settles down to sleep.

Infant Singing

Vocal exploration in the "babble" stage includes the infant's imitations of the "fluid/amorphous" singing and leads to two definite pitches the infant uses for "mama," "bobo," "dada," etc. The first pitch is higher than the second.

combined with normal sounds in the home, often creates such an overload of sounds that young children tune out, failing to build important listening and singing skills. As children get older they often do not have as many opportunities to engage in free play with peers; many of children's two- or three-note songs originate with free play— while children are swinging, bouncing a

Songs Arising From Children's Play

I'm swing-ing by my-self, by my-self, by my-self.

Bub - ble - gum, bub - ble - gum in a dish

How man - y pie - ces do you wish?

ball, or jumping rope with others (see 5.3). Many of the musical groups older children listen to do not model the type of singing and playing that foster solid musicianship. All too often, young children enter school lacking sufficient musical exploration, attention, and development. Therefore, it is especially important that young children have an opportunity to explore music freely in the classroom and that teachers introduce children to a wide array of music experiences.

The Key Experiences Included in Exploring Music

The first of the three broad categories in the High/Scope K–3 music curriculum is **exploring music,** which incorporates the following key experiences:

- Moving to music
- Exploring and identifying sounds
- Exploring instruments
- Exploring the singing voice
- Listening to and describing music

These key experiences help build the foundation for the child's initial comprehension of music through active participation. Classroom teachers will find that their guidance in music exploration activities provides opportunities for child-initiated experiences in a safe, supportive, interactive environment. *Exploring* implies that learning is an experience shared by teacher and child, that questions are welcome, that discoveries will be made, and that each learner's ideas will be considered and discussed.

Repeated activities related to the five key experiences in **exploring music** provide a firm foundation for developing the basic musicianship that each child needs for a lifelong involvement in and appreciation of music. Remember that *many and varied* experiences exploring basic music concepts are necessary if children are to understand and own the concepts. Because music is abstract, consisting mainly of sounds that exist only in the young child's memory, repeated experiences are necessary for the concepts to be understood and used. For example, children learn to sing by imitating a song. Once they have sung the song, it exists only in their memories. Nothing concrete remains.

The five key experiences in **exploring music** are discussed in this chapter. Following a short introduction to each key experience is a sequence of four or more *accents* (marked with >) showing the broad range of explorations that are possible for K–3 learners. Each child will bring his or her individual strengths, learning style, and preferences to each experience and will therefore progress in music at a unique pace. Observing the child's natural development will enable the teacher to assess and chart progress and thus provide parents with important information about the development of the child's musical intelligence, which is vital in the education of the whole child. A range of appropriate active learning experiences for exploring music with the K–3 learner are included in Chapter 8. These active learning experiences are designed to enable the teacher to observe student outcomes and effectively plan and guide sequential music experiences.

⌐ Moving to Music

Children need opportunities to use movement to freely express their thoughts and feelings about the music they are listening to or are singing (see 5.4). The movement enhances the exploration, develops attentive listening and thinking, and enriches the environment for all. In addition, moving to music develops children's ability to become better coordinated, improves their awareness of personal and general space, and increases their self-confidence as they volunteer to take the lead in sharing their movement ideas with others. As teachers guide those explorations, they begin to help each child develop ideas about the elements of a musical selection, such as its melody, **form** (see Glossary), tempo, style, and **dynamics** (see Glossary). Children can be encour-

Moving to music daily strengthens the child's musical- kinesthetic-cognitive link.

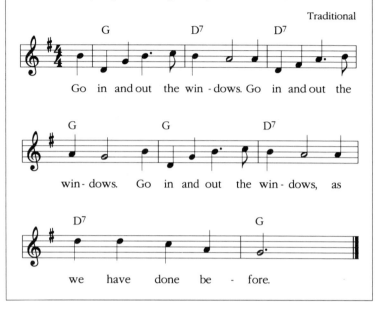

5.4

Go In and Out the Windows

Children freely express feeling as they move in and out.

Traditional

Go in and out the win-dows. Go in and out the

win-dows. Go in and out the win-dows, as

we have done be-fore.

aged to create their own songs and accompanying instrument sounds for their movement, as well as to create movement games. Their ideas can be shared and discussed in small groups or with the total group. Listening, feeling, and moving all affect children's ability to sing in tune and develop tonal memory, which includes the ability to remember pitched sounds.

The accents following each of the five key experiences in **exploring music** are sequenced for the K–3 learner. Each accent should be introduced with a range of musical examples. From the activities chosen, the teacher can observe the degree of proficiency each child has achieved.

Reading through the activities in Chapter 8 will help you to implement this key experience. The activities are planned with the classroom teacher in mind, so that what is initiated through music will be meaningful for the child.

> **Responding to different types of music.** As young children listen to music, they intuitively respond to the different types of music with distinctive movements. For example, when listening to Sousa's *Washington Post* march, they usually respond by marching or pretending to play an instrument; when a selection such as *Jimbo's Lullaby* from Debussy's *Children's Corner Suite* is played, children's responses are usually quite different. Folk songs evoke yet other kinds of responses while also increasing children's appreciation for different languages, instruments, and dances. The nine **Rhythmically Moving** recordings (RM1–RM9), compiled by Phyllis S. Weikart and published by High/Scope Press, provide beautiful short listening-selections. These selections increase the learner's appreciation and identification of musical elements and instruments. They also provide the teacher with many musical examples for introducing movement in steady beat for all ages, as well as folk dances for grades 2 and 3. There are many other high-quality recordings of various kinds of music that are suitable for use with young children (see the list in Appendix C). Using the **Rhythmically Moving** recordings or other selections from Appendix C as your starting point, plan to have young learners listen and respond to a musical selection for at least a few minutes each day.

Movement with objects (in this case, pretending to steer a car around the room) develops children's space and time awareness.

> **Using nonlocomotor and locomotor movements with music.** Children can use both **nonlocomotor** and **locomotor movements** to explore steady beat, musical phrases, and dynamics and to show their interpretation of the mood of a musical selection. Nonlocomotor movements (which are anchored movements performed in one's own space, with no full weight transfers) include twisting, bending and straightening, swinging, punching, and turning circles with wrist or arm. Locomotor movements (which are nonanchored movements performed in one's own space or in general space, *with* full weight transfers) include marching, jumping, galloping, hopping, and skipping. Through both types of movement, young children develop an awareness of space, language, and time, as well as an awareness of what motions various parts of the body are capable of. When music is added, the use of imagery also becomes a delightful addition to the movement.

When listening to a given selection, older children can explore nonlocomotor and locomotor movements for each melody they hear. For example, they can explore movements for the two melodies heard in *Salty Dog Rag* (RM9). Let children take a leadership role in planning appropriate movement ideas as they explore nonlocomotor or locomotor movement in different musical forms (such as AB, ABA, and rondo ABACA; see 5.5). As children explore, individuals can share their movement ideas with the class, thus increasing everyone's movement potential. Locomotor movement brings to music another dimension of a child's imagination. When several children are moving at the same time, they can develop an acute awareness of space; therefore, vision, planning, and anticipation become important adult considerations. Moving in one's own space can improve timing and balance; moving around the room continues to improve these two abilities and develops space awareness and coordination.

Parades, which never lose their attraction, can be led each day by a different child exploring new pathways—straight, zigzag, curved, or random. Movement maps (see 5.6; see also Chapter 8) can be used for exploring patterns of forward and

---

5.5

Different Musical Forms

AB: Musical selection having two melodic sections

ABA: Musical selection having two melodic sections, with first melody repeated

ABACA: (Rondo) musical selection having three melodic sections, with first melody returning after each new melody

5.6

Movement Maps

Mrs. Thompson's third-grade class had already explored and performed nonlocomotor and locomotor movement to *Peat Fire Flame* (RM2). They were aware of the two melodic sections that made up the AB form. Some musically sensitive students had noticed that each melodic section repeated, so the form was truly AABB. In four groups of seven students each, the students were planning designated pathways (movement maps) to fit the musical sections.

Group 1 chose to begin with a circle formation. They walked counterclockwise to the beat of the A melody, then clockwise to the repeat of the A melody. During the B melody, they performed four scissor kicks, then walked in four steps, did four scissor kicks, and walked out four steps. They performed this movement sequence twice before returning to the first plan.

Group 2 chose to begin in a line formation, with alternate students facing opposite directions. Each student walked eight steps forward, and then eight steps backward, performing this sequence twice. Each student then performed his or her own eight-beat nonlocomotor sequence four times during the B melody.

Groups 3 and 4 planned equally original and appropriate movement sequences that used nonlocomotor, locomotor, or integrated movements. Each group's performance for Mrs. Thompson's third grade was enthusiastically received.

Using a straight diagonal pathway, these girls perform a movement map to music.

backward movement, and movement in circles or squares. Combinations of nonlocomotor and locomotor movement increase music's exploration potential, to the delight of all. It is no wonder, then, that music and movement are vital components in the education of the total child.

> **Using coordination skills in performing action songs.** Action songs are a memorable part of childhood. Once learned, the movements to *The Wheels on the Bus* or *Hokey Pokey* are unforgettable, even when it has been years since we have performed them. Part of the attraction of these types of songs lies in a group's synchroniza-

tion of movements. Effective synchronization depends on the basic timing skills of each individual in the group. Phyllis S. Weikart, in her book *Movement Plus Rhymes, Songs, and Singing Games*,[2] pointed out that an action song is more successful if children experience the motor sequence *before* the song is added. Once learned, the motor sequence can "go on automatic," allowing children to concentrate on the words and melody. Try this strategy the next time you plan to lead an action song, such as *I'm a Little Teapot* or *Pizza Hut*. (*Pizza Hut* is explained on pp. 18–19). Make a game by having the students follow your motions visually and then recall the sequence. Turn it into an active learning experience by having students choose their own motions or create new motions and new accompanying words. The results may amaze you and are sure to delight everyone.

> **Illustrating expressive and dynamic qualities of a musical selection.** Young students are remarkably imaginative in using movement to express what they feel in a musical selection. After listening to a selection, such as Saint-Saëns' *The Elephant* from *Carnival of the Animals,* encourage children to explore the movements that they feel fit the music. Guide a discussion that elicits their awareness of tempo, their feelings of slow/fast and heavy/light, and their identification of particular instruments. Movement exploration used in this way gives children room to listen and to move as personal interpreters of the music. Then, during discussion, their listening/movement responses can help express ideas that are intensely personal and relevant to the music.

Listening experiences need to be short at first and should be presented in ways that capture the children's imagination. Music, the universal language, has very special things to share with those who develop a "listening ear."

> **Moving to phrases of a musical selection.** In music, a phrase is a group of sounds that expresses an idea, much as a sentence does in language (see 5.7). Songs have phrases that are alike and phrases that are not alike (see 5.8). As children recognize this, movement to represent phrases and their differences becomes a useful quest. Once children have explored phrases of various lengths, their singing begins to show a new awareness that all music is composed of like and unlike phrases. When children listen to *The Swan* from *Carnival of the Animals,* for example, movement to represent the song's graceful phrases is an enjoyable activity. As they explore, children may use only hand

---

5.7

Identifying Musical Phrases

One useful way to identify phrases of a musical selection such as *Sliding* (RM1) is to begin with both arms straight out in front. Move one arm slowly out to the side as long as you perceive the phrase (musical thought) to last. When the second phrase begins, move the other arm in a similar fashion. Continue listening carefully and moving one arm for each phrase. As *Sliding* is played, you will be aware that each phrase repeats, and that there are three different musical phrases within this selection before the sequence begins again.

5.8

Same and Different Phrases

When singing the chorus of *Looby Loo* to identify phrases, children will discover there are four phrases. Phrases 1 and 3 are the same. Phrase 2 and phrase 4 are each different. Each child can represent this information in his or her own way. The teacher can use their individual representations as one basis for developmental assessment.

Looby Loo

Teachers and students will want to plan specific listening activities that help to expand each child's ability to discriminate aurally. The sound concepts of high/low, same/different, loud/soft, and short/long can be explored through movement, and differences can be compared in a class discussion. Children can imitate sounds heard on a field trip as well as in the classroom, sounds such as sirens, train whistles, or animal sounds. This is an exciting way to build sound identification and discrimination. Students enjoy learning to identify other classmates by the sounds of their voices. Different types of speaking and singing voices, as well as the sounds of percussion, melodic, and invented instruments, provide a range of sounds to explore. Since the size and materials used in constructing an instrument affect its sound, children can experiment with sounds that they create and use in many different ways. Encourage children to talk

movement or they may use whole-body movement; scarves may be added to the movement. Occasionally, some students may wish to work further with moving to the phrases of a particular selection during the plan-do-review process.

⊶ Exploring and Identifying Sounds

Aural discrimination is vital to musical development. The barrage of sounds that today's children are continually exposed to may be one of the causes of poor listening habits, which can result in lack of attention and inadequate response to spoken information in the classroom. Effective listening requires thought and reasoning, and achieving effective aural discrimination requires many varied experiences that prompt students to want to listen and respond.

about their experimentation and discuss answers to their questions. Many successful experiences in aural discrimination are necessary before young students can imitate a melody accurately and with pleasure.

> **Making sounds with voices and instruments (musical and otherwise).** Opportunities to explore vocal sounds as well as sounds made by nonpitched rhythm instruments (such as wood blocks and finger cymbals) should be provided during the music class. Young children discover various ways to produce sounds and then remember the special feeling that goes with a specific tone. During story time, they can add sounds to enhance the narrative (see 5.9). As their vocal skill and imagination develop, these additions can become an irresistible complement to a story. Some children will create their own stories with accompanying sounds, thus providing creative extensions to class experiences. As children become comfortable using various rhythm instruments as accompaniments to their songs and recorded music, they may want to use instrument sounds to enhance stories, much as background music enhances favorite TV programs.

Exploring the maracas (left photo) and the vibraslap (right photo), these children discover that these two nonpitched rhythm instruments can be played in many ways.

Stories to Enhance With Sound Accompaniment

"Goldilocks and the Three Bears"

"Little Red Riding Hood"

"Three Little Pigs"

"Chicken Little: The Sky Is Falling"

"The Little Old Lady Who Wasn't Afraid of Anything"
by Linda Williams

"The Cloud's Journey"
by Sis Kock and Sigrid Heuck

"The Little Engine That Could"
by Watty Piper

> Working with percussion and melodic instrument sounds. As children explore **percussion instruments** (such as drums, tambourines, and wood blocks) and **melodic instruments** (such as xylophones and keyboards), they will learn to identify each instrument by its particular sound and name. Through this type of exploration, aural-discrimination games become a challenge for all. Children can move to represent an instrument's sound and then discuss how they chose to interpret the sound. Later, movement can be keyed to each child's discriminatory response; for example, a wood block can be the designated sound for one step forward, and the triangle, the designated sound for one step backward. Students can build and extend their musical skills, reinforcing memory, movement, choices, and aural discrimination!

> Exploring sounds to fit specific songs. As they build a repertoire of songs during the year, children will enjoy accompanying their singing with non-pitched rhythm instruments. Certain songs suggest specific instruments, while cumulative songs (such as *Old MacDonald Had a Farm* or *I Bought Me a Cat*) suggest using a variety of instruments—a different one for each animal. Children can also accompany recorded music with rhythm instruments, choosing contrasting sounds when two different melodies are heard, as in *La Raspa* (RM3).

> Exploring lower/higher and same/different sounds. Once children can identify a specific melodic instrument's sounds and once they have explored its range of tones, a particular range of tones can be classified from lower to higher. In doing this, children can respond through movement as well as with vocal responses to each specific tone played. Through personal exploration of an instrument, children actively display knowledge of low/high or same/different sounds. Since children's attention will first focus on producing sounds with an instrument, they will need many opportunities to work with an instrument in order to identify same/different sounds.

Short tone games in which students are asked to identify whether two tones are the same or different can be added very easily to any music class. Each child can be given opportunities to be the leader. Regular use of tone games (see Chapter 3, p. 35) will help children develop acute listening skills while also having fun. Create a movement code for *same* and *different,* and enjoy the challenges that will follow. Simple beat-keeping accompaniments to **pentatonic songs** and **rounds** can be devised by alternately striking a low C-bell and a high C-bell for the macrobeat (see 5.10). Pentatonic melodies use scale degrees 1, 2, 3, 5, and 6 (do, re, mi, sol, la). Try this with songs such as *I Bought Me a Cat,* or *Row, Row, Row Your Boat,* or *Are You Sleeping?.*

5.10

A Pentatonic Song

This pentatonic song uses scale degrees 1, 2, 3, 5, 6, and 8 of the C-major scale.

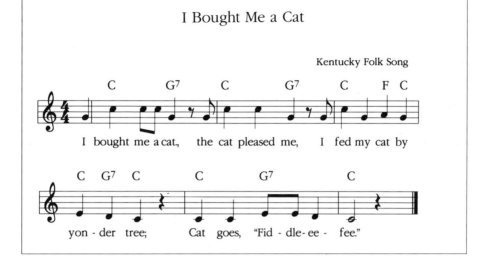

I Bought Me a Cat

Kentucky Folk Song

I bought me a cat, the cat pleased me, I fed my cat by yon - der tree; Cat goes, "Fid - dle-ee - fee."

⚷ Exploring Instruments

By the time children enter kindergarten, most of them probably have had some experience with simple musical instruments. Through exploration, they can discover various ways to create sound or pitch from an instrument. Through continued experiences and observation, they begin to understand that there is usually a preferred way to play each instrument. Children should be encouraged to invent instruments from everyday materials and containers found in their environment and to compare instrument sounds. Children can select sounds that best fit a specific type of song, such as a lullaby or a march. Children should be encouraged to play an instrument while they sing, to join with others to form simple bands, and to accompany recorded musical selections. All of these experiences stimulate musical growth. Gross- and fine-motor coordination are enhanced through exploring and playing instruments. As children have more and more experiences hearing and recognizing particular sounds, their aural discrimination is challenged and refined.

> **Trying out ways to play instruments.** Even without help, most students are quick to try out instruments and to discover ways to play them. Children need to explore playing—how loud, how fast, how soft—and they need to discover how many sounds are possible before they are ready to refine their technique. Experience and practice are necessary in order for them to play to a steady beat while singing a song. Encourage interest in discovering how instruments are made: with wood (wood blocks or log drums, rhythm sticks, and temple blocks), with shakers or rattles (tambourines and maracas), with skins (drums), or with ringers (triangles and finger cymbals). Discuss how string instruments are plucked, bowed, or strummed; how resonator bells and Orff instruments are struck with a mallet; and how keys on a keyboard are pressed down by individual fingers.

> **Discovering ways to play percussion, harmonic, and melodic instruments.** Working in pairs can help kindergartners play rhythm instruments: One child holds the triangle, drum, or tambourine while a partner strikes it. In striking an instrument, bilateral (two-hand) and alternate hand motions should be explored before a favored hand is used, since many young children may not yet have a preferred hand by age 5. Also, before the age of 7 many children are unable to inhibit movement; that is, they are not able to hold one side of their body still (holding the triangle, for example) while moving the other side (striking the triangle). Unless a partner holds the instrument, being able to inhibit movement is a necessary skill for playing many of the instruments. Therefore, children should be given the choice of working alone or with a partner. Instrument playing can be refined after age 7, when motor coordination matures through experience.

The autoharp can provide harmonic accompaniment for songs. It works well initially with partners, since one child can press the chord bar(s) while the other strums the macrobeat. Cross-hand strumming is an excellent way to help children learn to cross the midline, an important playing skill that can be further developed after age 7.

Resonator bells can be used to play part of a melody, or

A 7-year-old both holds and strikes her triangle (top photo), but two kindergartners find it easier if one holds while the other plays the drum (bottom photo).

they can be grouped to provide a chord accompaniment to a song for third-graders (see "Discovering Chords" in Chapter 8). Step bells help children understand tonal relationships. Some children, through tone games and step bells, will discover how to play familiar melodies, such as *Twinkle, Twinkle, Little Star.* A child might choose to work on such an activity during plan-do-review time. If a small keyboard with an individual headset or Orff instruments are available in the classroom, these can also be used for accompanying songs and for individual exploration of how to play melodies.

> **Discovering pitch range and labeling the sound quality of instruments.** At the same time that children are discovering how to play instruments, they become aware of **pitch range** and **sound quality.** The classroom

Tonal relationships become "real" to children as they explore high and low with step bells.

teacher or music educator can encourage children to find out about certain instruments by asking questions that require them to compare and contrast the ranges and sounds. As children talk about what they are learning and hearing, they *remember,* because they have brought their thoughts to a level of conscious awareness. Students may graph pitch ranges of instruments, an excellent task for small-group workshop time.

> **Playing melodic phrases and known songs.** Melodic instruments (keyboard, step bells, resonator bells, Orff instruments) provide fixed tones for children to work with as they "sound out" a specific instrument and its pitch range. For example, students may first find the two tones they have sung for *Rain, Rain, Go Away* and then proudly play that. The teacher can strengthen this major discovery with tone games, by singing G (scale degree 5, or sol) and then showing a static motion on the shoulders and by singing E (scale degree 3, or mi) with a static motion at the waist (see "The Body Scale" in Chapter 3). When students have copied sound and motion enough times to be comfortable, tone games begin (see "Developing Melody Through Tone Games" in Chapter 3). Children can take the lead in these tone games and will delight in the opportunity to shape, sing, or play back. From simple two-tone games, the teacher can progress to three-tone and four-tone games, and then to melodic fragments that end a song, such as the tones for "rolling home" in *This Old Man* (see 5.11).

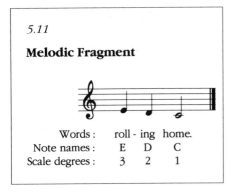

5.11

Melodic Fragment

Words :	roll - ing	home.
Note names :	E	D	C
Scale degrees :	3	2	1

Tone games should continue throughout the K–3 years to broaden children's singing range. These games also build kinesthetic and tonal relationships within a key system (key of C, key of D), making it easier to transpose a song. Students strengthen their attending skills and their aural discrimination when tone games are continued, and definite pitches then have kinesthetic tuning within a specific song. When tone games are carried out consistently, playing and singing a melodic phrase or even a simple song becomes a memorable accomplishment.

⚷ Exploring the Singing Voice

Children need a broad range of vocal experiences to understand highs and lows, to move their voices stepwise (one note at a time) from low to high, and to sing a melody consisting of tones that skip around. Through these experiences, they learn to pay attention to how tones are produced and how to differentiate between singing and speaking. Opportunities to imitate sirens, trains, machines, birds, animals, and other sounds should precede and accompany tone games involving matching pitch. Children need to sing many simple songs, to make up their own songs, and to lead songs they know (see Chapter 3, "Developing Melody in the 'Primary Learning Center'"). One child may begin a song in his or her tonal range, and then the group may join in. Because an adult's vocal comfort range is sometimes not the best vocal range for the children, it is often easier for children to follow another child's lead in singing than to follow an adult's. It is helpful for children to experience adults and other children following their lead.

Melodies that contain repetitive phrases are useful in helping children develop the ability to match pitch. Nursery songs, action songs, singing games, nonsense songs, and folk songs build a repertoire for enjoyable group singing experiences and provide the basis for creating new verses to familiar songs (see 5.12). Children must learn to hear their own voices and to realize that we each have a *singing* as well as a *speaking* voice. Songs are important for children's language development because they provide experiences that improve speech-flow and enrich vocabulary. Singing also develops the lungs and vocal cords in healthy ways.

> **Making pitched sounds.** Although children often lack experience in how to manipulate their voices to match specific tones, they will progress quickly once they understand what is expected. To match pitched sounds, children must realize that they can start with any comfortable tone, high or low, and "zoom into" the tone being sung or played. A simple game can be developed for matching tones: First, the child produces a tone for the teacher to match; then the teacher takes a turn. Eventually, the learner realizes that singing uses the "head voice," and he or she must learn to remember how that feels and sounds, so it can be found and used for all songs. Making and matching vocal sounds, combined with the tone games mentioned earlier, will help young children begin to sing with confidence.

> **Exploring the singing and speaking voice.** Young children who have not had many singing experiences may not realize that the speaking voice and

the singing voice have different functions. The teacher can help children discover this difference by using vocal explorations, singing lots of songs, and helping children to identify whether a voice is speaking or singing. A simple game that has been used with success in small groups is to have each child pronounce his or her name or favorite word and then sing that name or word in any way. By focusing on the differences heard and felt, children can learn to use their singing voices more appropriately. We cannot expect young children to sing in tune unless they have been given many opportunities to sing. (See "Sing or Speak" in Chapter 8.)

When children are able to explore and use their singing voice consistently, they develop into young singers who energetically display joy and confidence in their new-found ability.

> **Exploring the broad range of the singing voice.** As stated earlier, vocal exploration should include opportunities to imitate *environmental* sounds as well as *musical* sounds. Imitating a siren, or pretending to make "elevator sounds" when zooming from the basement to the 10th floor, will enable children with limited vocal ranges to "take" their voice from low to high. As you play this game, let the children choose where the elevator will stop, and accompany the sounds with movement. The beginning goal of this game is not so much to match the pitch for each floor as it is to explore the highs and lows of the vocal range and to provide an opportunity for each child to lead and make choices. (It also helps with control and balance as children slowly reach the basement!) Exploring ghost-like sounds, high to low, is another interesting activity. Later, this exploration can be refined by incorporating the body scale with tones 1–8, and starting or stopping on a specific floor.

> **Initiating singing alone and singing in tune with others.** A child may be able to sing *Happy Birthday to You* perfectly within his or her personal vocal range yet have trouble matching the teacher's pitch. In most cases, this indicates that the child needs more singing experiences or needs a reminder about matching the leader's pitch. Some children need to concentrate on tuning in to the pitch. When a singer feels comfortable with the song, he or she can then concentrate on matching the pitch of the leader. Repeated experiences build abilities and confidence in singing. Some children are natural song leaders and

---

5.12

Songs for Group Singing

Songs With Repetitive Phrases
> *Hokey Pokey*
> *Pizza Hut*
> *Make Your Own Music*
> *Old MacDonald Had a Farm*

Nonsense Songs
> *Polly Wolly Doodle*
> *Found a Peanut*
> *I'm a Nut*
> *Willoby Walloby Woo*

Action Songs
> *Tony Chestnut*
> *Little Cottage in the Wood*
> *Eensy Weensy Spider*
> *Six Little Ducks*

Singing Games
> *Blue Bird, Blue Bird*
> *Go In and Out the Windows*
> *Sally Go 'Round the Sun*
> *I've Been to Harlem (Turn the Glasses Over)*

need no encouragement to initiate singing. Teachers should provide opportunities for all children to lead, thus building success for everyone.

When singing in tune with others is the goal and no instrument introduction sets the beginning pitch, the teacher may find that providing the **anchor pitch** (beginning pitch) helps. The anchor pitch is sung four times, using the macrobeat and singing "One, two, ready, sing." Then all join in on the beginning pitch and sing together. The anchor pitch provides a "tonal safety net" for listening and responding and enables singers to begin the song together (see 5.13).

5.13

The Anchor Pitch

Sometimes the beginning tone of a song is something other than the tonic or scale degree 1. In that case, for example, when singing the anchor pitches for *Farmer in the Dell*, the teacher may sing scale degrees 1 and 5_1 in this order:

One, two, ready, sing, The far-mer in the dell.

⌖ Listening to and Describing Music

Active listening is an important prerequisite for understanding any musical concept. Listening can be directed to the melody, the instruments, the mood, the form, or the type of voice. The teacher's role is crucial in guiding the listening experience to help children organize their observations about what they have just heard. Open-ended questions allow students to verbalize thoughts about how the music makes them feel; what instruments were heard; or whether the music causes them to think of a story, a special season of the year, or some other important aspect of their school experiences. Live performances by classmates, guests, or parents will create a different dimension for active listening and provide additional opportunities for discussion and participation. To appreciate and value music, students need to be introduced to musical examples of enduring quality. Examples selected must be chosen for the students' level of experience and understanding. Listening is the foundation for perceiving all musical experiences and is necessary for musical growth. Listening is essential for developing auditory awareness, sequencing, memory, discrimination, and appreciation.

> **Recognizing music versus sound.** The simplest things can sometimes be the hardest to discuss! What is music to the child? Is the kindergartner's definition of music still valid in third grade? How do children differentiate between sounds and music? How is music recognized? Is a bird's call musical? Is the sound of a car horn musical? By making a list of *sounds* versus *musical sounds,* the first steps are taken toward understanding the difference. Children easily recognize songs, recordings, and various types of music; drawing their attention to what is and what is not music helps tune their ears to the world around them.

Adults or older children knowledgeable about specific instruments are usually glad to share their expertise. Here a group of children have an opportunity to learn about a melodic instrument, the clarinet, and how to blow through its mouthpiece.

> **Talking about voices and instruments heard or the feelings expressed in the music.** Young learners are quick to point out the feelings they have for the music they hear or the obvious aspects of a song being sung. Simply asking children "What did you hear?" will initiate their responses as to whether the music used only instruments or a combination of voices and instruments; whether it made them feel happy, excited, or quiet; and whether one voice or a group of singers sang the melody throughout. Children may identify

specific instruments, especially those they have had some hands-on experience with. Talking about their feelings helps children understand that music is indeed the universal language, communicating to each of us through ears, instruments, voices, thoughts, and feelings.

Starting a discussion with "I wonder what the composer wanted to express" often works well in eliciting thoughts from older students. Having the students draw during a listening session also works well if they are already familiar with the music.

> **Identifying previously heard or sung musical selections.** Much of music's magic lies in recognizing a song by its introduction or in identifying music previously heard. Being able to recognize music is a sign that musical thought and memory are developing. Although musically sensitive students will quickly identify various selections, all students can develop this ability when guided by a classroom teacher who feels it is important to incorporate many musical behaviors into each lesson. Help students recall important melodies and the stories connected with the music or places where they heard or sang a particular musical selection. Sensitivity to the sound of music and musical memory are skills worth cultivating for a lifetime.

> **Discussing the type or style of the music.** Music is so accessible to us in the twentieth century that children will need little encouragement to identify broad categories they recognize and enjoy. Their categories might include marches, lullabies, dances, songs they have sung, seasonal music, instrumentals, vocals, commercials, religious music, and background music used in children's TV programs or movies. Young learners will enjoy compiling lists of selections that fit these types of music.

As the teacher continues to guide musical growth, attention may be drawn to a specific type of music performed by large musical groups (orchestras or bands), medium-sized groups (folk groups, blues ensembles, rock bands), or small ensembles consisting of two to four performers. Examine aspects of rhythmic, melodic, harmonic, or instrumental interest. Ask open-ended questions such as these: How did you respond to the overall mood? Why? What did you like or not like about this selection? What else have we listened to that expresses the same mood? Specific stylistic qualities will be understood as children grow older, but the foundation for perceptive listening and appreciation is best laid during the K–3 years.

Summary

Exploring music will be a rewarding experience when the classroom teacher approaches it with great enthusiasm. Teach songs you know; guide the children through active learning experiences in Chapter 8; assess their ownership. The music key experiences are a framework for helping children develop a firm foundation for lifelong musical development.

ENDNOTES

[1]L. Davidson. *The Young Child and Music: Preschool Children's Tonal Knowledge: Antecedents of Scale* (Music Educators National Conference, Reston, VA, 1987), p. 25.

[2]P. S. Weikart. *Movement Plus Rhymes, Songs, and Singing Games* (Ypsilanti MI: High/Scope Press, 1988), p. 2.

Chapter 6

Using the Elements of Music

An education enriched with participation in lively arts encourages students to reach for the best within themselves. The self-esteem they develop from this experience builds the confidence to reach for the best in our society. . . . The investment in a fine arts curriculum is repaid many times over by the quality of life it fosters in the community and by the growth it encourages in our most valuable asset: our children.

William E. LaMothe
Chairman of the Board Emeritus
Chief Executive Officer
Kellogg Company

Because music is one of the natural languages that young children use to express feelings and events important to them, opportunities to use the elements of music abound throughout the K–3 years. When educators develop and facilitate growth through this natural language by including music experiences throughout the day, they reinforce the fact that music and all its elements are important not just to children's *musical* growth but also to their *overall intellectual* growth. The classroom teacher and music educator have many opportunities to help build a solid foundation for each child's emerging musical literacy as well as to increase his or her confidence in and appreciation of the art. When children are able to participate in a variety of musical activities, a treasured bond can be created between classroom teachers and students, with quality musical experiences long-remembered (see 6.1).

Regardless of the extent of their prior musical experiences, children bring natural musical abilities into the classroom. Young children like to sing and move to music. They enjoy experimenting with sounds and playing rhythm instruments. They like to add sound effects as they move about or accompany songs and stories. Listening to musical recordings and sharing ideas about what the music represents broadens the experience for all and creates in children the desire to request such listening experiences again. In addition, the social and emotional climate in the classroom is greatly enhanced when children share songs, instruments, and musical games from home. Recognizing and appreciating children's efforts to spontaneously use music gives them the needed encouragement to continue. The High/Scope educational approach emphasizes *shared learning experiences,* with both teachers and children initiating ideas for musical activities.

This chapter focuses on **using the elements of music,** the second general category in the High/Scope music curriculum. The key experiences within

An Experience to Remember

Ms. White's afternoon kindergarten class loved to sing. The majority of the children came from homes where there was little opportunity to sing or learn to play an instrument, so Ms. White often played her guitar to accompany their favorites, when they "really sang well." She quickly learned that singing or other musical activities could change her classroom climate from lethargy or rowdiness to a positive focus. She began to motivate her students with a song, *We'll Do the Best We Can Today,* which became a daily request. Individuals contributed ideas for other verses: "We're cleaning out our desks, hurray!" . . . "We're marching to the bus this way" . . . "Juanita has a birthday today" . . . "We've done a lot of work today." They brainstormed to complete the text of each new verse. The class had over 20 verses for this one melody by the end of the year! Now, years later, when students from this class bring their own children to Ms. White's class, many of them ask her, "Do you remember all the fun we had when I was in kindergarten and we made *We'll Do the Best* our song?" What is loved, valued, and *sung* is never forgotten.

We'll Do the Best We Can Today

Grace C. Nash
Used With Permission

this category are designed to introduce children to the following musical elements, which form the base from which musical literacy and proficiency are derived:

- Steady beat
- Tone color
- Melody
- Form
- Tempo
- Dynamics
- Meter
- Rhythm
- Harmony

These musical elements, which are as distinct and interesting as each individual child, combine to bring meaning to the overall music curriculum. Active experiences related to these elements, combined with individual reflection, can help build a solid foundation for success.

The Key Experiences Included in Using the Elements of Music

The following key experiences are described in this chapter:

- Feeling and expressing steady beat
- Identifying tone color
- Developing melody
- Labeling form
- Recognizing the expressive qualities of tempo and dynamics
- Feeling and identifying meter
- Expressing rhythm
- Adding harmony

Within each key experience are the various musical *accents* (marked with >), which have been designed to provide measurable outcomes. These accents can be used by teachers to become familiar with all aspects of a key experience and to build the knowledge that children need for a solid foundation in music. Although *many* experiences are needed for learning to take place, this in no way implies that drills are necessary. Rather, repeated music experiences, such as the singing of favorite songs followed by reflective questions or comments, enable important discoveries to take place.

The first step in implementing the key experiences in this chapter is to provide time for each child to freely *explore* each of the elements of music. During this exploration time, the classroom teacher can assess each child's developmental level of music understanding. Later, active learning experiences that focus on a specific musical element can be introduced during the block of time devoted to music each day. In addition, music activities can be initiated at the beginning of the day, during plan-do-review, as part of small-group time or outside time, or during transition times throughout the day. By introducing the various elements of music, classroom teachers can help each child develop an awareness and curiosity that can lead to a lifelong interest in music.

Feeling and Expressing Steady Beat

Steady beat refers to the consistent pulse that occurs throughout a rhyme, song, or recorded musical selection. As an example, the underlined syllables in the text of the following song represent the steady beat:

> *Yan*-kee *Doo*-dle *went* to *town*,
> *Rid*-ing *on* a *po-ny*.
> *Stuck* a *fea*-ther *in* his *cap* and
> *Called* it *ma*-ca-*ro-ni*.

Although the terms *beat* and *rhythm* have sometimes been used interchangeably, they actually mean very different things. While steady beat is the underlying pulse of music or speech, rhythm refers to the action *within* and *among* the beats.

While recorded music plays, one child pats his tummy to lead the group in a beat-keeping motion. In this beat-keeping game, the children take turns as leaders.

A child's ability to respond consistently and accurately to a steady beat is a reflection of his or her ability to listen and focus, or attend. Often, children will attend and keep a steady beat with their hands or feet for the first part of a rhyme or song, but they are not able to continue throughout the entire selection. In other instances, children will copy the teacher's demonstration of beat accurately, but when the teacher is no longer the model, their accuracy disappears. True competence in beat-keeping includes being able to *independently* find, feel, express, and keep the steady beat in with one's hands or feet throughout a rhyme or song (see 6.2). Success with this simple task seems to be directly related to a child's aural processing ability, that is, to how accurately he or she generally attends and responds to spoken information in the classroom.

When working with beat, the teacher will guide various activities (such as walking to various tempos) that allow children to feel the steady beat. As mentioned in Chapter 3, this regular, walking beat is the **microbeat;** there is also a beat that organizes microbeats into groups of two or three, and this is the **macrobeat,** the first beat of each of these groups (see 6.3). Calm rocking or patting motions to the macrobeat help children feel and respond with accuracy as they listen to rhymes, songs, or recorded music. Dr. Edwin Gordon developed these concepts of beat to help us feel these important anchors in music.[1] Applications of macrobeat and microbeat are made in this text as they relate to building a secure musical foundation with timing as the base. For K–3 students, this hearing-feeling connection is critical for all they will experience in music.

Phyllis S. Weikart, in *Round The Circle, Movement Plus Music, Movement Plus Rhymes, Songs, and Singing Games, Movement in Steady Beat,* and *Teaching Movement and Dance,* has combined the microbeat and macrobeat concepts with movement, so children may develop both the music and movement aspects of steady beat, thus improving processing skills in music, movement, and speech. A study conducted by Phyllis S. Weikart in the Romulus, Michigan, schools in 1981 concluded that children who possess ability to use steady beat have the timing base (inner anchor) necessary for

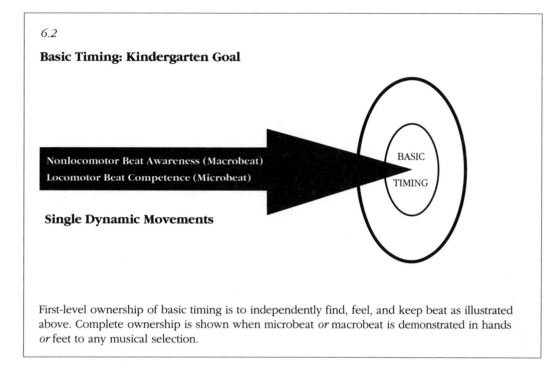

6.2

Basic Timing: Kindergarten Goal

Nonlocomotor Beat Awareness (Macrobeat)
Locomotor Beat Competence (Microbeat)

BASIC

TIMING

Single Dynamic Movements

First-level ownership of basic timing is to independently find, feel, and keep beat as illustrated above. Complete ownership is shown when microbeat *or* macrobeat is demonstrated in hands *or* feet to any musical selection.

proficiency with fundamental motor skills, musical concepts, and speech-flow.[2] *(Feeling and expressing steady beat* is also one of the key experiences in movement; see Chapter 8 in *Round the Circle* or Chapter 4 in *Teaching Movement and Dance.*)

In grades 2 and 3, children should be able to express microbeat *and* macrobeat independently by using their hands or feet, and they should be able to move in beat sequences (see Chapter 3, pp. 28–34). Proficient demonstration of these skills shows evidence of **basic timing,** the goal of *feeling and expressing steady beat.* The following rhyme can help kindergarten children or beginners to remember the difference between macrobeat and microbeat:

> *Keep macro in our hands*
> *Keep micro in our feet.*
> *Big beat, little beat,*
> *Will keep our music neat.*

The **beat competence** goal for kindergartners is to feel and express the macrobeat by synchronized rocking or patting ("Keep macro in our hands"); they feel and express the microbeat by matching it as they step in place or travel in general space ("Keep micro in our feet").

The first beat of every two beats is the naturally accented beat. However, at ball games and rock concerts, audiences commonly clap on the second beat of a chant or song instead of the first, which places emphasis on the unaccented beat. This is often referred to as "off-beat clapping." Because off-beat clapping distorts the flow for the underlying beat and inhibits natural development of steady pulse and precise rhythm, it is important that young children learn to respond to the *first,* naturally accented beat in a musical selection (see 6.4).

Microbeat and Macrobeat

Underlined syllables represent microbeats:

<u>Jack</u> be <u>nim</u>ble
<u>Jack</u> be <u>quick</u>
<u>Jack</u> jump <u>o</u>ver the
<u>Can</u>dle<u>stick</u>

Bold underlined syllables represent macrobeats:

<u>Jack</u> be nimble
<u>Jack</u> be quick
<u>Jack</u> jump over the
<u>Can</u>dlestick

In this example the macrobeat organizes the microbeats into groups of two:

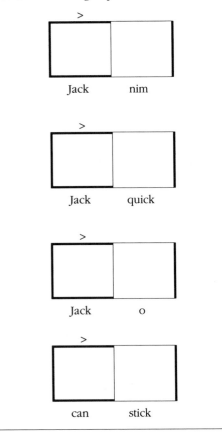

6.4

Responding to the Natural Accented Beat

For the words of *Bingo*, the accented bold represents the preferred clapping response:

>   >   >   >
<u>B</u> - <u>I</u> - **<u>N</u>** - G - <u>O</u>, **<u>B</u>** - <u>I</u> - **<u>N</u>** - G - <u>O</u>
>   >   >
<u>B</u> - <u>I</u> - **<u>N</u>** - G - <u>O</u> and **<u>Bing</u>**o was his
>
<u>name</u>-<u>o</u>.

The microbeat is best used with simple locomotor movements such as walking, marching, or jumping. When children are seated, the macrobeat, the natural rocking beat, should be used. By second and third grade, children should be expressing macrobeats and microbeats independently with feet *or* hands, so experiences with rhythm can be added successfully. Activities that allow children to express beat in *both* ways provide the foundation needed for developing proficiency with steady beat, the organization of beats, and using rhythmic patterns with precision and understanding.

Teachers may wish to incorporate some of the following suggested active learning experiences for using beat throughout the year:

- *Listen and respond with steady beat.* By focusing on and listening to the beat of a rhyme, song, or recording, children do not have to think about words or melody. This simple focus helps them respond accurately.

- *Link beat-keeping movement to simple language to strengthen the cognitive-motor bridge.* Children chant, "March, march," and respond with a marching step for each word spoken. They chant, "Swing, swing," and simultaneously swing their arms. (Learner SAY & DO)

- *Rock and pat to the steady macrobeat while saying rhymes and singing songs.* (Part of kindergarten goal for *beat competence*)

• *Keep the steady macrobeat on rhythm instruments or while strumming an autoharp.*

Additional beat activities may be found in the active learning experiences in Chapter 8.

> **Moving to one's own steady beat**. Each child has a natural, internal beat. It is our goal to help each child refine that beat in a steady way and to express it naturally. *(Steady* means not changing within a specific experience.) Each activity will have its own steady tempo. Children will discover that *steady* when one is excited may be faster than *steady* when one is tired. *Steady* may be slightly different for each rhyme, song, or recording, but it is consistent for that particular example at that given time.

Children often find it easier to demonstrate their own steady beat (usually microbeat) by stepping in place or patting their hands on their knees or chest in an alternating manner. Children should have many repeated opportunities to demonstrate steady microbeat *on their own* by walking or patting. In the classroom, begin by having each child step in place; then have a few children march or walk about to their individual steady beats before all children do so simultaneously. When all move at once, it is more difficult for each child to keep his or her own beat, but it is important that each child learns to *independently* keep a steady walking, marching, or patting beat.

The rocking beat (macrobeat) will be felt as children rock calmly from side to side or front to back while listening to a rhyme, song, or musical recording. Later, they can transfer this rocking macrobeat to a two-hand patting motion on knees or other parts of the body. Rocking while speaking or singing brings flow and comprehension to the thoughts being expressed, and it carries over into reading with flow and comprehension. Proficiency with both of these aspects of steady beat develops the child's "inner anchor," which is so important for reading comprehension, problem solving, attending, and responding to directions. Patting the macrobeat while speaking often helps students who stutter resolve their speech problems.

> **Matching someone else's beat.** Children often find it helpful to work as partners, with each watching and then matching the other's steady beat by using nonlocomotor or locomotor movements (see 6.5). From this visual-matching experience, they can move on to explore matching a beat that is slower or faster than the one just experienced, always focusing on keeping a *steady* beat. Watching

---

6.5

**Steady Beat:
Leading and Following**

(Kindergarten or Grade 1)
Sam and David are taking turns leading and matching each other's steady beat. Sam says, "Watch me and copy when you're ready." Then he pats the steady microbeat on his chin with one hand and then the other. David watches and copies the example. When David is the leader, he alternates patting his elbows, which Sam matches with the same steady beat. Sam says, "Copy this, David," and begins to walk quickly in a straight pathway. David matches this new tempo of Sam's steady beat. Then David asks Sam to match his slower steady beat, as he creeps around the chairs in the computer area.

someone else's steady beat is an easy way for children to reproduce that beat correctly, but the process requires concentration. To help concentration, encourage a cognitive response from the "follower" once the "leader" has begun movement to a steady beat. For example, the child who is watching the leader's movement might say "Pat, pat, pat, pat" or "Walk, walk, walk, walk" in time with the leader's steady beat and then add his or her own movement to the label when ready. When children label a steady-beat movement and then synchronize their own movement to that label, they are *directing* the movement, and thus their attention to it is strengthened. *They are assimilating the observed steady-beat movement at a cognitive level.*

Another technique is to have one child (the leader) begin a steady beat by supplying a label for a movement, spoken in a steady chant (SAY). The follower then joins the steady chant before beginning to move to the steady beat (SAY & DO). The leader may join the movement or observe the partner's response (see 6.6).

Extensions in this category can include moving to the macrobeat of spoken words, such as names, favorite foods, companion words ("*ted*dy bear"), or rhyme phrases ("*hic*kory dickory *dock*"). In these extensions, it is important to pronounce the words as they are naturally spoken and to start the patting movement on the accented syllable (see 6.7).

> **Matching the steady beat of recorded music, songs, and rhymes.** Daily opportunities to listen to music and feel the natural beat need to be offered to children during the K–3 years. Because a child's beat-keeping ability affects competence in all areas of the curriculum, it is important to introduce relevant activities in as many ways as possible. When steady macrobeat or microbeat movement accompanies songs and rhymes, it is helpful to set the tempo for the desired movement response by using an **anchor word.** This is a word spoken by the teacher several times before the song or rhyme is begun, to synchronize the group's movement. (See "Anchoring the Beat" in

---

6.6

Partners Using SAY & DO

Judy and Joy are partners. Judy says, "Let's gallop together like this," and she sets the tempo by chanting "Gallop, gallop, gallop, gallop." Joy chimes in, saying "Gallop, gallop, gallop, gallop" and begins to gallop in time with the chant (SAY & DO). Judy then begins to gallop at the same tempo.

To strengthen the cognitive-motor link, Phyllis S. Weikart's progression described in *Teaching Movement and Dance* (3rd Ed.) is helpful.

> Learner SAY
> *(should be omitted for K–1)*
>
> Learner SAY & DO
>
> Learner WHISPER & DO
>
> Learner THINK & DO
> *(should be omitted for K–1)*

6.7

The Macrobeat of Spoken Words

Two-syllable words:
  *Bri*an, *Bri*an, *Bri*an, *Bri*an

Three-syllable words:
  E*le*na, E*le*na, E*le*na, E*le*na
  spa*ghe*tti, spa*ghe*tti, spa*ghe*tti, spa*ghe*tti

Five-syllable words:
  ele*men*tary, ele*men*tary, ele*men*tary, ele*men*tary

Chapter 8.) Later, **anchor pitch** may replace the anchor word, when singing in tune is the focus. (See Chapter 5, p. 76.)

When using recorded music, help children listen to the song's introduction, which always sets the tempo. As their abilities to distinguish macrobeat and microbeat develop, children may choose which of these beats they want to keep. Children enjoy leading the beat, and they often find many ways to use hands or feet in this task.[3] In grades 1–3, children can share their ideas and plan the order of the musical selections (see 6.8). They often remember very clearly which children's beat-keeping ideas were used. With this active learning approach, children are able to make relationships to learning that enable them to think, sequence, and remember.

Children who have developed independent beat competence by grade 2 will be able to extend their ability to activities such as international folk dance. Folk dance incorporates many music and movement abilities, in addition to increasing multicultural and aesthetic appreciation. There is a special joy evident in young children who can join older family members in ethnic dances, such as the Greek *Hasapikos* or the Israeli *Hora.* The bond that unites all ages in such a musical activity is memorable for all involved. (A wealth of folk dance material is found in Phyllis S. Weikart's *Teaching Movement and Dance,* 3rd Ed.)

> Performing single nonlocomotor movements to the steady beat. Young learners enjoy rocking to the macro-beat, either alone or with a favorite stuffed toy or doll. Often, on their own, they will accompany the motion with a song or lullaby, giving the teacher an opportunity to observe the child's comfort level in keeping the beat. Children can rock together in pairs, or in groups of four or five. A song such as *Row, Row, Row Your Boat* is a natural choice for such an activity (see 6.9). For a child

This child demonstrates basic timing as she independently finds, feels, and expresses the macrobeat by "helping" Curious George to pat his knees.

6.8

Children Plan Their Beat-Keeping

Mrs. Johnson's second-grade class discovers a way to enjoy a lively orchestral arrangement of *Jingle Bells.*

Working in small groups of eight, each child creates his or her own way to keep the macrobeat with brightly decorated paper plates. The children determine to keep the macrobeat during the verse, and the microbeat during the chorus. Then they determine who will lead the beat-keeping first, second, and so on. They decide that each person will lead for eight macrobeats. After two students have led, they march around in a circle and keep the microbeat with feet and their plates, each in his or her own way. There are four repetitions of the song, therefore eight leaders are needed to lead the macrobeat. What fun! What a wonderful demonstration of the relationship of macro- and microbeat!

> 6.9
>
> ### Rocking to the Macrobeat
>
> Macrobeat is underlined:
>> _Row_, row, _row_, your boat
>> _Gent_ly down the _stream._
>> _Mer_rily merrily, _mer_rily, merrily,
>> _Life_ is but a _dream._

> 6.10
>
> ### Selections for Rocking to the Macrobeat
>
> _Apat Apat_ (RM4)
>
> _Sellenger's Round_ (RM7)
>
> _Gaelic Waltz_ (RM1)

having difficulty feeling the macrobeat, it is helpful to rock between two strong beat-keepers.

Rocking to the macrobeat leads easily into rocking and patting the macrobeat softly, with both hands, on knees, chest, or head while reciting rhymes or singing songs. When children are secure in using the macrobeat, they can discover how to keep the microbeat by alternating their motions to the faster pulse. Opportunities for working alone, in pairs, in small groups, and as leaders of the whole class will be easy to incorporate into the daily schedule and will be initiated by young learners. Selections from various high-quality recordings, such as those found in **Rhythmically Moving** and **Changing Directions,** may be used daily (see 6.10). Remember that instrumental recordings (those without vocals) are better for young children to work with. Listening to the words as well as the music often distracts children, making it difficult for them to keep the beat.

> **Performing single locomotor movements to the steady beat.**
Children need _many_ experiences with locomotor movement before they can be expected to move accurately and consistently to the steady beat. When all class members are moving to the beat at the same time, a child has to attend to space and others' pathways as well as to his or her own movements to the music. One way to help children stay on track is to have a small group perform locomotor movements around the room while the rest perform locomotor movements by stepping in place. Another solution is to divide the class into four groups and let each group decide on a special pathway in their own area of the room. When all children are working at the same time on locomotor movement to the beat of the music, it is helpful, for the first section of the music, to have them begin moving their feet to the beat while seated in chairs. During the next section, the children may stand and choose a locomotor movement (walk, jump, hop), performing it in place; during the repeat of A, they may travel, keeping the beat (see 6.11). The musical selection can be temporarily stopped if the children seem to lose their concentration.

> **Playing instruments in steady beat.** Children should be allowed to explore all types of musical instruments as they learn to play the beat with comfort, confidence,

> 6.11
>
> ### Plješkavac Kolo (RM3)
>
> The selection includes eight repetitions of AB form:
>> Section A: "Walk" while seated, 1st time;
>> Actually walk on repeats of A.
>>
>> Section B: "Walk" (or other locomotor movement) standing in place

Partners pat the macrobeat on each other's shoulders for the A section of a recorded musical selection. During the B section, each child will choose a way to travel around the room, keeping the microbeat.

and consistency. Often, instruments become extensions of a child's arms, and playing motions are not always symmetrical. Some instruments, such as the triangle, require the ability to *inhibit* (to hold one side of the body still while moving the other side), a skill that many children do not attain until second grade. Children may become frustrated as they concentrate on "doing it right," thereby completely tuning out the music. When working with children below the age of seven, one strategy that has been successful is to have each child work with a partner; for example, one child can hold the hand drum or triangle or press chord buttons on an autoharp while the other child strikes or strums the instrument. This cooperative arrangement provides reinforcement and encourages children to help one another.

> **Combining nonlocomotor and locomotor movement to the steady beat.** When children in second or third grade are comfortable in expressing and leading sequenced macro- and microbeats with their hands and feet, they may be ready to integrate movement. Many exploratory activities are needed before children are able to have their hands do one thing while their feet do another. Start with

simple challenges, patience, and humor. Practice a simple sequence for the arms (such as a windshield wiper motion, back and forth). Then try out a simple, in-place alternating foot pattern, such as "HEEL, STEP." Put the language of the feet with the arm motion. Begin the foot pattern with SAY & DO, and layer on the arm pattern while continuing the language and foot pattern (see 6.12).

When the class is ready, try singing *Are You Sleeping?* or any simple round. Or try this integrated movement to *The Hustle* (RM9). Integrated movements are also employed in many folk dances, such as *Bannielou Lambaol* (RM8) or *Kendime* (RM5). Integrating movement to the beat presents many opportunities for making cognitive-kinesthetic links, links that may help develop higher-level thinking and coordination skills. (For further information on sequencing movement to the beat and integrating movement, refer to *Teaching Movement and Dance,* 3rd Ed.)

6.12

Integrating Foot and Hand Movements

Marla uses learner SAY & DO by saying "HEEL, STEP" as her feet begin the movements. She continues to say this sequence as her arms layer the windshield wiper motions to the tempo of her speech and feet.

⚍ Identifying Tone Color

In music, **tone color** refers to the specific characteristics by which a particular sound, voice, or instrument can be identified.

For example, experience in listening to instruments helps us to identify the sound of the flute as being very different from the sound of the trumpet. Just as the flute and trumpet can be identified by their unique qualities, so can individual voices or specific sounds. An infant readily identifies and turns toward the sound of its mother's voice even when there are several people talking at once. Children's abilities to aurally discriminate begin to develop even before birth and should continue to be fine-tuned in as many ways as possible. Identifying tone color in a musical sense helps children identify specific instruments within the categories of strings, woodwinds, percussion, and brass, as well as untuned rhythm and homemade instruments. Children also strengthen the ability to identify low and high tones, specific pitches, melody patterns, and songs.

> **Distinguishing different persons' singing and speaking voices.**
This accent was introduced in Chapter 5, under the key experience *exploring and identifying sounds.* Here, we take it a step further. Now, the task is to assist children in identifying a particular person's speaking or singing voice by its very own tone color. Several factors, such as enunciation, dynamic level of the voice, and resonance, enter into one's ability to identify a particular voice. Developing aural discrimination at the K–3 level presents children with problem-solving challenges. Of course, students will try to disguise their own voices in order to increase the challenge for their classmates. The thinking and responding involved in aural discrimination activities demand children's best

vocal and speaking abilities. Discover how delightful these aural discrimination games can become. (See Chapter 8 for related activities.)

> **Hearing the differences in voices and percussion instruments.** In this accent, attention is called not only to responding to directions or specific questions but also to hearing specific differences in voices and instruments and attending to what is unique about the tone color. Because each person breathes, supports sound production, uses the vocal cords, and uses the body's own resonating chambers in a unique way, each voice has a characteristic quality. The voice is animate and changes as a person matures, expresses feelings and emotions, describes or recalls an important event, or responds to a state of health. A person controls how his or her voice is used. The voice has a much broader capacity for producing sounds and variations than a musical instrument has.

Musical instruments owe their characteristic sounds to the materials used to construct them (brass, wood, skin, etc.). When children explore ways to play instruments, they remember the particular instrument sound and how it changes when played in different ways. The instrument is inanimate. The sound produced depends on how it is played. When opportunities are provided in natural ways for instruments to be heard and explored, children find they can identify the different sounds easily. This leads to the following accent.

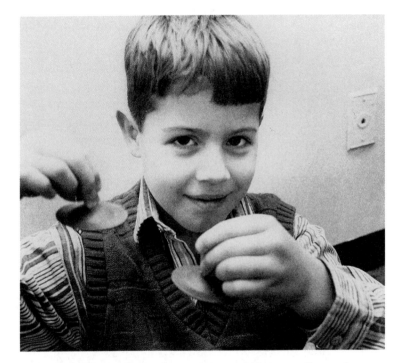

Finger cymbals have a distinct characteristic sound. Their tone color can be compared to that of the triangle yet cannot be imitated. Children can describe similarities and differences between these two types of "ringers."

> **Distinguishing the different instrument sounds.** Instruments are grouped into families. The instruments young children usually come into contact with first are those classified as **unpitched percussion instruments.** Examples include drums, tambourines, triangles, finger cymbals, maracas, and wood blocks. Each of these is classified as unpitched because it does not produce a variety of specific pitches.

Active learning experiences can provide opportunities for children to explore each instrument and for teachers to pose questions about the sound or pitch capability of each specific instrument. For example, have the children move first to the sound of the wood block and then to the sound of the triangle. Ask the children about the movement they chose for each sound and if they had a reason for moving in that way. Guide the children to describe their movement and the tone color of the related instrument. Because it is difficult to express a reason for moving to the sound of only one instrument when one has nothing to compare that movement and sound to, try using two different unpitched instruments (e.g., wood block and finger cymbals) or two pitched instruments (e.g., recorder and autoharp) with movement exploration activities. Then ask for the children's descriptions and comparisons.

Instruments that are classified as **pitched instruments** are grouped as follows:

> *Strings*—guitar, autoharp, violin, viola, cello, double bass
> *Woodwinds*—recorder, flute, piccolo, clarinet, saxophone, oboe, bassoon
> *Brass*—trumpet, french horn, trombone, tuba
> *Percussion*—marimba, chimes, xylophone
> *Keyboard*—piano, organ, synthesizer

As children construct their knowledge about instrument sounds, help them make their own charts of the instruments, draw and find pictures of the instruments, discover ways to play the instruments, and decide which instruments to use to accompany favorite songs. In so doing, classification, representation, and seriation are also incorporated.

> **Matching an instrument's sound with its picture.** Children need to see, hear, touch, try out, and associate a sound with a specific musical instrument. Often instruments can be borrowed from the band or orchestra director, or older students can demonstrate them. If exploration time is well spent, children can easily identify an instrument's sound with that experience and its appropriate picture. The classroom teacher will find it valuable to assess the knowledge-base of each child as he or she begins to make this identification naturally. Identification requires visual and aural discrimination, recall, and classification. There are musical recordings that introduce children to specific instrument sounds, as well as some that use a specific instrument as the solo in the musical selection. (Both *Bowmar Orchestral Library* and RCA's *Adventures in Music* contain excellent examples of specific instrument sounds. See Appendix C for a list of recommended listening selections.)

> **Identifying voices and instruments heard in a recording.** When instrumental recordings are used in the classroom, children can learn to identify a specific instrument. Instruments that children have played and those that have been identified for them will be the easiest to recognize. In general, percussion instruments (drums, tambourines) are easier to identify than wind instruments; brass instruments are easier to identify than strings. Any invited guests (parents or older students) who can visit the classroom and share a live performance should be welcomed. All of the **Rhythmically Moving** and **Changing Directions** recordings provide excellent resources for listening to a variety of instruments. Recordings that do not have vocals permit each child to more easily attend to the specific instruments played.

To help K–3 children identify voices heard on a recording, the teacher can draw attention to whether there is a group of singers or one solo voice. As ears become able to discriminate, K–3 listeners can distinguish between two singing voices (duet), three voices (trio), or four voices (quartet); between a man's, a woman's, or a child's voice; and even between individual singers by name.

> **Identifying special characteristics of tone color within the music.** When music is used as an important part of the daily classroom routine, children will discover that certain selections appeal to them more than others do. Consequently, the ability to identify the characteristics that make a particular selection memorable can lead to a lively discussion. A certain song may bring a feeling of calm, joy, or excitement; certain instruments may be the attraction; or perhaps the melody or rhythm of the selection links very special feelings together. The music may be unusually descriptive, reminding the listener of a favorite story or subject, real or imagined. As children begin to articulate these special characteristics, their "musical ear" begins to be linked to the effect that music has on individuals, and they fine-tune their ability to aurally discriminate. Relationships are made that create the desire for more understanding of the elements of music. Learning how music is created, used, and shared by people in every culture helps them to understand that all cultures rely on music to fill many important needs.

⌒ Developing Melody

Melody is a pattern of musical pitches within a key system. Arranging these pitches creates a specific tonal and rhythmic succession of sounds that makes each piece recognizable and expresses a musical idea.

The element most quickly associated with music is melody. We often are able to recognize the title of a song by hearing its melody, without having to hear its words. The song *Happy Birthday to You* is a good example of this. Also, when we read the words to a song, the melody (or at least part of it) invariably comes to mind. We respond to the theme songs of TV shows and commercials; to seasonal, sacred, and patriotic songs; and to many other types of music because of the melodies involved. We often hear people hum or whistle a certain tune when they are happy. People sometimes complain that they can't get a melody out of their head—for them, *melody* and *music* are synonymous.

A melody is based on a group of tones or pitches *within a scale.* Melodies are divided into *phrases,* which might be thought of as musical sentences. A piece may contain melodic phrases that have the same pitches in the same order (this is the **shape** or **contour** of the melodic phrase), and it may contain melodic phrases that have different orders of pitches (see 6.13). This adds variety and form to the piece. Melody also incorporates beat, rhythm, and tempo. Each new melody we learn adds to our vocal repertoire, aural discrimination, and lifelong association with music.

Some children are not able to distinguish singing a song from simply chanting its words on a single pitch. Rap is an example of the latter skill. When a song is presented to children without using the **simplify** strategy of the Teaching Model (see Chapter 2), young learners have difficulty attending to the melody and text simultaneously, unless the phrases are very short. Because words are within their immediate experience, they attend and respond to the text, but they miss the contour of the melody. We can help them develop ability to follow melodic contour with their singing voices by guiding their experiences in the following accents and by using the teaching guidelines found in Appendix A, "Teaching Model for A New Song."

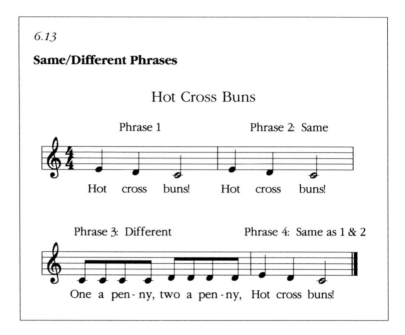

6.13

Same/Different Phrases

Hot Cross Buns

Phrase 1   Phrase 2: Same

Hot   cross   buns!   Hot   cross   buns!

Phrase 3: Different   Phrase 4: Same as 1 & 2

One a pen‑ny, two a pen‑ny, Hot cross buns!

> **Identifying higher and lower pitches.** Movement can help children understand the differences first between high and low pitches, followed by the range of high*er*-low*er* pitches. Active experiences in comparing high/low movements support children in learning to make and identify high and low pitches. The teacher can help children create movements that represent "low," "high," by using corresponding pitches for each motion. Adequate exploration will encourage children to volunteer to share their movement and sound. The teacher or student leader can then extend to singing a pitch that the class identifies through movement; the student leader can also do the reverse—show through movement what sound his or her classmates should make (see 6.14).

When enough experiences have been shared with single vocal or instrumental pitches, children will naturally combine two pitches, such as "low-high," "high-higher," "low-lower." Children can carry out this activity as partners or in small groups. Soon, three, four, or even more pitches can be combined before a

6.14

High and Low Movements for Sounds

After children have explored high and low movements and sounds, Steven shares his movement representing "high"—stretching his arms straight overhead. Classmates copy his movement and add their high-pitched sounds. Steven then curls up on the floor. Children copy his movement and add sounds representing low.

Caitlyn makes a high vocal sound, and other students show their own movements representing "high." Then David wants to challenge the class, so he says, "Give me an answer in movement to my three sounds." He sings a high pitch, a low pitch, and then the original high pitch again. Classmates answer by showing high-low-high movements.

movement response is sought, or the demonstrated movement can precede the vocal response. Children's aural attending and memory will be strengthened by such an activity, and more tuneful singing will result.

> **Identifying the direction of the melody (upward/downward).** Once children's ears are attuned to hearing a range of high and low pitches, attention can be drawn to the **tonal direction** of each part of a melody. As children sing *This Old Man,* for example, the teacher can call attention to the upward direction of "give a dog a bone," and the downward direction of "came rolling home." These are good examples of upward and downward tonal direction, respectively. Encourage children to sing "give a dog a bone," and accompany their singing with a motion that shows how the melody moves upward. Do the same with the downward "came rolling home," and then discuss and compare their findings. Further "melody sleuths" will detect the shape of "he played knick knack on my shoe" as one that starts higher, goes down, and then goes back up (see 6.15).

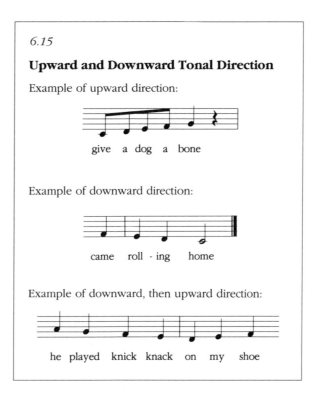

6.15

Upward and Downward Tonal Direction

Example of upward direction:

give a dog a bone

Example of downward direction:

came roll - ing home

Example of downward, then upward direction:

he played knick knack on my shoe

Children and parents use yarn to lay out "pathways" showing how melodies move up and down. One child and parent represent their melodic contour in 3-D space.

Some major-scale songs, such as *Wise Old Owl* (see Chapter 8), are fun to sing with movement, and they reinforce this important concept while strengthening children's voices. Young children often enjoy creating major- or minor-scale songs, which are vital to their understanding of how pitches are organized. *Gloomy Boomy Day* (see Chapter 8) is an example of a minor-scale song.

> **Matching intervals and repeated pitches.** An **interval** is the distance between two different pitches. Movement is very useful in helping children match intervals. Ask them to follow you visually as you place both hands on your shoulders. While your hands remain in this position, sing the pitch for G (scale degree 5 in C-major key system) using a neutral syllable such as "bom," and have them match the pitch. Place your hands on your waist; they copy. Sing the pitch for E (scale degree 3) on a neutral syllable. Sing the two pitches in a sequence several times, as the children sing the pitches associated with shoulders (G) and waist (E). Encourage students to SING & SHAPE various patterns of these pitches, such as G, G, E, or G, E, E, or G, E, G. Place your hands on your shoulders and recall the G pitch; place hands on knees; they copy. Sing the pitch for C (scale degree 1), again on a neutral syllable. Repeat these movements and pitches several times. Sing the two pitches (G and C) in a sequence, and have the children echo with movement *and* sound. Create other combinations of these pitches, such as G, G, C or G, C, G.

Begin on G each time, and continue to use a neutral syllable. Such questions as "How does it feel inside your body when you sing each of those pitches?" help them focus on the vocal production of specific sounds. See the tone games in Chapter 3, and proceed accordingly. Moving your hands to different body locations for pitch association (using the **body scale**) strengthens pitch recall and provides a kinesthetic-cognitive link. Major- and minor-scale songs also reinforce these step-wise pitch relationships.

Because a child's voice is his or her own personal musical instrument, it is most important that it be developed with care and used well. When teachers help children find and use their singing voices, they are giving them a most precious gift indeed, for the K–3 years are critical in developing vocal ability. Young children need to realize that they can focus their voices to match specific pitches. (See "Exploring the Singing Voice" in Chapter 5 for the early experiences that precede this accent.)

> **Imitating three- and four-note melody patterns.** This accent builds on the procedure begun in the preceding accent. As a first step, sing three different pitches of equal length, such as G, E, C (scale degrees 5, 3, 1) on a neutral syllable. Pause after the third pitch, to give students time to organize what they have heard before they echo it. (See "Developing Melody Through Tone Games," Chapter 3.) This is another logical place to employ the Teaching Model's **simplify** strategy (see Chapter 2), because it enables children to concentrate only on *pitches,* without the encumbrance of rhythm. Immediately after singing the third pitch, motion to them with both hands, so they know to begin. They echo back with motions *and* pitches in *steady beat.* Once they understand the activity, individual students should have the opportunity to volunteer to lead

in singing the pitches for others to echo. Four-pitch patterns in steady beat are the next strategy to use. These brief, "warm-up" melody patterns help young children to refine their pitch discrimination and to warm up their vocal cords for singing the melodies of songs.

> **Distinguishing *same* and *different* in short melody patterns.** Short **melody patterns** are fragments of the musical phrase. In *This Old Man,* for example, the first phrase consists of a twice-repeated melody pattern. "This old man" and "he played one" both have the same melodic shape (see 6.16). In *Twinkle, Twinkle, Little Star,* the second long phrase consists of a twice-repeated melody pattern, "up above the world so high" and "like a diamond in the sky" (see 6.16). Encourage students to become "melody detectives" in discovering same and different patterns in the songs the class sings. Young children are always surprised to discover that songs have special organization, or order, and

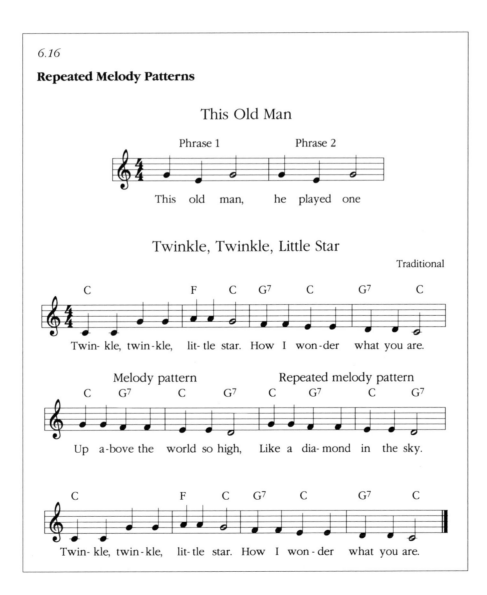

6.16

Repeated Melody Patterns

that they can detect these interesting patterns. Children will be motivated to create their own songs when they realize that they can make and follow a plan for composing a song in much the same way that they can make a plan and carry it through during plan-do-review!

> **Responding to the shape of the melody.** Active learning experiences can easily be introduced by encouraging children to use movement to respond to the **shape,** or **contour,** of the melody being sung. For example, the shape of *Looby Loo* might be described as having lots of ups and downs, with repeated notes generally occurring in the beginning of each phrase (see 6.17). Children can use whole-body movement, arm motions, or body scale placements to respond to the shape of the melody. *Hot Cross Buns* (see 6.13 again) has a "step" shape, with three repeated patterns. The shape of *Wise Old Owl,* a major-scale song, has many repeated notes, with each phrase moving higher until the last phrase of the song, at which point the phrase fragments begin lower (see Chapter 8, p. 245).

When presenting a new song to be learned, use this **simplify** strategy: Sing each phrase on a neutral syllable; then have the children use movement to respond to the contour of the phrase as you sing it one more time; next they can echo your pitches as they perform the movement. This strategy will help uncertain singers to strengthen their pitch discrimination.

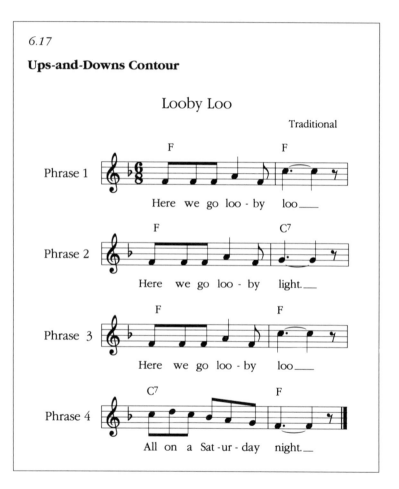

6.17

Ups-and-Downs Contour

Looby Loo

Traditional

Phrase 1 — Here we go loo-by loo____

Phrase 2 — Here we go loo-by light.____

Phrase 3 — Here we go loo-by loo____

Phrase 4 — All on a Sat-ur-day night.____

> **Identifying and singing phrases in the melody.** As children develop proficiency in the preceding accents, it becomes natural to have them respond to the shape, or contour, of a melodic phrase (see 6.18). They can pretend to draw the shape of a specific melodic phrase with finger paint, for example, or pretend to draw the shape on an invisible chalkboard. By observing children in activities such as these, the teacher can assess each child's level of understanding of melodic shape.

Contour and Notation for
Mary Had a Little Lamb

Melodic contour:

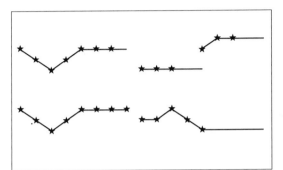

Phrase 1 and Phrase 2 begin the same but end differently:

Most simple songs have two or four phrases. As children respond to each phrase with movement, draw attention to phrases being alike or different. The children might notice that some phrases begin the same way but end differently. Making such interesting comparisons helps children understand that melody is organized musical thought and that they themselves have the ability to create simple songs. From a student-made chart listing the songs the class knows, a classification code can be developed showing how each song's phrases are organized. *Twinkle, Twinkle, Little Star,* for example, has three long phrases, organized as ABA (see 6.19).

6.19

Musical Notation

> **Recognizing patterns and sequences in melodies.** Once children can identify melody **patterns,** they will notice that often, immediately after a melody pattern is first introduced, it is repeated beginning one pitch higher or lower. This is a **melody sequence.** The melody pattern for "up and down" in *The Wheels on the Bus,* for example, is followed by one sequence and one repetition of that pattern (see 6.20).

Sequences are often used in children's songs because they make songs easier to sing. After all, once a lovely pattern has been created, why not use sequences to gain full enjoyment of the musical idea? A more challenging activity for musically sensitive learners is to ask them to find upside-down patterns **(inversions)** of a melody, or variations of the pattern.

> **Singing and shaping phrases and songs.** When children are able to sing and shape phrases of songs, they are showing their ability to integrate four concepts at once: **melodic direction, melodic rhythm, pitch relationships,** and **in-tune singing.** Their demonstrated ability indicates that their prior experiences have given them the knowledge to use melody in a manner that will provide the basis for ownership in many additional musical encounters. Their tonal (pitch) memory may be developed enough to play melodies on the keyboard or xylophone and may lead to additional study of the piano, guitar, or violin.

⊶ Labeling Form

In music, **form** refers to the organization of a musical composition according to its sections of melodic repetition, contrast, variation, or development. The form of a musical composition can be compared to the blueprint of a classroom. Some aspects of the room may be repeated more than once, such as a given window size or a given wall length. Closets and doorways might make some walls different from others. The similarities and differences fit together into a whole unit, the classroom.

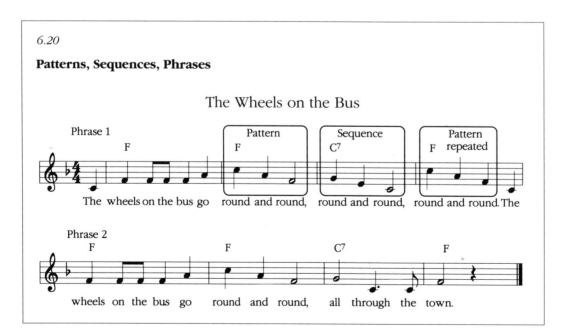

6.20

Patterns, Sequences, Phrases

The Wheels on the Bus

As they listen to recorded music, children raise their right hands to demonstrate the length of the first phrase of the musical selection. When the next phrase begins, they will represent its length by raising the other hand. In this way, they will "signal" the beginning and ending of all phrases.

The form of a musical composition can be understood in much the same way. The form for *La Raspa* (RM3), for example, is AABB; A is the first section, which repeats itself; B is the second section, a contrasting melody to A, which also repeats. On **Rhythmically Moving 3,** the AABB form is played six times. The B sections of *La Raspa* are quite different from the A sections. When the A and B sections are combined, they create the musical composition known as *La Raspa*. Even something as complicated as the first movement of Beethoven's Ninth Symphony can be analyzed for its form. **Form** provides a succinct organizational representation of a musical composition, so we understand how it is put together.

As children learn songs that grow in range and length, they can be guided to recognize like and unlike phrases that make up a melody. For example, through singing them, children will notice that some songs have several verses and a chorus that is repeated after each verse. In this case identifying the musical form can mean labeling the verse as "A" and the chorus as "B." *(It's a Small World,* for example, has this AB form).

Listening selections often will have the following forms:

ABA: Melody #1, melody #2, melody #1 (e.g., *Tant Hessie,* RM7)
ABC: Melody #1, melody #2, melody #3 (e.g., *Sliding,* RM1)
AABB: #1, #1, #2, #2 (e.g., *Rakes of Mallow,* RM2)
AABA: #1, #1, #2, #1 (e.g., *Spanish Coffee,* RM4)
ABACA: #1, #2, #1, #3, #1 (e.g., *Hineh Ma Tov,* RM4)

Third-graders are capable of identifying this last form (ABACA) as **rondo** form. Children can be challenged to listen for and respond to this organization of music.

> **Identifying the beginning and end of a song or rhyme.** Kindergarten children often join in after a song or rhyme is already begun. They may not always begin speaking or singing with the first word or note. The teacher can naturally ask questions that help children focus on the first and last words of the song or rhyme and urge them to begin speaking or singing together. Providing an anchor pitch is a useful strategy here. An enjoyable activity in grades 2 and 3 is for the entire class to speak only the first and last words of a rhyme or sing the first and last notes of a well-known song. The teacher can challenge the class to sing "inside our minds" and still stay together for the very last word and pitch. If children suggest singing special words that occur within the song, add them as well (such as all the rhyming words or all the words that begin with a specific letter).

> **Identifying the verse and chorus of a song.** When singing a familiar song, most children realize that there are sections where words and melody remain the same and repeat (the **chorus**) and sections where the melody repeats but the words are different (the **verse**).
This Land Is Your Land and *Yankee Doodle* are familiar examples. The classroom teacher can reinforce this basic concept by asking questions that allow children to describe and label the verse and chorus of familiar songs. Children should be encouraged to create new verses to familiar songs and to share their creativity. Some of the best verses to familiar songs have been written by K–3 students. Consider, for example, the second-grader's Halloween version of *Hokey Pokey* presented in Insert 6.21.

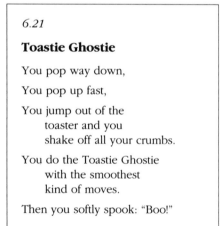

6.21

Toastie Ghostie

You pop way down,

You pop up fast,

You jump out of the
toaster and you
shake off all your crumbs.

You do the Toastie Ghostie
with the smoothest
kind of moves.

Then you softly spook: "Boo!"

> **Identifying same and different phrases.** This accent, which was introduced earlier in the chapter under the accent "Identifying and singing phrases in the melody," can now be extended to listening to songs or recorded music and identifying phrases that are the same and different. Often, a musical phrase will begin like a preceding phrase, only to end differently. Examples of songs with such phrases include *The Wheels on the Bus* (see 6.20) and *Muffin Man* (see 6.22).

With enough listening experiences in identifying same and different phrases, third-graders can develop even greater listening skills by recognizing phrases that begin alike but end differently (see 6.23). This helps them understand that music is indeed a universal language and that musical phrases, like sentences, communicate ideas.

6.22

Muffin Man

Kum Ba Yah

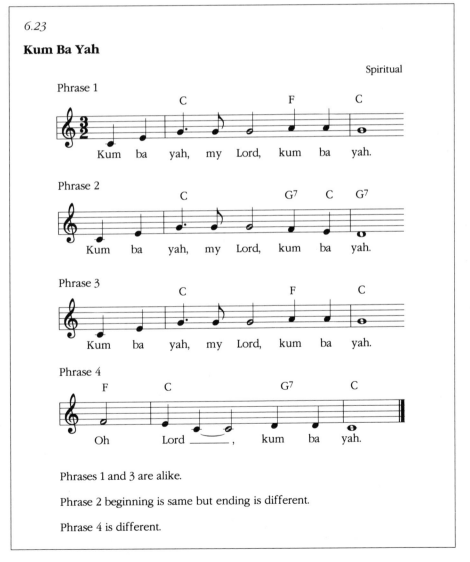

Phrases 1 and 3 are alike.

Phrase 2 beginning is same but ending is different.

Phrase 4 is different.

> **Identifying and responding to different sections of recorded music.** When certain selections of instrumental recordings are repeated several times, listeners have an opportunity to distinguish and identify the form of a particular selection because they hear it more than once. For example, *Yankee Doodle* is in AB form and is played six times on RM2. After children listen to two or three repetitions of the music, encourage them to identify the form and create a movement for each section. As the recording continues, they will be able to use their first movement during the A section and a contrasting movement for the B section, because they have listened and prepared the motor response and are now ready to show that they hear and can respond accurately to the two distinct sections.

In children's initial work with this concept, the recorded music you choose should have *distinct* differences between sections, such as in *Yankee Doodle, D'Hammerschmiedsgsell'n,* (RM7), or *Blackberry Quadrille* (RM2). Other beginning listening suggestions for this accent are *Southwind* (RM1) and *Bannielou Lambaol* (RM8). More sophisticated selections, such as *Bele Kawe* (RM3) or *Hineh Ma Tov* (RM4), can be presented later, in grades 2 and 3. Since aural discrimination tends to be one of young children's weaker learning modalities, the teacher should encourage activities that build positive responses to listening and singing. Developing alert listening skills is worth the effort.

> **Labeling and using AB, ABA, and ABC forms.** As children develop listening skills and begin identifying the forms for songs or recorded selections, it may be helpful to use visual cue cards, such as a square of one color for the A section and a square of a different color for the B section. Using two different nonlocomotor movements for the two sections is another way to reinforce their difference. Children can also create a different static pose for each section and later add beat-keeping, using a different body part to keep the macrobeat for each section. Children need to be given time to listen attentively to the recording and keep the macrobeat, because there is great value in listening to a melody to distinguish its form.

ABA is a common three-part song form, just as ABC is a common three-part dance form. Charts listing songs, recordings, or dances in each of these forms can provide a useful way for children to classify musical selections. Children often enjoy comparing these forms to familiar foods (see 6.24). AB is like an open-faced sandwich (bread, cheese), ABA is like a sandwich cookie (cookie, filling, cookie), and ABC is like a pizza (crust, sauce, topping)!

Once children have had experiences identifying melodies and labeling musical forms, you will begin to see them incorporating this musical knowledge into other academic areas, for example, in pattern work in mathematics, in poetry writing, or in art projects.

> **Labeling and using rondo form and simple theme and variations form.** Once ABC form is easily identified, children in third grade may be ready for ABACA **(rondo form)**. *Hineh Ma Tov* (RM4) is a good example. *Mexican Mixer* (RM3), with its AABBACA form, is an example of "rondo deluxe"! Children are intrigued by **theme and variations** form. The piano recording of Mozart's *Variations on Twinkle, Twinkle, Little Star* provides children with a favorite listening experience.

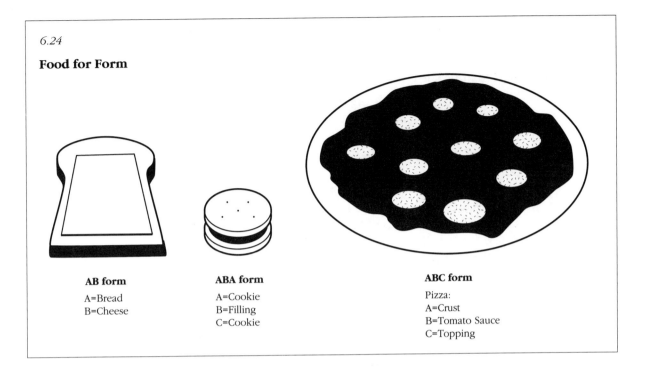

6.24

Food for Form

AB form
A=Bread
B=Cheese

ABA form
A=Cookie
B=Filling
C=Cookie

ABC form
Pizza:
A=Crust
B=Tomato Sauce
C=Topping

Children can experience beginning understanding of variation by changing only one or two notes (not the beginning or ending notes) of a well-known song such as *Twinkle, Twinkle, Little Star* (see the accent in Chapter 7 on melody improvisation, p. 156). Provide for children's learning by giving them enough time to choose how they will vary the melody. After they have explored and are satisfied with their variations, several children may volunteer to sing their *Twinkle* variation for the class.

⚬ᴈ Recognizing the Expressive Qualities of Tempo and Dynamics

The term **tempo** refers to the pace of a musical selection—whether the steady beat moves quickly or slowly. Tempos are expressed in Italian and include *lento* (very slow), *adagio* (slow), *moderato* (moderate), *allegro* (lively), *presto* (fast), and *vivace* (very fast). (See Glossary for pronunciations.) The tempo of a march is often marked *allegro*. The term **dynamics** refers to sound level—the relative softness or loudness of the music; it includes the dynamic shaping of the musical phrase, such as soft/getting louder/getting softer, or loud/growing louder. Dynamic indications are expressed in Italian or with Italian abbreviations. For example, we might say that a march was played loud, or *forte*. Lullabies are always soft, or *piano.*

Experiences in this accent enable young children to use musical terms easily; they should be encouraged to incorporate the terms in their vocabulary whenever appropriate. Movement is again a natural complement to these elements, because it is through movement responses that cognitive connections are made to tempo and dynamics.

> **Identifying slow and fast through movement and vocabulary.** Since children have a general sense of these concepts, this is an excellent time to add

the musical terms for **slow** *(lento)* and **fast** *(presto).* Have the children demonstrate lento and presto through slow and fast movements of their choosing. A musical selection excellent for experiencing both lento and presto is *Hora Hassidit* (RM5). Section A is lento and section B is presto.

> **Identifying *loud* and *soft* through movement and vocabulary.**
Musical terms for **loud** *(forte)* and **soft** *(piano)* can be added to children's vocabulary, once their cognitive understanding of loud and soft is already in place. The teacher might ask, "What movement would you show for forte footsteps?" "For piano footsteps?" "For forte punches?" "For piano finger-snaps?" Activities can be extended to forte/piano voices, and many other aspects of opposites in dynamics. A song excellent for reinforcing the concepts of forte and piano is *John Jacob Jingleheimer Schmidt.* Other musical selections excellent for experiencing these two concepts are Saint Saëns' *Carnival of the Animals* (forte: *Royal March of the Lions;* piano: *Turtles*) or Haydn's *Surprise Symphony* (the story is delightful).

> **Identifying *slow, medium,* and *fast* through movement and vocabulary.** Once opposites in tempo have been established through movement and musical terms, the metronome may be introduced. The action of the traditional wind-up metronome with its pendulum movement intrigues children while reinforcing musical vocabulary, and it provides a concrete example of each particular steady tempo.

Young children who have experienced the concepts of lento and presto through movement and music are now ready to understand *moderato* (medium) tempo. Children should be given time to use movement in exploring musical selections that include passages ranging from slow to fast. Experiencing the concept of moderato with a specific musical selection, such as *Bulgarian Dance* (RM8), can provide the necessary concrete experience. Also, *America (My Country 'Tis of Thee)* is usually sung with moderato tempo.

Special projects can now be undertaken by the whole class or by a small group to provide reinforcement of the terms for tempo and dynamics throughout the year; songs and musical selections the children have loved can be grouped and classified by tempo as well as by dynamics. As children hear these authentic musical terms used over and over again, everyone's vocabulary is enriched!

> **Identifying *loud, medium,* and *soft* through movement and vocabulary.** Rarely are sounds classified only as soft or loud. Children can also learn that the term for the medium dynamic level, for example, is *mezzo,* and their attention can also be called to the concepts *mezzo forte* (medium loud) and *mezzo piano* (medium soft). To provide visual reinforcement for the terms used in dynamic classification, the terms for dynamic levels—from *pianissimo* (very soft) to *fortissimo* (very loud)—can be graphed. Then all sounds heard during a particular time period, such as large-group time or outside recess, can be listed and graphed according to these musical terms. Children can use movement to reinforce their ownership of these concepts. It is important for teachers to facilitate development of listening skills and aural discrimination in every way possible.

> **Identifying getting faster and getting slower.** Young children are fascinated by musical selections that deliberately get faster, and they love to use the term for this— *accelerando.* Eliciting children's movement responses again provides important kinesthetic-cognitive links and is sure to bring smiles when the steady beat becomes faster and faster (see 6.25).

Passages that get gradually slower, termed *ritardando,* are often found at the end of a selection. Keen listening and motor responses are needed for children to move with a steady beat that consistently slows down. Using imagery, such as imagining a train slowing down at the station, often helps. Children need to be aware that slowing down (tempo) and getting softer (dynamics) are two entirely different concepts. Fine examples of ritardando that are suitable for beginning listeners are *Zemer Atik* (RM4) and *Sham Hareh Golan* (RM9). The ritardando occurs at the end of the final repetition of the AB form in each selection.

> **Identifying *getting louder* and *getting softer.*** Familiarity with the concepts of forte and piano should be in place before working with the gradual increase in dynamics known as *crescendo* (getting louder). The written symbol for crescendo (see 6.26) provides a concrete example of the gradual increase, and children easily relate it to the math symbols for the concepts less than (<) and greater than (>), if they have been introduced. Relating crescendo to an increase in vocal volume is another way to reinforce the concept. Children can make the *crescendo* symbol with their arms, and vocally "activate" the symbol. A fine musical selection that reinforces this concept is Grieg's *In the Hall of the Mountain King* (from the *Peer Gynt Suite*).

The reverse of the above concept, gradually decreasing the volume, is known as *decrescendo.* This concept can be developed in much the same way that crescendo was developed. Children can use their arms to illustrate the decrescendo symbol (see 6.26 again), as their voices show the gradual decreasing of a tone's volume. Note that the symbol is the reverse of the crescendo symbol. Because children have all experienced what happens when the volume of the radio or tape player is gradually turned louder or softer, they find crescendo and decrescendo understandable. What

---

6.25

Fjäskern (RM2)— **Accelerando**

During section A, walk the micro-beat counterclockwise. When section A is repeated, walk clockwise. During section B, walk **IN** four steps (microbeat), then touch knees, shoulders (macrobeat). Walk **OUT** four steps (microbeat), then touch knees, shoulders (macrobeat). Repeat this as section B repeats. Each repeat of the AB form is a little faster and challenges learners to keep the beat as they enthusiastically discover the concept of accelerando.

6.26

Getting Louder and Softer

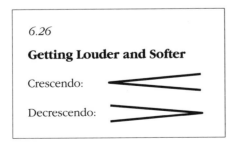

Crescendo:

Decrescendo:

does confuse children is being asked to turn the radio or TV "up" or "down" instead of the more correct "louder" or "softer"! A fine example to include for a listening experience that illustrates crescendo and decrescendo is *The Oxcart,* from Moussorgsky's *Pictures at an Exhibition.* One can easily imagine the tired farmer leading his ox and cart home from the distant field, passing right beside the listener, and continuing down the road until out of sight—a most memorable picture.

> **Selecting suitable dynamics and tempo for a song or instrumental piece.** The opportunity to choose the dynamics and tempo for familiar songs or instrumental pieces is exciting and powerful, and it makes use of each child's full range of understanding of these musical terms. With many opportunities to sing and play, expressive singers or players will develop. A sensitive, caring classroom teacher can nurture and support children's potential as they make their various choices about dynamics or tempo. Children can shape each phrase dynamically and realize that each phrase has a point of emphasis. The teacher can encourage wise choices daily for suitable dynamics and tempo to be used in singing particular songs. In this manner, critical listening, choosing, and performing abilities are refined for all children as musical interpretation skills develop and grow.

⚷ Feeling and Identifying Meter

Meter can be defined as the grouping of accented and unaccented beats in a pattern of two (ONE, two, ONE, two) or three (ONE, two, three, ONE, two, three) or in combinations of two and three. Meter gives internal organization, consistency, and flow to music. Feeling the macrobeat prepares for the kinesthetic understanding (feel) of meter.

For example, such marches as Sousa's *The Washington Post* or *Stars and Stripes Forever* were composed in a duple meter (two beats in each measure). Lullabies, such as Brahm's *Lullaby,* and waltzes, such as *Dance of the Sugar Plum Fairies* (from Tchaikovsky's *Nutcracker Suite)* or *Tales from the Vienna Woods* (Strauss), were composed in triple meter (three beats in each measure).

Duple meter is the easiest for children to work with initially, because it correlates with walking to the microbeat. When children walk to the microbeat, one foot consistently steps on the first beat (accented beat), and the other on the second beat, making this a natural, even movement-flow.

Most of the early childhood songs, poems, rhymes, and jump-rope chants are in duple meter. Children should be secure with walking to the microbeat in duple meter before they work on proficiency with triple meter.

Music in triple meter is excellent for rocking. The use of the macrobeat in triple meter provides calm and peace. The graceful flow of triple meter seems to expand the human need to reach out and to cooperate with other people. Our national anthem and *America (My Country, 'Tis of Thee)* are in triple meter.

Understanding meter and rhythm involves recognition that *pulses, or beats, are always grouped in twos or threes or multiples thereof.* When important concepts concerning meter are presented and experienced, the musical organization we are able to hear and understand is based on this fundamental concept of beat.

> **Identifying and moving with macrobeats and microbeats.** Since the macrobeat is the organizational beat of the song, rhyme, or musical recording, it is easily identified if children are challenged to *listen, feel,* and *express* quietly this first beat of every two- or three-beat grouping. Often, closing their eyes helps students concentrate on finding and feeling the macrobeat, and this gives the teacher an opportunity to assess the accuracy and attention span of the class as a whole. As students rock to the macrobeat, suggest that they keep the beat with a "spider pat" or "piano (soft) pat" so as not to interrupt one another's concentration.

Children often can feel the macrobeat, but if they rock to it for very long, they may lose the beat because their rocking gets out of control. One solution to this problem is to have children rock to the macrobeat and pat on the floor simultaneously, so that their rocking motion has a tactile endpoint, for balance. Another helpful strategy is to have two partners face each other, join hands, and rock back and forth. If PVC pipe is available, have the students hold between them two 24-inch pieces of pipe, to form the "sides of a boat." Then a third student can sit between the pipes to feel the macrobeat as he or she is rocked inside the "boat."

Third-graders who are accurate with the macrobeat in duple meter can bounce a tennis ball on the accented beat (beat 1) and catch it on the next beat. They may also work in pairs with a tennis ball, bouncing it to the partner on the accented beat. Using balls as objects to reinforce macrobeat in triple meter is also an important learning experience. The bounce occurs on beat 1, the catch occurs on beat 2, and a rest occurs on beat 3. When the ball goes high enough following the bounce, the catch occurs on beat 3, with the rest on beat 2.

Moving with the microbeat in duple meter develops increased proficiency and has already been discussed in the key experience *feeling and expressing steady beat.* Kindergartners can begin to perform alternating hand motions to the microbeat, a skill that is usually fine-tuned in grades 1 and 2. Students in grades 1 and 2 can also conduct the microbeat with a simple down-up conducting pattern, using both hands at the same time (see 6.27).

Third-graders will enjoy conducting triple meter with both hands,

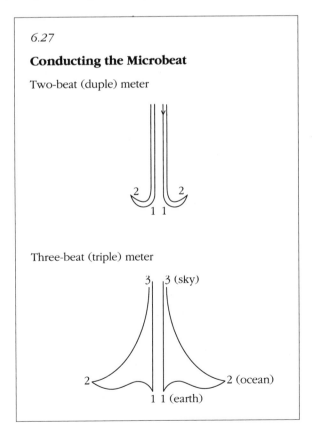

6.27

Conducting the Microbeat

Two-beat (duple) meter

Three-beat (triple) meter

using Grace C. Nash's word cues of *earth* (arms down), *ocean* (arms wide apart), and *sky* (arms up).[4] (See 6.27.) They will also find it challenging to walk to the microbeat in triple meter. They will discover that the right and left foot alternate stepping on the accented beat. This task requires concentration! Skating to represent the macrobeat in triple meter helps second- and third-graders build strength, balance, coordination, and therefore knowledge of the metrical concept.

Using hands or feet to move to the macrobeat and microbeat in duple or triple meter is a skill that all children should be able to exhibit independently by the end of third grade. When daily musical experiences are a natural part of the schedule, this ability will be secure and will help develop skills needed for singing, reading, thinking, understanding directions, and problem solving.

> **Identifying same and different meter.** When children feel and move to the macrobeat, the classroom teacher can guide them to recognize that not all macrobeats are the same. Some macrobeats are the first of two beats (duple meter) and some are the first of three (triple meter). Compare familiar songs and recorded music to strengthen this understanding of same and different meter. Sing *America (My Country, 'Tis of Thee)* and *This Land Is Your Land*, for example. Are the meters the same or different? (Students should answer "different.")

The focus of this accent is on *feeling* same and different meters. A way to clarify these concepts is through movement—through rocking to the macrobeats, stepping to the microbeats, and organizing the information that is experienced.

> **Identifying and moving to duple meter.** When children feel and understand that some macrobeats organize the microbeats into groups of two, and when they can keep the beat by walking in personal and general space consistently to a number of selections of various tempos, then they have ownership of the concept of duple meter. Some children may choose to rock to the macrobeat and show microbeat groups of two by patting their hands. Others may rock the macrobeat for the A melody, and walk the microbeat during the B melody. All of these activities demonstrate that the listener can accurately identify macrobeat and microbeat in duple meter, which is a necessary proficiency for **basic timing.**

> **Identifying and moving to triple meter.** When third-graders feel and identify that the macrobeat in triple meter organizes the microbeats equally into groups of three and can show this microbeat by walking in personal and general space consistently to a number of selections of various tempos, then they have ownership of the concept of triple meter. Some children may choose to rock to the macrobeat and express the microbeat groups of three by touching the fingers of each hand together in a continuous pattern. Others may rock to the macrobeat for the A melody while touching chin, ears, ears, in a pattern on the microbeats. Still others may rock to the macrobeat for the A melody and walk to the microbeat while conducting triple meter during the B melody. Each of these activities demonstrates that the listener can accurately identify macrobeat and microbeat in triple meter, which is a necessary proficiency for **basic timing.**

> **Differentiating between duple and triple meter.** Once children can identify duple and triple meter for individual selections, they are ready to experience musical selections that use more than one meter. Detecting changes of meter can be quite intriguing. The meter may differ in various sections of the music. In *Danish Masquerade* (CD4), for example, section A is in a moderate duple meter; section B flows in a graceful triple meter; and section C is composed in a brisk duple meter.

Strategies for differentiating duple and triple meters within a selection are consistent with preceding discussions and are a natural extension of the expanding musical repertoire of third-graders. Quick and accurate differentiation of changing meter within a piece prepares children to be able to work in uncommon or unusual meters of 5/4 (one triple plus one duple, or vice versa) and 7/8 (one triple plus two duples, or vice versa) in later grades.

⟳ Expressing Rhythm

Rhythm is the distinctive element that gives life to sound—the action of tones or sounds within and among the beats. Rhythm is made up of longer and shorter durational patterns or of even and uneven patterns. It includes everything that pertains to the durations of musical sounds. Grace C. Nash tells us that rhythm "permeates the entire fabric of music; it magnetizes all the musical elements, drawing them together into a vibrating, breathing whole which occupies a specific length of time."[5]

Rhythm is an irresistible element of music. It captures the ear and draws our attention immediately to a song or musical selection we find appealing. Rhythm is as unique to a specific song as each child is unique in the classroom. The rhythm of *If You're Happy and You Know It*, for example, is always the same, no matter when or where you sing it. It is unlikely that any other song has exactly the same rhythm or melodic organization.

Repetition, variation, syncopation, and creativity are rhythm's essential factors, as are beat, tempo, and meter. Because it represents the distinct personality of language and of music, we respond to rhythm automatically by imitating what we hear. However, if we encourage children to clap rhythms before they are secure with steady beat, they will not have had adequate preparation in hearing, singing, or speaking rhythms against the steady beat expressed in movement. The result will be that their motor responses to rhythm will lack precision. A helpful rule is this: Children's movement responses should be **in time to steady beat** until around the age of seven, or until children are secure in **beat competence.** The rhyme presented earlier is appropriate again here:

> *Keep beat in the body,*
> *Speak rhythm in the mouth.*
> *It's just as plain as*
> *North and south.*

Second- and third-grade students who are secure with steady beat can and should respond to music's rhythms through basic locomotor and nonlocomotor movements, movement with objects, creative movement, and rhythmic dramatizations. When children have waited until second grade to play rhythmic patterns to accompany songs or rhymes, they are ready to begin to clearly understand basic rhythmic relationships and will be able to play rhythms precisely and musically.

> **Listening for longer and shorter sounds.** As young children respond to the macrobeat, they can also be guided to listen for specific long or short sounds. *Sunrise,* from Grofé's *Grand Canyon Suite,* is an example of a selection filled with long sounds. Short sounds may be heard in *Irish Washerwoman* (RM3). Often there is an opportunity to identify long and short sounds in the same selection, such as in *Seven Jumps* (RM2). Section A contains many short sounds, and section B includes long sounds of varying durations. The class may be guided to use one hand signal when they hear the long sounds (perhaps the fists slowly opening) and another hand signal for the short sounds (finger tips of both hands touching each other). Many and varied identification experiences will enable them to recognize long and short sounds quickly and easily.

Patterns of long and short sounds also provide a listening challenge. *If You're Happy, Looby Loo,* and *This Land Is Your Land* are fine examples. Students in grades 2 and 3 will want to begin to represent these long/short sound patterns with manipulatives and to play these on unpitched instruments. They should be encouraged to do so. Their discoveries become the catalysts for others to listen for the secrets rhythm holds.

> **Moving to sounds of longer and shorter duration.** Young children have more success responding to sounds of longer and shorter duration when beginning experiences provide sounds that are close to their internal timing. For example, at first, a wood block that is played consistently to produce sounds of short duration would be a simple percussion instrument to use for movement. (See Chapter 8, "Magic Eight," p. 268.) Then, when finger cymbals struck together to create sounds of longer duration are introduced, more-sustained movements would be natural for these sounds. When listening to sounds that are twice as fast, such as those played on a tambourine, several children can explore running lightly as a way of representing their understanding of this faster concept.

Layering two instrument sounds seems to reinforce the relationship of the concepts of longer and shorter durations, especially when children have time to discuss and compare what they have heard. If some class members respond to the sounds of longer duration while others respond to the sounds of shorter duration, the relationship of longer to shorter duration becomes even clearer. When their comparison of the two durations indicates that they perceive and understand the relationships, they are beginning to have ownership of these concepts. One child can lead in deciding when each instrument will be played. To further challenge children's aural discrimination responses, the instrument players can be hidden from the group.

When sounds of longer duration (such as the sounds of the triangle being played) are the consistent focus, children can engage in movement exploration that is either nonlocomotor or locomotor. Some students may experiment with a slow walk; others with a swing of both arms. Children will discover that movements of longer duration (for the longer sounds) require balance, strength, coordination, listening, and thinking.

Many experiences are needed in order for young children to listen and respond with confidence to repeated sounds of longer and shorter duration.

> **Moving to rhythm patterns.** Students in kindergarten and first grade can move their bodies **to the steady beat** as they say rhythm patterns (see 6.28). They also may echo rhythm syllables back to the leader while keeping the macrobeat.

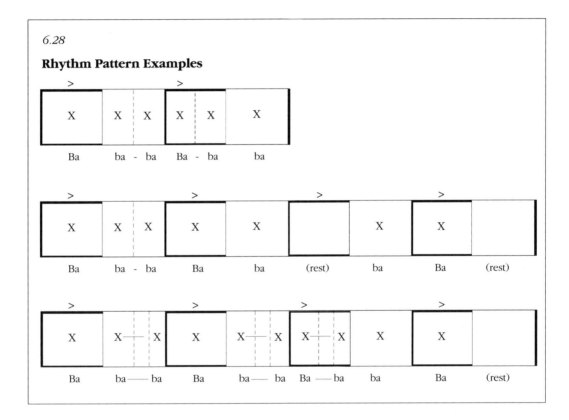

6.28

Rhythm Pattern Examples

When students have developed proficiency with the movement key experiences and *secured* basic timing with daily beat-keeping experiences throughout grade 1, they are ready to represent rhythm patterns through movement combinations. For example, the movement combinations shown in Insert 6.29 might be explored. Children can create other rhythm patterns. Some **rhythm patterns** (long, short, long, short) call for a gallop, or skipping, response, and the hand drum works well to represent this rhythm pattern. Children will enjoy the opportunity to create their own combinations of long and short sound patterns and will develop movement ideas for them that they can share with the class.

When the children learn a new rhythm pattern, it works well to perform the pattern at least four times. Instruments mentioned in the preceding accent can be played to aurally reinforce these patterns. Students in grades 2 and 3 will

6.29

Movement Combinations to Explore

walk	walk	walk	walk	jump		jump	

jump		jump		walk	walk	walk	walk

walk	walk	run ┆ run	run ┆ run

run ┆ run	run ┆ run	walk	walk

gallop	gallop	gallop	gallop	gallop	gallop	whoa	

skip	skip	skip	skip	skip	skip	skip	

have the motor and mental abilities to create extended patterns of longer and shorter duration. They should be encouraged to create as many as possible and to play them with understanding and coordination.

In keeping with the spirit of active learning, there should be plenty of time to explore and to share ideas about movement rhythm patterns. When a student creates a movement rhythm pattern for the class to copy, there should be time for each child to practice it at his or her *individual* tempo, with SAY & DO, before trying to bring the pattern to a group beat with instruments added. If music is to be added so that the pattern is repeated a number of times, students should have the opportunity to listen to the tempo and to concentrate on how the movement rhythm pattern will fit the music before attempting to do it. The "safety net" will be in place when students try out the SAY with the music several times before adding the DO. (See the Teaching Model in Chapter 2.)

Many opportunities for second-graders to move to rhythm patterns in duple meter should be included throughout the year. For a secure foundation, patterns in triple meter can be added in third grade.

> **Distinguishing same and different rhythm patterns.** Aural discrimination and thinking skills are activated when students try to identify same and different rhythm patterns in rhymes, songs, and recorded selections. For example, as the class recites "Humpty Dumpty," help them discover whether any of its parts have rhythms that are the same (see 6.30). If so, which parts?

In kindergarten and grade 1, play spoken-echo rhythm games. One such game involves the leader (a teacher or child) thinking of a four-beat rhythm pattern in which the last beat is a rest, such as one of the two patterns shown in Insert 6.31. The rest, for beginners, allows just enough time to organize before having to respond with the echo. After the leader gives two of these rhythm patterns and others echo them, the class determines whether the patterns were the same or different. In later grades, three or four patterns may be given before the class is asked to determine which were different and which, if any, were alike. (For an activity that uses this concept, refer to Chapter 8.)

6.30

Humpty Dumpty

Humpty Dumpty sat on a wall,

Humpty Dumpty had a great fall.
(Same rhythm as line 1)

All the king's horses and all the king's men

Couldn't put Humpty together again.
(Same rhythm as line 3)

6.31

Four-Beat Patterns With a Rest

When singing familiar songs, encourage children to listen carefully to the rhythm patterns and to identify those that are the *same*. *Happy Birthday* is a nice one to begin with (see 6.32). Then, the children can become *real* "rhythm detectives" by identifying the rhythm pattern that is *different*.

When rhythm patterns include *specific durations* (in grades 2 and 3), we suggest implementing Dr. Edwin Gordon's rhythm syllables.[6] His system provides learners with a way to understand, read, and write rhythm. The beat is always "du"; the division of the beat in two is "de" (pronounced "day"), and division of the beat into three is "da-di" (pronounced "dah- dee"). "Ta" (pronounced "tah") represents the *subdivision* (division of the division) of beat. (Unusual meters are not dealt with here because of our K–3 focus.) Dr. Gordon's consistency has taken much of the confusion out of reading and understanding rhythm. Examples in Inserts 6.33 through 6.37 on the following pages show how rhythms are read using this approach.

6.32

Same and Different Rhythm Patterns—*Happy Birthday*

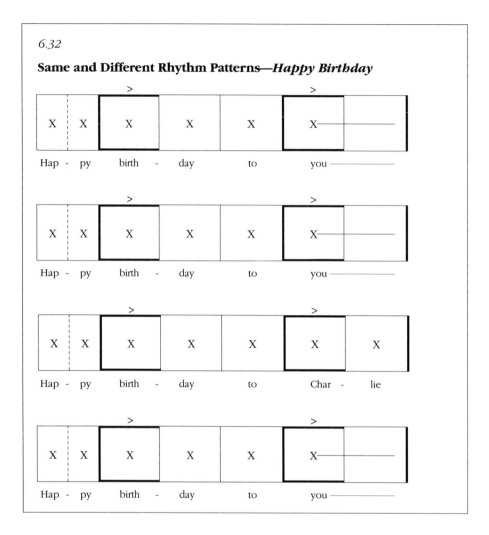

Children in grades 2 and 3 will be able to play extended versions of the echo rhythm game. First, they listen. Then, they repeat the pattern back with SAY. Finally, they SAY & DO the pattern. Children can be encouraged to lead these echo rhythm games.

> **Recognizing and playing even and uneven rhythm patterns. Even rhythm patterns** are those that repeat the same duration, such as "du, du, du, du" or "du-de, du-de, du-de, du-de." Even rhythm patterns have a special place in the learning sequence. Pachelbel's Canon in D, which uses an even pattern for the bass melody, would not cause us to listen twice without the interesting uneven rhythm patterns that decorate the melody and occur in the supporting instrumental parts.

Uneven rhythm patterns combine different rhythmic durations. These patterns can be as short as the phrase "little lamb" in *Mary Had a Little Lamb,* or as long as the uneven pattern repeated five times in the first two phrases of *If You're Happy and You Know It, Clap Your Hands* (see 6.38). Uneven patterns also include ones for skipping or galloping (also shown in Insert 6.38). Once children recognize even and uneven rhythm patterns, they should be

6.33

Duple Rhythm Patterns

1. When a microbeat is divided into two parts:

2. When a microbeat is divided into three parts:

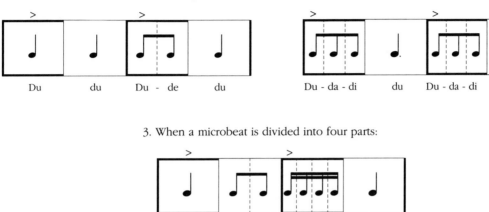

3. When a microbeat is divided into four parts:

6.34

Triple Rhythm Patterns

1. When a microbeat is divided into two parts:

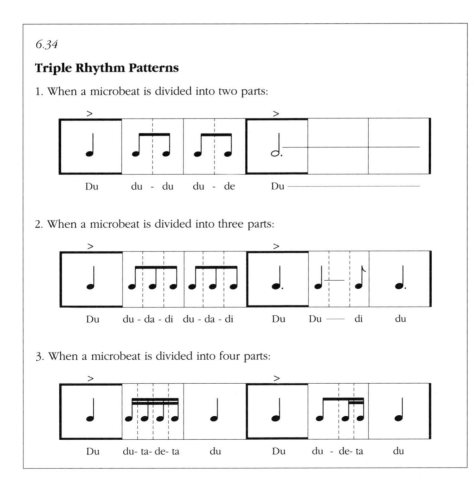

2. When a microbeat is divided into three parts:

3. When a microbeat is divided into four parts:

6.35

Hot Cross Buns (Duple)

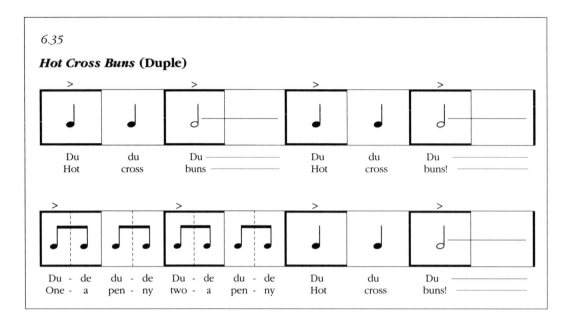

6.36

Happy Birthday (Triple)

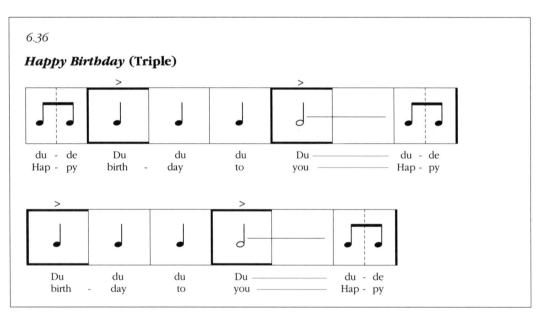

encouraged to play them while the class sings. Rhythm patterns may synchronize with the melody or may complement the melody. One strategy, "operation rhythm," is useful with students in grade 3. To begin "operation rhythm," start with a familiar song. Then dissect its even and uneven rhythm patterns; even patterns may be played on triangles, and uneven patterns, on sticks. (See Chapter 8.)

Rather than being heard one note at a time, music is heard in groups of notes called phrases, or musical sentences. Beginning experiences in discovering even and uneven rhythm patterns are very closely associated with identification of melodic patterns students have sung. Listening experiences are also filled with opportunities to find these even and uneven rhythm patterns. The more experiences young children have with detecting them, the more proficiency they

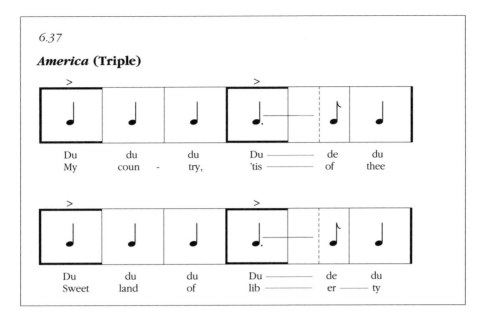

6.37

America (Triple)

Du	du	du	Du ——— de	du
My	coun - try,	'tis ——— of	thee

Du	du	du	Du ——— de	du
Sweet	land	of	lib ——— er ——— ty

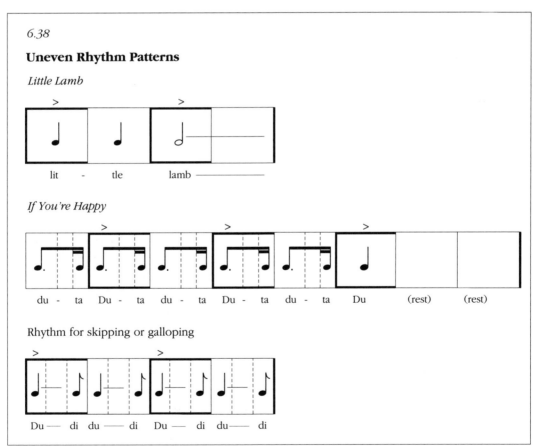

6.38

Uneven Rhythm Patterns

Little Lamb

lit - tle	lamb ———

If You're Happy

du - ta Du - ta du - ta Du - ta du - ta Du (rest) (rest)

Rhythm for skipping or galloping

Du — di du — di Du — di du — di

will exhibit in discovering even and uneven rhythm patterns in rhymes, in speech, and in the written word.

> **Reading, writing, and performing rhythm patterns.** Writing rhythm patterns generates excitement, and one way to "write" is with manipulatives!

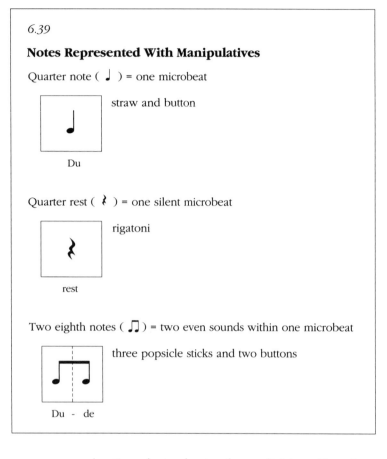

6.39

Notes Represented With Manipulatives

Quarter note (♩) = one microbeat

straw and button

Du

Quarter rest (𝄽) = one silent microbeat

rigatoni

rest

Two eighth notes (♫) = two even sounds within one microbeat

three popsicle sticks and two buttons

Du - de

For example, in the music room, one music teacher kept a box full of manipulatives that students could use to create rhythm patterns. This box was filled with small paper bags containing drinking straws, medium-sized buttons, popsicle sticks, and uncooked rigatoni.

In March, after many experiences with moving to different rhythm patterns, one of the second-grade children expressed an interest in writing musical notation, so the teacher brought out the box and gave each child a bag of manipulatives. From their prior movement experiences, all the students understood the duration of microbeats, of even division of beat into two, and of silent beat. It took them only a matter of minutes to decide that the rigatoni could represent the beat of silence called a quarter rest, each straw and button could represent the quarter note, and three popsicle sticks plus two buttons could represent the equal division of microbeat into two faster sounds, two eighth notes (see 6.39). Everyone sat on the floor and the teacher began speaking simple rhythm patterns like those shown in Insert 6.40. The children would repeat the teacher's pattern twice and then "write" with their manipulatives. Then they would read them in unison together, as a volunteer set the tempo.

The children requested more work with these manipulatives, which they thought of as rhythm codes. They eventually began to create longer rhythm patterns for one another to "write." Within 2 or 3 months, the children could "write" patterns of 12 and even 16 beats. This experience was reinforced by having the children choose a locomotor movement to represent each duration in a pattern (see 6.41).

When the foundation is laid with movement, it then becomes natural to progress from writing simple, basic rhythm patterns to writing longer patterns that may include additional durations. Later, students can be led to an understanding of how notes convey both pitch *and* rhythm in this universal language.

> **Recognizing and using note and rest values (quarter ♩, two eighth ♫, half ♩, dotted half ♩., and whole o).** When children use movement to represent

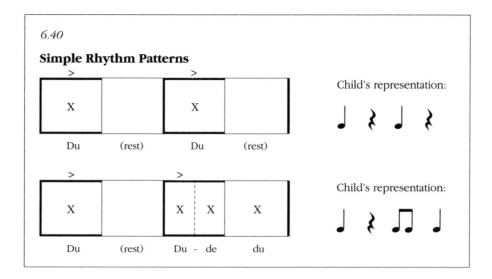

6.40

Simple Rhythm Patterns

>		>	
X		X	
Du	(rest)	Du	(rest)

Child's representation:

>		>		
X		X	X	X
Du	(rest)	Du	- de	du

Child's representation:

specific durations, they are already recognizing and using note values, even though they have not read actual music notation. When movement experiences precede an activity such as the one involving writing patterns (just described), children are using icons for further rhythmic problem solving. The previous accent used manipulatives to represent the quarter note, quarter rest, and two eighth notes. Continuation of this rhythm writing can extend to include patterns that use the half note, dotted half note, and whole note, as

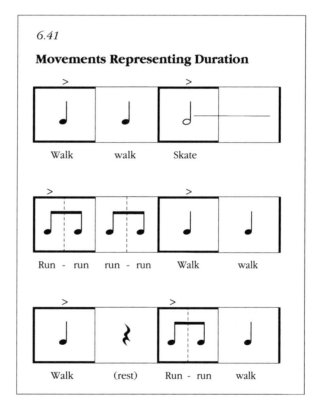

6.41

Movements Representing Duration

>		>	
Walk	walk	Skate	

>		>	
Run - run	run - run	Walk	walk

>		>	
Walk	(rest)	Run - run	walk

explained in Insert 6.42. Because students had experienced these additional durations through movement first and because they were actively involved in the natural problem solving that goes with the writing and creating of new rhythm patterns, they never tired of this activity.

The transfer of this aural-kinesthetic knowledge (enactive) to a visual display (iconic) becomes the next natural step, followed by the desire to draw the various types of notes (symbolic). The applications of Bruner's learning cycle

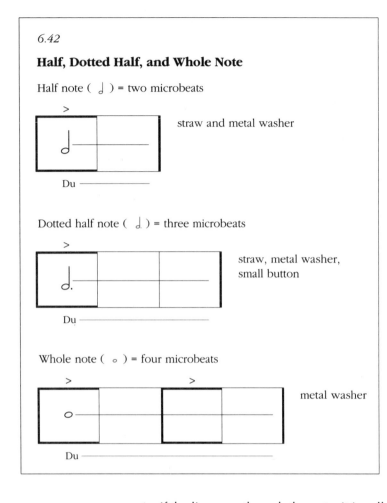

6.42

Half, Dotted Half, and Whole Note

Half note (♩) = two microbeats

straw and metal washer

Du

Dotted half note (♩.) = three microbeats

straw, metal washer, small button

Du

Whole note (○) = four microbeats

metal washer

Du

described in Chapter 3 can now be better understood as it occurs naturally with children throughout this key experience. At this point, learners will want to know about the musical staff and about the information represented by **line** and **space notes.**

> *Each note has a name, a place, a sound,*
>
> *Each note is special!*
>
> *Each note must be found!*

Each note in music has a name (quarter note, half note, etc.); a place (on the music staff); a sound (a specific pitch). A note drawn on the staff that is placed *in* the space between the lines is called a

space note. If the line goes through the note, it is called a **line note** (see 6.43). It is *important for students to discover for themselves* that a basic understanding of each musical element provides a foundation for incorporating these elements in ways that enable them to use, create, enjoy, and appreciate all that music offers.

⚷ Adding Harmony

In music, **harmony** refers to a simultaneous combination of sounds that enhances or supports the melody. For example, harmony may be added to the song *Hush, Little Baby* when one child strums the autoharp chords as the rest of the class sings. If a group of students plays chords on the resonator bells, a different quality of harmonic accompaniment is heard. When the class sings *Down by the Bay,* holding

6.43

Notes on the Musical Staff

Line Note

Space Note

Before learning to write music with conventional notation, children can use manipulatives to create various rhythms. Here two girls use straws and buttons to create a four-beat rhythm made up of a quarter note, two eighth notes, a quarter note, and a quarter note.

the last note of each phrase, and a small group of volunteers sings the echo response, another kind of harmony is heard. Harmony, whether vocal or instrumental, provides rich texture to any song, rhyme, or musical selection.

One of the most pleasant sounds to hear is that of young children singing in unison and in tune with no accompaniment. This should be the goal for classroom singing across the nation. Young children need *many more* opportunities to sing than are afforded in a single 20- or 30-minute music class each week. Singing, for young children, should be as natural as speaking. The classroom offers many things to sing about, and music can and should be incorporated in many ways throughout the day.

Once children can sing a song well, adding harmony can develop, or broaden, the musical experience. How this is done depends on the type of song. For songs such as *Little Sir Echo, Down by the Bay,* or *I'm on My Way,* which are found in most music books for young singers, echo responses by two or three strong singers are appropriate. These echoes provide beginning vocal harmony. Children themselves can play the autoharp accompaniments for rounds, because only one chord needs to be played on the macrobeat. Resonator bell maps (see 6.44), as well as autoharps, can be used to create the two or three primary chords needed for many other song accompaniments. (The chords accompanying songs printed in this text are autoharp chords.) Rhythm instrument accompaniments are another possibility for adding harmony. Generally, accompaniment by one or two instruments is sufficient. Of course, such songs as *I Bought Me a Cat* or *Old MacDonald* require several instruments—one to represent each kind of animal.

6.44

Resonator Bell Map

Each player has a bell and plays when the leader indicates which column of bell pitches should be played. For example, the chords played for the macrobeat of *This Old Man* are these:

	F
G	D
E	B
C	G
C-chord	**G⁷-chord**

This	man	he	one	He	knick	on	drum
C	C	C	C	G⁷	G⁷	G⁷	G⁷

knick	paddy	give	bone	This	man	roll	home
C	C	C	C	G⁷	G⁷	G⁷	C

> **Recognizing the difference between unison singing and singing accompanied by instrument(s).** Although most children can recognize when instruments are being used to accompany singing and when they are not, the classroom teacher's facilitating questions can elicit a discussion about what specific accompanying instruments are being used or could be used. After children listen to a recording, for example, the teacher can guide a discussion of what instruments they heard accompanying the singers and what differences they heard when the music involved only the singers' voices.

> **Using chords to create harmony. Chords** result when two or three pitches that sound good together are played at the same time. When used with skill, chords can add to the melody a supporting sound texture that enhances the effect. Almost all children's songs can be harmonized quite nicely by using the three main chords—I, IV, and V in any key system. The I-chord uses scale degrees 1, 3, 5 (or C, E, G) in the C-major system. The IV chord uses scale degrees 4, 6, 8, (or F, A, C) in the C- major system. The V chord uses tones 5, 7, 2 (or G, B, D) in the C-major system. A song such as *Mary Had A Little Lamb* needs only two chords—I and V—to construct basic harmony (see 6.45).

The autoharp may be used quite nicely to provide chord accompaniment, because each chord is automatically fixed on a specifically named chord button on the instrument. Many children's songbooks have the chord information written above the melody (as this book does), so teachers will be able to know what chords to play.

> **Singing call-response and echo songs. Call-response songs** are those in which young singers have a very simple response to sing at specific places in the song. Their response may be only on one pitch, as in

6.45

Mary Had a Little Lamb

Scale	F	G	A	B♭	C	D	E	F
Scale Degrees	1	2	3	4	5	6	7	8

C	G
A	E
F	C
I-chord	**V-chord**

Mary	had	a	little	lamb,	little	lamb,	little	lamb
I	I	I	I	V	V		I	I

Mary	had	a	little	lamb,	Its	fleece	was	white	as	snow	—
I	I	I	I		V			V		I	I

Who Can? (see Chapter 8), and it may consist of only one or two words or syllables. The fun of singing call-response songs lies in being able to respond with the needed words or syllables at just the right time. *Who Can?* and *She'll Be Comin' 'Round the Mountain* are call-response songs everyone should have the pleasure of singing.

Call-response songs work well with singers who are age 7 or older. Before that age, the focus needs to be on getting children to sing well as a group and to enjoy knowing they can sing. After age 7 or 8, they can begin to build a repertoire of good-quality songs that can be enhanced with instrumental or vocal harmony.

Echo songs usually have a phrase to be echoed by a solo singer. *Little Sir Echo, Bill Grogan's Goat, Charlie Over the Ocean, Down by the Bay,* and *When the Saints Go Marching In* are examples of this type of song. In this book, *Charlie Over the Ocean* has been adapted to *Now It Is December* (see Chapter 8, p. 288).

> **Adding melodic chants.** Children often find it easier to add a **melodic chant** to a known song by using the chant as introduction and *continuing* throughout the song. Insert 6.46 shows an example of how a chant uses only one pitch.

These first attempts to enhance a song with harmony should be gradual and should only be attempted if the teacher feels comfortable guiding the adventure. The chant can be repeated to beat-keeping movement until several strong singers are ready to be "harmony pioneers" and try it. Be patient. This requires tonal memory, patience, and cooperation, as well as independent, timed, and tuned singers.

> **Singing rounds.** A round is a song that is imitated at the same pitch by a second (or third) group of singers who begin at a designated time. Second- and third-graders are ready to begin singing rounds. All of the singers should know the song well. To prepare the children for this new idea, the teacher can at first layer the sound by beginning the round at the appropriate later time while they are singing. This will leave the teacher finishing the song last. Then discuss what happened, and ask for a few volunteers to sing with the teacher in "rounding" the song. This strategy provides a safety net for first attempts at singing in rounds. Keep in mind that a few strong singers will be needed to lead the first group of children who attempt to layer the sound, so the

---

6.46

A Melodic Chant for *Skip to My Lou*

Key of C: Beginning song pitch is E.

Scale degree 5 (G) is used for the chant because that tone is common to both the I-chord and the V-chord.

Skip to my Lou	(This chant is sung four times as a vocal introduction. On the fifth repetition, class members begin singing the song while a small group of four to five students continues the chant.)
G G	

group does not falter in singing their independent part. Some rounds to use are *Are You Sleeping?, Row, Row, Row Your Boat,* and *Make New Friends.*

> **Finding and using ways to add harmony to a song or instrumental selection.** Learning experiences that involve adding harmony provide a critical thinking environment in which budding musicians can develop. During plan-do-review time, individuals may choose to work with the autoharp or some other instrument to add harmony to a known song. The results of these creations may be shared with the larger group.

There are numerous ways to add harmony and richness to a song or instrumental recording. Remember that the ideas young children have for enhancing a song or recording

Young students are usually eager to suggest musical ideas for enhancing a song, rhyme, story, or musical recording. An idea thus shared often becomes the catalyst for many appropriate creative variations, and this enriches everyone's listening experience!

are often far better than any ideas adults have. Cooperation and respect for young learners' ideas for adding harmony can provide rich aural experiences for all.

Summary

There are so many opportunities for classroom teachers and music educators to introduce young children to music's various elements. The key experiences and accents described in this chapter can develop and facilitate each child's natural musical intelligence, especially when relevant activities are provided in an environment of active learning. Once children have had many experiences in using the elements of music, they will be ready to create and perform their own music, a topic further explored in Chapter 7.

ENDNOTES

[1] E. Gordon, *Learning Sequences in Music* (Chicago: GIA Publishing, 1984).

[2] P. S. Weikart, "Movement Curriculum Improves Children's Rhythmic Competence," *High/Scope ReSource,* Vol. 6, No. 1 (Winter 1987), pp. 8–11.

[3] *Movement Plus Music* by Phyllis S. Weikart has many lessons prepared for teachers to use in matching the beat of recorded music.

[4] G. C. Nash. *Creative Approaches to Child Development with Music, Language, and Movement.* (New York: Alfred Publishing, 1974).

[5] G. C. Nash. *Creative Approaches,* p. 4.

[6] E. Gordon, *Learning Sequences in Music.*

Chapter 7

Creating and Performing Music

. . . Music education can provide students with a strong sense of determination, improved communication skills, and a host of other qualities essential for successful living.

Edward H. Rensi
Chief Operations Officer, President,
and Chief Operating Officer
McDonald's Corporation (U.S.A.)

The previous two categories of music key experiences, **exploring music** (Chapter 5) and **using the elements of music** (Chapter 6), included many opportunities for children to show initiative in *figuring out something new.* Children who have had opportunities to "figure out" music—to explore and be actively involved in using its elements—are often eager to use their growing musical abilities by **creating and performing music.** For such children, figuring out familiar songs; creating original melodies, instrumental accompaniments, or movement sequences choreographed to music; and performing musically for their peers become a natural part of the daily process. Together, everyone supports, discovers, and delights in the many ways music can be incorporated into the various aspects of learning. Children's interest in, and thus their knowledge of, musical concepts grows as they create original musical thoughts and relate them to existing knowledge. The results of an active learning approach can be seen in the ways children schooled in this approach naturally use music throughout the day—singing, using instruments, creating music, and listening to recordings. In many ways, the High/Scope educational philosophy develops in young children what is already inherent in them—the urge to use music as a natural language, a true means of expression and communication.

This clearly observable outcome of children's **individual growth in musical abilities** is of particular importance. Just compare this outcome of the High/Scope educational approach with psychologist Howard Gardner's description of the outcomes of some other approaches to music education that are prevalent in the United States: "For many children, the start of formal musical instruction marks the beginning of the end of musical development. The atomistic focus in most music instruction—the individual pitch, its name, its notation—and the measure-by-measure method of instruction and analysis run

Building a musical foundation together, two students play the autoharp and finger cymbals while others sing. The students are developing separate but interdependent musical responsibilities and skills.

counter to the holistic way most children have come to think of, react to, and live with music."[1]

Some children will not have an opportunity to develop their musical intelligence unless classroom teachers and music educators provide the experiences that form the basis of music literacy. While children, on their own, may become aware of how music affects people's everyday lives, a teacher's guidance can assure that children's basic music experiences are not left to chance. Moving, singing, and listening to good selections from all genres of music will help children to improve the quality of their lives and to realize the deep effect music can have on them. Regularly offering children opportunities to explore, make choices, learn cooperatively, and initiate activities will enable them to share their musical interests, questions, performances, and creative efforts with one another and with their families.

Children who enjoy making music will want to figure out how to play familiar songs on musical instruments. (*Rain, Rain, Go Away; Hot Cross Buns;* and *Mary Had a Little Lamb,* for example, are songs for them to begin with.) As children begin to create original melodies that they want to be able to recall, they will develop a desire to read and write music using their own symbol system, and they will want to use the tape recorder to record their creations. Some will be interested in reading "real" music notation. This holistic approach feeds each child's desire to use music's rare capacity to express, through pitch and rhythm notation, those feelings for which there are no words.

We cannot overemphasize the long-term significance of including music in the classroom's daily schedule. Music speaks to all of our senses, moods, and attitudes. The classroom teacher, who knows each child and also has a sense of the overall class personality, will want to take responsibility for helping children achieve their potential for musical growth and development. At times, the teacher may sense that either the general class mood or an individual child's problem is hindering the learning at hand, and thus a change of lesson plan may be in order. Very often, a well-chosen instrumental selection can change the classroom climate (see 7.1). Often, students' attitudes can be changed by marching to *Soldier's Joy* (RM2), or skipping to *Sellenger's Round* (RM7), or moving to other appropriate musical selections.

In this chapter, we explore the key experiences that make up the third and final category in the High/Scope approach to music, **creating and performing music.** These key experiences, which develop naturally from those in the first two categories, **exploring music** and **using the elements of music,** focus on each child's emerging abilities to use, perform, and appreciate our musical heritage. The following key experiences are described in this chapter:

- Responding to various types of music
- Playing instruments alone and in groups
- Singing alone and in groups
- Sharing music by performing
- Moving creatively and choreographing movement sequences and dances
- Creating and improvising songs and instrumental music
- Reading music
- Writing music

As in the previous two chapters, within each key experience are various musical *accents* that are designed to provide measurable outcomes on a continuum throughout the K–3 years. These accents should enable the classroom teacher to become familiar with all aspects of the **creating and performing** music key experiences and to guide children in their pursuit of musical adventures.

The Key Experiences Included in Creating and Performing Music

⟿ Responding to Various Types of Music

Responding to various types of music provides children and teachers with opportunities to open their ears, minds, and hearts to important experiences. *Quality choices of all types of music need to be included,* because each composer and selection has something worthy to offer. Teachers already have the basic tools to guide children's musical understanding. Introduce children to a variety of music, including the classics, the semiclassics, and the rich array of folk music. A secure foundation has its base in musical diversity, where children also have the opportunity to choose the type of music they want to work with during plan-do-review.

> **Showing through movement the differences heard in music.**
As children's listening skills and imaginations develop, they may surprise adults with their interpretations of music that is being played. First, give them time to listen to a selection before asking for their movement response, but keep these listening experiences short and relevant to the group. Until children have had many experiences listening to music and expressing their reactions through movement, their movement responses may be somewhat inhibited. The more a teacher values and supports the creative thoughts children express, the more sensitive and intricate the children's musical interpretations will be. Also, the more often children listen to a requested musical selection, the more expressive their movements will become. Like the singing voice, the listening ear is developed only through repeated experiences.

> **Responding to *same/different* in songs children sing.** As children's vocal repertoire grows, they will express such things as pride, joy, excitement, love, sadness, multicultural understanding—and even nonsense—as they respond spontaneously and naturally to the text, mood, and melody of each particular song they sing. Teachers can appeal to children's natural curiosity by asking questions like these about the music:

- Do any of the songs you know sound almost the same? (scale songs like *Wise Old Owl* or *I Know a Little Puppy*)
- Do you know songs with the same melody but different words? (*Mary Had a Little Lamb* and *Merrily We Roll Along*)

7.1

Peaceful Listening Suggestions

Southwind (RM1)

Leor Chiyuchech (RM8)

Al Gemali (CD4)

Scheherazade—
　　Nicolai Rimsky-Korsakov

Eine Kleine Nachtmusik—
　　Wolfgang Amadeus Mozart

New World Symphony,
Second movement—
　　Antonin Dvořák

- Can you think of any songs that have some parts that are alike? (*The Muffin Man* and *All Night, All Day*)
- In what ways do all patriotic songs sound alike? (majestic music and text, memorable melody, feeling of pride and loyalty)
- Is melody the only thing that makes one song different from another? (also, rhythm, harmony, text, tempo, etc.)

Guide children to discover that the musical elements all combine in various ways to create differences among songs. Every category of music includes some songs that sound alike and some that sound different. How many different types of music can be explored and categorized within a given year? The answer depends only on the possibilities presented and the imaginations of children. Types of songs to introduce to children include songs to begin (or end) the day, songs about animals, happy songs, sad or thoughtful songs, spooky songs, songs of America, songs of other countries, seasonal songs, work songs, songs of the sea, songs of the West (or South, North, East), canons and rounds, camp songs—the list is endless.

There are many ways that music learning can influence other areas of learning. In a developmentally appropriate classroom, encourage students to take the lead in discussing the differences they hear and feel in various songs, and encourage them to show these differences through their singing. Help children compare and classify these differences. Look and listen for each child's understanding of various music elements. Connections made through active music experiences have long-term significance across the curriculum.

> **Responding to *same/different* in instrumental music.**

Discussions about what children hear in specific musical selections can lead to same/different instrument recognition

A child who enjoys music will often want to figure out how to play the melody to a simple song on a musical instrument.

as well as to insights into the overall mood, dynamics, tempo, and style of various selections. Being able to articulate their responses to music through movement can be a boon to shy children. When partners or small groups respond together to music, dynamic interaction can result. Groups can select adventures such as "Listening Treasure Hunt" (How many different instruments can you identify in the recording?), "Instruments: Listen and Name," "Differing Dynamics" (How many different dynamic changes did you hear in this recording?), or "Tempo Police" (How many times did the tempo change? or Was the tempo the same or different in each or all of these pieces?). These music games help children develop acute listening skills, as well as cooperative and integrated learning strategies. Listening skills developed through music experiences can lead to better peripheral hearing and refined aural discrimination. The teacher may be surprised to discover just what children can and do hear when they are motivated to listen carefully.

> **Responding to different moods of a musical selection.** This accent is included because each child needs to experience group and individual responses to the whole spectrum of music's various moods. For example, we may respond automatically to the patriotism expressed in Sousa's *Stars and Stripes Forever* (while marching), to the reverence so evident in Gruber's *Silent Night* (while singing), and to the uplifting beauty of Holst's Second Suite (while listening). When children are given the chance *each day* to listen and respond to music's many moods, the quality of the day's learning can be greatly enhanced. Listen to *Mindrele* (CD5) and its haunting, mysterious mood. *Santa Rita* (CD5) brings a Mexican fiesta directly into your classroom! Many other valuable musical selections are listed in "Children's Selected Listening," Appendix C.

> **Responding to a repertoire of different types of music.** If only one type of music is played for children, their corresponding movement, cognitive, and aesthetic responses will be rather narrow. Therefore it is important that children be exposed to a well-balanced variety of music. They will enjoy listening to classical selections, marches, jazz selections, folk music, waltzes, easy-listening selections, and the "golden oldies." Easy-to-use teacher guides accompany the excellent classical selections in the *Bowmar Orchestral Library* series and the RCA *Adventures in Music* series listed in Appendix C. Prokofiev's *Peter and the Wolf,* Saint-Saëns' *Carnival of the Animals,* and Korsakov's *Flight of the Bumblebee* are also favorite selections of many young children. Appendix C lists further selections appropriate for K–3 listeners.

The types of music used in the classroom should reflect **children's interests** as much as possible, but it is up to the teacher to guide the listening/responding adventures so the elements of **quality** and **scope** are considered, as well.

⚡ Playing Instruments Alone and in Groups

For young children, music is an abstract, aural experience when the focus is on singing, listening, and moving to music. When children have the opportunity to play instruments, however, this provides a chance to work with music and sounds (unpitched or pitched) in a concrete way—to construct or reconstruct simple songs and accompaniments. Once children discover ways to play various instruments, they will want to choose specific instruments to play for accompaniments to particular songs, poems, or stories. Their first instrumental

accompaniment choices will be simple. Later, as their experience and confidence grow, they may use two or more instruments for accompaniment, or they may plan ways to represent specific parts of a song, poem, or story by instruments. "Decorating" a song with sound becomes an exciting project that continues through the K–3 years and beyond.

Playing various instruments provides music with a concrete aspect that allows children's musical literacy to develop holistically. When children have

A teacher supplies support and encouragement as these children use percussion instruments to play a simple song together, keeping a common steady beat.

sufficient experiences and encouragement in playing musical instruments, they will want to play together in groups, to accompany simple songs, and even to perform alone to share known or original songs with others. Tonal memory— the ability to remember the specific order of musical pitches in a phrase or song—will develop as children work with the **body scale** and **musical intervals** (see *interval* in Glossary). Knowing that they are playing a musical selection in a specific key (in the key of C, for example; see *key system* in Glossary) will begin to give them a sense of how the body scale and the musical scale provide the framework for melody and chords. In addition, students can begin to understand why music theory and harmonization are necessary parts of music education. The practical need to know about each new aspect of music drives children's interest and gives them incentive to figure it out.

> **Playing an instrument alone or in a group, using steady beat.**
Playing a steady beat alone is easier than playing a steady beat with instruments in a group. When several children plan to play together, they will need to think about who will lead, how they will all stay together, and how they will all stop at the same time. The learner SAY & DO four-step process will link cognitive to motor, so the group stays together. Preparation for keeping steady beat with instruments will have occurred earlier, when children learned to keep the beat on their bodies. Of course, children will also need to have explored playing an instrument before they join an instrumental group.

Some children may volunteer to demonstrate that they are ready to play alone with steady beat. Encourage them to take the lead in this way by providing a safe environment—one that is supportive of each child's musical efforts.

A positive comment or a smile may be just the encouragement a child needs to do it alone.

> **Playing an instrument in steady beat while others sing.** Playing a steady beat simultaneously with someone else's singing requires the integration of two different kinds of abilities. It also requires the instrument players to choose to keep either the macrobeat or the microbeat. Many prior experiences with singing and keeping the macro- and microbeat, as well as with exploring various instruments, are needed for children to successfully play and sing together. Encourage individual children to volunteer to play an accompanying instrument, so you can observe outcomes based on each child's own choosing. A child's ownership of accompaniment skill will be evident if he or she is able to play a steady beat for *any* familiar song. That child's feeling and playing beat will then show his or her ability to adapt steady beat to each particular song's tempo.

> **Playing an instrument in steady beat while singing alone.** Compared with accompanying other singers, playing an instrument in steady beat to accompany one's own singing involves an even more difficult integration of abilities. This accent incorporates a child's ability to *play* a steady beat while also keeping to the tempo of a song or rhyme with *words and melody*. The **simplify** strategy works well here: First, without an instrument, a child should sing many songs and accompany the singing with movement on two sides of the body at the same time. Then add the unpitched percussion instrument. Children should already have explored the instrument, so attention can be focused on both playing the instrument and singing.

Since young children are natural performers, singing and playing an instrument alone is a natural part of the music key experiences. This accent offers regular opportunities for children to develop musical proficiency in singing, playing, and listening.

> **Playing an instrument in a rhythm pattern.** By second grade, children who have experienced the High/Scope K–3 approach to learning music will understand the concept of beat competence and will be able to use rhythm instruments to play patterns that they have previously spoken or sung in echo fashion. Because of their continuing involvement with the K–3 music key experiences, and because they have had enough rehearsal time, children understand how rhythms relate to beat. They will be able to choose which rhythm pattern or patterns best fit a given song, rhyme, or recorded music selection, and they will understand why. (The magic of rhythm can be employed much more musically after the age of 7, when children's motor coordination and cognitive development are more advanced.)

To introduce children to this accent, begin by playing a simple rhythm accompaniment pattern for well-known songs such as the ones in Insert 7.2. *In beginning experiences with rhythm patterns, simplicity is always best.* Give children time to enjoy the simple repeated patterns, with a thoughtful choice of instrumental accompaniment.

> **Playing instruments together using rhythm patterns.** Children may naturally progress from playing one repeated rhythm pattern to layering a

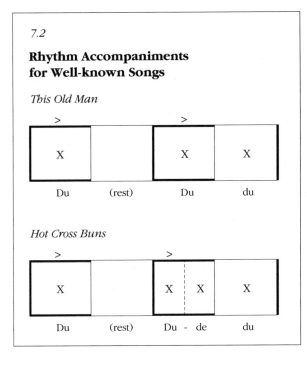

7.2

**Rhythm Accompaniments
for Well-known Songs**

This Old Man

>		>	
X		X	X
Du	(rest)	Du	du

Hot Cross Buns

>		>		
X		X	X	X
Du	(rest)	Du -	de	du

rhythm pattern to a beat-keeping accompaniment. Later, in grade 3, two rhythm patterns can be layered over the beat-keeping accompaniment (an example of this is shown in Insert 7.3). The possibilities for such musical rhythmic ensembles are limitless. Children's enthusiasm will grow as their skills expand, and their skills will multiply *if* the foundation in steady beat has been securely laid for all students by grade 2.

> Creating and planning instrument parts for a song or ensemble. Creating and planning instrumental parts for songs, rhymes, or recorded music is a natural part of the active, hands-on learning that characterizes the music key experiences. Small groups of three to five students can plan instrumental parts for favorite or familiar songs during plan-do-review. By third grade, children will be able to make charts showing rhythms they have created. These charts can utilize the children's own symbol systems or Phyllis S. Weikart's beat-box notation, used throughout this text.

7.3

Layering a Rhythm Pattern Over Beat-Keeping Base

This Old Man

	>		>	
Microbeat base	X		X	
First rhythm	X		X	X
Second rhythm	X X	X X	X	

Strategies children develop as they participate in cooperative learning experiences, reflect on and review their activities, and share their ideas with peers and adults will fine-tune their ensemble performance. In addition, the whole class can plan a musical program for parents; small groups can decide on the appropriate balance of singers and instruments; student leaders can be responsible for the theme, program order, and rehearsals. It is important to

Several students perform a song that they have together created. Three students accompany the group with metallophone, autoharp, and tympani.

remember that the focus for K–3 musical performances is *not* perfection, nor is it repetitive drill. The goal is to promote children's enthusiastic participation in singing, moving, and playing musical selections, so they can experience the joy, delight, and confidence that result from such activities.

⚙ Singing Alone and in Groups

Children should have the opportunity to sing with others at various times during the school day. Times for singing may occur at the beginning or end of the day, during circle time or outside time, or when the social studies/math/language arts/computer lesson includes a song for that particular concept. Children's singing abilities begin with the simple songs of kindergartners and progress in a sequential manner through the grades. Therefore, choose songs that are developmentally appropriate to each student's vocal range and rhythmic background. For example, *Zip-a-dee-doo-dah* is a wonderful song, but it is not appropriate for the average kindergarten class. The song's melodic range is too wide, and the musical pitches are difficult to sing rhythmically in some of the phrases. Young singers are apt to tune in only to the words, since they can speak more easily than they can sing. Because they can't attend to both melody and text at the same time, they may become "droners."

When teaching a song, use the "Teaching Model for a New Song" in Appendix A. If most of your students are having difficulty echoing the words or melody phrases, that is a red danger flag sending an important message. Choosing an easier song may be helpful, and there are thousands to select from. Song sources in Appendix B may provide a starting point. Set up a safe, consistent way for the class to join the song leader in singing a known song. Use an **anchor pitch**—sing the beginning pitch of the song four times in macrobeat:

"One, two, ready, sing." The class will then hear and join in with the *beginning word and pitch* instead of joining in at random. (See Chapter 5.)

Students who love to sing may spontaneously begin singing during plan-do-review or at workshop time. Young children do sing when absorbed in a task they enjoy, and they should usually be encouraged to do so. If a student's singing is distracting others, remind that student of times when singing *is* welcome. A quiet reminder to sing to one's self may be sufficient. Children demonstrate *ownership* of this key experience when they sing spontaneously, volunteer to lead a song, create verses for melodies they like, or create new songs when involved in their work.

> **Singing simple songs alone and with others.** When a young child sings a simple song alone, the teacher has an opportunity to listen for *tonal replication* of that particular melody, and also for that child's *natural tonal center.* Does the child sing comfortably, using pitches normally associated with beautiful singing, or does the tonal center more closely resemble that of a "chest" or "stomach" voice? Singing with others in a group is a common experience for most children. Singing *in tune* with others is the desired outcome of this accent. The teacher may lead the group, or a student may volunteer to lead. Every child should develop a song bank by accumulating songs and adding new musical skills to them in each successive school year. In addition, students may choose to share songs learned at home, at church, at camp, or in scouts. If they choose to teach a song to the class, this leadership experience gives them an opportunity to strengthen musical abilities while giving the teacher another occasion to encourage student-initiation and shared learning. Children in the K–3 years usually tend to teach both the words and melody of a song at the same time, repeating the whole song over and over until the group has learned it. They most likely will not spontaneously employ the strategies of the Teaching Model—**separate, simplify,** and **facilitate** (see Chapter 2 and Appendix A).

Singing solos should be encouraged and supported. Keep in mind that some young children will volunteer easily; others may never volunteer in class yet may sing confidently at home. Whenever a child volunteers to sing for the class, the teacher can listen for consistent pitch, rhythmic accuracy, and clear enunciation. The child's level of confidence and joy in the performance can also be observed. Children will gradually accept the challenge of singing a solo as their confidence in singing increases throughout the year. When the teacher and the other students provide comfort and support for each individual, even a shy singer may decide to sing for others.

> **Singing a short solo phrase during a call-response song or a single verse when the class sings the chorus.** As children are having more and more fun and their vocal confidence is growing, individuals may volunteer to sing a solo response during a call-response song such as *Who Did Swallow Jonah?* or they may volunteer to sing a solo verse in a song such as *Looby Loo.* The holistic approach inherent in the music key experiences especially encourages young children to feel comfortable singing a solo, because the approach *allows children to make their own choices about when they are ready* and because the approach encourages children to support one another's learning.

> **Singing songs of increasing length and difficulty with others.** When the music key experiences occur in both child-initiated and teacher-initiated ways and

when children are introduced to songs that are developmentally sequenced over the K–3 years, children will gradually become able to sing, in tune, *songs of increasing length and difficulty;* they will not fall into monotone chanting of a song's words in rhythm, which results when children are expected to master difficult songs before they have had adequate experiences in singing simple songs in tune. Because children who are faced with a too-difficult song attend to what is easiest for them (the words and rhythm), the result is omission of the melody. One way to avoid this problem is to use the **simplify** and **facilitate** strategies from the "Teaching Model for a New Song," Appendix A. No child needs to go through life remembering the well-meant but humiliating advice "Please don't sing out loud in the performance—just mouth the words."

Guide the children in developing a repertoire of songs they can skillfully sing and enjoy singing again and again. One classroom, for example, had on the wall a large picture of an elephant surrounded by cutouts of seven large peanuts—one for each K–6 grade. The display's caption "I Never Forget!" reminded the class to keep feeding mastered songs into the appropriate peanut, so on days when a substitute teacher was in charge, the entire class could perform these songs, with a student as song leader. As children progress through the grades, they can decorate songs they learned in earlier grades with instrumental accompaniment or vocal melodic chants. They can also use simpler songs to invent rounds sung in two and three parts, or they can enhance the songs with movement patterns or hand jives. Asking "What else can we add?" provides the incentive to think creatively about extending the experience to include instruments and movement. With the active learning approach in place, students will challenge *themselves* to accomplish more than any teacher can challenge them to do.

A short weekly or monthly time for music sharing can be an opportunity for individuals to sing or play a solo for groups of various sizes to perform. When performances regularly include everyone in some way, opportunities to listen, sing expressively, support others, and discriminate wisely become the standard.

Every child needs a repertoire of songs that he or she can skillfully sing and enjoy singing again and again.

> **Singing a solo with musical competence and confidence.** Having frequent opportunities to listen to music and sing increases children's individual

competencies and skills and increases their joy in participating in something that they love and others appreciate. Students will eagerly volunteer for a solo if they feel comfortable in their classroom music experiences. Singing a solo may never occur to a young child unless the child's prior music experiences are ones associated with feelings of safety, happiness, and camaraderie.

⚷ Sharing Music by Performing

Musical performance has traditionally been thought of as something for a special occasion, something requiring much practice and precision. While this may be true for concerts or special performances in the *adult* world, musical performance for children in the K–3 classroom need not be restricted to an all-school, once-a-year event. Rather, young children can be involved in daily, weekly, and monthly performances in which the focus is on individual children *sharing* their own musical interests with others.

The active learning model assumes that children will have many casual opportunities to share what they know or can do musically. Since music is a natural language for young children, their desire to share musical information and abilities is to be expected.

Some children will exhibit a strong musical intelligence, just as others may exhibit strong logical, verbal, kinesthetic, spatial, linguistic, or social intelligence. In educating the *whole child,* High/Scope endeavors to provide opportunities for *every* child to strengthen all of his or her ways of knowing. For some children, in particular, sharing through music and *relating music concepts to academic concepts* will become their strongest contribution to the active learning of the whole class. For every student, involvement in music concepts and activities (singing, listening, playing instruments, and moving) will provide a viable way to enhance overall learning and communication.

> **> Creating and singing a new verse to a known song.** When children enjoy a song and sing it well, they often continue to sing it on their own or to request it in whole-group activities. There is an obvious skill-level attained when the song is sung well. Ownership of this skill can be extended when individuals or small groups create a new verse for that melody and share it with the class. For example, many new verses have been created by kindergarten singers for the well-known song *Hello, Everybody, Yes Indeed* (see 7.4).

7.4

Creative Verses for
Hello, Everybody, Yes Indeed

1. We're going to the circus, yes indeed.

2. Today is Carolyn's birthday, yes indeed.

3. Today is "purple day," yes indeed.

4. It's almost Christmas, sing hurray.

When a song has rhyming words, creating new verses gives children an opportunity to use specific language arts skills. The *Clementine* folk song, in particular, has been the basis of countless variations. One favorite is *Oh, My*

Monster *Frankenstein* (see 7.5). Also, the song *Who Did Swallow Jonah?* has been transformed to *Who Did Eat the Turkey?* by some first-graders (see 7.6). Assessing observable outcomes for this accent is fun for both students and teachers. Some of children's favorite songs will be those in which new verses have been created by children themselves.

> **Creating and sharing an instrumental piece on percussion or melodic instruments.** Children who are studying an instrument such as the piano, violin, or guitar in private or group instruction outside of school may volunteer to share with the class a selection they've learned. These opportunities to share, which will be welcomed by all, may provide incentive for others to study a musical

A student shares his new musical composition, explaining how the ending phrase differs from the previous phrases by ending on the home, or key, tone.

instrument. Such performances offer starting points for discussions of many musical topics that can enrich the class.

Plan-do-review time may be used by some children to learn to play a familiar melody on an instrument. When students choose this task, they are activating their **tonal memory**—they know how the melody goes and want to figure out how to play it. Choosing to work with this task helps each child realize that songs are composed of same and different melody patterns, which ties into their understanding of **form** as a musical element. Such songs as *Hot Cross Buns* or *Twinkle, Twinkle, Little Star* have simple melodies that children can easily figure out how to play.

Children may also choose to compose, or create, their *own* melodies or percussion pieces on an instrument. The use of a xylophone or keyboard provides a concrete set of pitches with which to work in creating a melody, whereas creating a vocal melody is a somewhat more abstract process. Young children often take a holistic approach to creating their own compositions, and for some, this may work well. For other young composers, some guidance may be necessary. Hands-on experience with various musical elements (beat, rhythm, melody, tone color, meter, form) can lead them to an understanding of how musicians compose.

> **Playing a musical instrument while the group sings.** This accent focuses on playing a **pitched musical instrument,** such as the xylophone, autoharp, guitar, or small keyboard, while the group sings. A high level of concentration is required for a student to play a musical instrument while the group sings. If one is playing a *repeated pattern* on the xylophone, success is fairly well assured, because the pattern is a repeating one and can complement the singing. For example, the class may be singing the well-known round *Make New Friends* while the player is repeating the microbeat-keeping pattern F, C, D, C throughout the singing (see 7.7). This simple melodic accompaniment enhances the singing and brings success to the player.

7.7

Melody and Microbeat-Keeping Pattern

Make New Friends

1. Make new friends, but keep the old,
2. (A) Cir - cle's round, it has no end,

Pattern to accompany:

One is sil - ver and the o - ther gold.
That's how long I'll be your friend.

Pattern to accompany:

When playing chords on the autoharp or guitar as accompaniment to a folk song, a repeated chord pattern is followed. In the example in Insert 7.8, *The More We Get Together* in the key of F, after five steady introductory strums of the F chord, the accompanist would play the chords printed above the music.

When playing on a small keyboard, a child may be playing the melody alone, the chords alone, or the chords and melody together. If that player makes

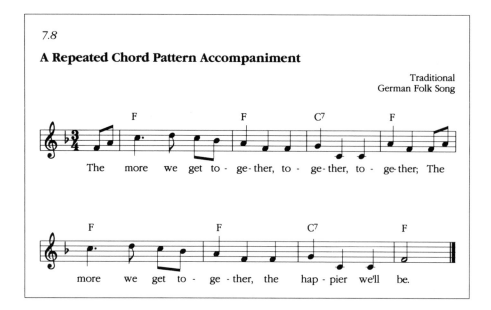

7.8

A Repeated Chord Pattern Accompaniment

Traditional
German Folk Song

The more we get to-ge-ther, to-ge-ther, to-ge-ther; The

more we get to-ge-ther, the hap-pier we'll be.

a mistake, he or she can easily correct it. When the player is accompanying a group, however, the group keeps singing, making it difficult for the player to recover and keep going after making a mistake. It takes great concentration on the part of an accompanist to keep on playing in spite of a mistake. One's first urge is to go back and fix it—in some cases, to go back to the very beginning and start all over.

Students can always be encouraged to play accompaniment to group singing. The challenge of doing this successfully builds tremendous concentration skills that have great value in other areas of academics. It also enables some students to take a leadership role in music.

> **Sharing songs created by students.** To create original songs, children may need teacher guidance and support. Because it involves the voice as an instrument, singing is a rather abstract skill that requires a sense of **singing in tune** as well as good **tonal memory.**

At first, children may create beautiful songs and then record them on a tape recorder in order to remember them to sing another day. Composing in this manner often leads children to want to use music notation to write down their original composition(s). When the desire to learn about music notation emanates from the child, then that desire can be addressed. Here, the classroom teacher who is not a music specialist may wish to seek help from a music specialist or from a parent with music training. There are also computer programs that notate original compositions.

> **Sharing an instrumental ensemble created by students.** When working in an active learning environment, cooperative learning partners often are able to create miniature impromptu instrumental ensembles. This is a natural outcome of the High/Scope approach to music—one in which every child can be successful. The ensemble may be as simple as having one child play a pattern on the drum while another plays a pattern on the finger cymbals, as the example in Insert 7.9 illustrates. Extensions from this can lead to ensembles such

as the one in Insert 7.10, created by third-grade students using ABA form.

Introductions and fade-outs are usually included when the group performs for the class, and often a vocal improvisation is layered for a more complete effect. Teachers who have never experienced such a level of creativity through music in the classroom can be assured that ensembles such as these are not

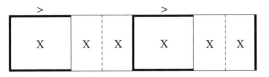

7.9

A Simple Ensemble

Wesley plays this pattern on the drum:

His partner plays this pattern on the finger cymbals:

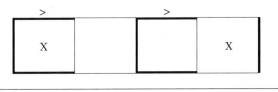

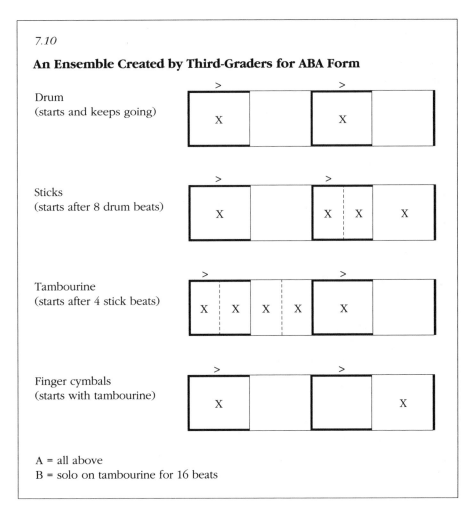

7.10

An Ensemble Created by Third-Graders for ABA Form

Drum
(starts and keeps going)

Sticks
(starts after 8 drum beats)

Tambourine
(starts after 4 stick beats)

Finger cymbals
(starts with tambourine)

A = all above
B = solo on tambourine for 16 beats

only possible but also probable and natural when a musical foundation has been developed.

⚬ⱬ Moving Creatively and Choreographing Movement Sequences and Dances

When kindergartners are able to explore various ways of moving to music and then discuss how and why they moved in that manner, they are building their personal interpretative idea bank. The classroom teacher and music educator can help children succeed by motivating them to listen and respond thoughtfully. Such questions as "How can you describe your movement?" or "What were you thinking of as you moved to the music?" will help children to express their reasons for responding in particular ways.

Many repeated creative movement experiences will be needed consistently throughout the K–3 years if children are to own the concepts embedded in this key experience. Some children will find creative movement and choreography natural and easy. All children will benefit from regular opportunities to move creatively, to analyze their creations, to share the movement responses of others, and to exhibit their own movement ideas in choreography and dance.

Members of a small group try out a movement sequence they have created for a specific musical selection.

> **Moving creatively alone or with a group.** Most children feel safe to explore movement when they are in a large group. This "safety net" provides children with the opportunity to develop body, space, language, and time awarenesses while listening and responding to their own thoughts. Even shy children will risk sharing a movement idea when they realize that each person's ideas are valued. Take time to discuss why a certain child moved in a particular way. Invite responses from the group that encourage cooperative learning. Provide experiences where individual volunteers move alone while others describe their movement. Design movement experiences in which the whole class moves during the A section and individuals move alone during the B section of a musical selection. Then, discuss and recall how movement helps us discover the meaning within each musical selection.

> **Creating movements and variations for a specific musical selection.**
When children have explored a favorite musical selection through movement and then have been engaged in a discussion leading to sharing their movement

ideas, the next logical step is to have the class as a whole try out the shared movement ideas. The children themselves can decide how to order, or sequence, the movements they choose to perform.

Including child-choice is of the utmost importance in this accent. One teacher spent many hours planning a beat-keeping movement sequence for an instrumental arrangement of *Rudolph the Red-Nosed Reindeer*. In teaching the sequence to her class, she became frustrated when some members of the class had trouble with parts of the sequence. Then, remembering the importance of child- choice in working with movement sequences, she asked the children to explore their *own* movement ideas while the music played. A lively discussion followed, during which the students came up with eight movement ideas of their own that they wanted to use. Then, *they* decided how to order the movements, making up several sequences of equal length to match the musical phrases. The result was a stunning performance, full of energy! When the children suggested using objects to dress up the performance, the teacher and class prepared shiny red and green disposable plates (two per child), each with one jingle bell attached with yarn. What fun everyone had keeping the beat!

Children can choose specific movements and explore variations to create a movement theme and variations. For example, in one class, 7- and 8-year-old children were comparing the nonlocomotor movements of *swinging* and *rocking*. After exploration, the class discovered that the difference between these two movements had to do with the axis of each movement—*swinging* involves an axis at the top of the movement, and *rocking* involves an axis at the bottom of the movement. After several volunteers demonstrated movements they enjoyed performing to *Peat Fire Flame* (RM2), a plan was made to swing both arms across the body to the macrobeat during the A section, and to rock, standing in place, on the B section the first time through. Listening to the music revealed that each section repeated four times, so the class created three variations each for *swinging* and *rocking* and then decided what order they would perform them in. After trying out their plan with the music, they made changes where needed and then performed the movement themes and variations successfully to the music! Children's ownership of movement ideas and AB musical form is clear when such an activity occurs as a natural part of active learning (see 7.11).

7.11

Peat Fire Flame: **Theme and Variations**

First time, section A: Macrobeat—Swing both arms across the body.

First time, section B: Macrobeat—Rock side to side, standing.

Variation 1: Swing arms back and forth during section A. "Rock the baby," pretending to hold infant cradled in arms during section B.

Variation 2: Swing one leg back and forth during section A. "Rock the baby," pretending to hold infant upright on one shoulder during section B.

Variation 3: Sit in chair and swing both legs back and forth from bended knees during section A. Rock side to side while seated in chair during section B.

Class experiences prepare children for small-group adventures in this accent. These adventures, in turn, help children create movements and variations for a favorite musical selection. Again, the process insures success for all, and the teacher initiates, guides, supports, and interacts with the children in providing the experiences that permit memorable learning to flourish.

> **Creating and using different movements for AB music.** Another way to elicit movement ideas from the class is to have the class explore macrobeat motions to a particular selection. For example, *Machar* (RM5) has two main sections, A and B. After listening to the recording, children may be guided to individually explore at least two strong movements suggested to them by the music and then each choose their best idea to share with the group (see 7.12). Depending on the age and experience level of the learners, these movements could be nonlocomotor, locomotor, or a combination of the two (for example, a combined upper- and lower-body movement). When children are familiar with the A and B sections of *Machar,*

7.12

Possible Strong Movements to Explore for *Machar*

slash (karate-style)	leap	push/pull
punch	jump	stomp
flick	swing	twirl

---

encourage each child to prepare one movement idea that the group can imitate. Carry this out with the music playing, so each child has an opportunity to express his or her movement idea accompanied by the music.

On another day, one movement can be used for the A section and another for the B section of *Machar.* Now the focus shifts to changing from one movement (for section A) to the other (for section B) and then back again (when section A repeats). This is a good opportunity for the teacher to assess the listening and movement skills of the total group. With repeated experiences in this accent, individual children will be able to successfully create and use different movements to correspond to the different sections of AB music in both macrobeat and microbeat. They will become musically sensitive to the mood, dynamics, and style of a particular selection and be responsible for changing their movement according to each musical section.

> **Creating patterns and moving creatively.** As their listening abilities develop, children are able to identify and move to melodic or rhythmic sections of the music. Often, when asked why they moved in a particular way, children will answer, "Because the music told me to." As children repeat their movements, the teacher may notice that some children have refined individual phrases and patterns of their movements. Labels can be given to the movements, using learner SAY & DO, so a group of children can create a movement sequence that uses each person's own movement idea for the introduction, one child's idea for the A section, and another child's idea for the B section. These small groups may perform for each other, showing what possibilities there are within the class for interpreting the music through movement. Expressing ideas

in this manner creates a rich environment for everyone and provides the teacher with independent outcomes for assessing children's musical interpretation and style.

There will be occasions when the teacher will share a musical selection and guide the learners to listen and move as the music's *title* suggests, as in Grieg's *In the Hall of the Mountain King* or Saint Saëns' *Aquarium* from *Carnival of the Animals.* Such experiences are valuable because titled compositions provide children with a broad framework for movement ideas. Discussions that follow such an experience can bring interesting ideas and insights to all. Through opportunities for natural, thoughtful response to musical selections, children's aural discrimination and identification are strengthened.

> **Planning and using different movement and dance sequences for a specific song or recording.** As regular opportunities are provided for creating and sharing movement ideas, children may begin to create foot patterns and arm movements for song phrases or instrumental selections. These movements can evolve into dance sequences, especially if folk dances are a regular part of the movement activities for children in grades 2 and 3. Folk dances provide a unique way to experience our world's rich ethnic heritage and to learn to move with coordination. The learner SAY & DO process for becoming successful with beginning folk dance helps to build children's concentration, listening, and appreciation skills. (See Chapter 8, "Movement Maps, Level 2," p. 193.) *Teaching Movement & Dance,* 3rd Ed., by Phyllis S. Weikart contains a wealth of folk dances appropriate for this accent. Incorporate beginning folk dances into your daily movement and music time for second- and third-grade students.

Using the learner SAY & DO process, these girls learn the folk dance Djurdjevka Kolo *(RM2). Here, they observe how the foot pattern of the B section repeats four times.*

⎈ Creating and Improvising Songs and Instrumental Music

Creating and improvising are natural outcomes of singing and playing, thinking and doing. Creativity can be defined as working with something known (melody, tones, rhythms, instruments, choreography) in new ways. When active learning experiences, such as those in Chapter 8, are used throughout the K–3 years, children will begin to show creativity in musical thinking in this key experience. Abilities begin to develop when learners are asked to change only one or two notes of a song or musical selection. Instrumental improvisation is usually easier than vocal improvisation, because the musical instrument provides a concrete medium. Experience with improvisation can initially be provided with rhythm instruments. When the preparation has been initiated in movement, creating and improvising is an important, natural problem-solving step in children's music-making.

> **Choosing instruments to play and accompany.** When children discover ways to play various instruments, they will want to choose specific instruments to play for accompaniments to songs, poems, or stories (see 7.13). Their first choices will be simple, but as their experience and confidence grow, they may plan for two or more instruments to play a pattern or for specific parts of the song, poem, or story to be represented by a specific instrument. This is the beginning of improvisation. Most students will approach improvisation holistically. There are no rules—no right or wrong ways to go about it. The task is to represent, through voice or instruments, what the words convey, in order for that selection to be enhanced tonally beyond the spoken words.

7.13

Accompaniment Examples

1. Play a beat-keeping accompaniment on rhythm sticks or wood block for *Hickory Dickory Dock.*

2. Create an order for accumulating non-pitched percussion sounds that uses the crescendo concept for accompanying *Gloomy Boomy Day* (in Chapter 8).

A child's choice of a specific instrument to accompany a particular song can indicate ability to discriminate as well as ability to choose the characteristic instrument sound. Decorating a song with sound becomes an exciting project that continues well beyond the K–3 years, activating one's imagination and tonal memory.

> **Creating simple melodies vocally.** Before children are ready to create simple songs individually or in a small group, they need to have the appropriate musical readiness. Daily singing sessions in which they listen to and sing many songs are the best preparation. They should also have opportunities to use their voices to represent and enrich texts of poems and stories, and they should have experiences creating new verses for familiar songs. Creating a simple melody becomes possible when children have a repertoire of familiar songs as models. One way to start them creating simple melodies is to sing a song for which students supply an original last phrase, such as in Activity 75, Chapter 8.

Some children may just create a simple melody naturally, without thinking about how they did it. Other students will want to create a melody but will not know how to do it. This is where the classroom teacher can be of great help. An explanation follows.

In language, we communicate through questions and answers or through narratives developed on a particular subject. There is no communication possible unless answers or narratives relate to or clarify the questions. So it is with music. A musical question is always followed by the musical answer. In *Merrily We Roll Along,* for example, the musical question is the first half of the song. Notice how the first half of the song does not end on a resting tone (scale degree 1); hence, it is a musical *question* (this is similar to a spoken question ending with an upward vocal inflection). The musical answer copies the first part of the melody but ends on the resting tone (scale degree 1), thereby giving the melody closure. Because the answer copies the question's beginning melodic pattern, we say it is a **parallel answer** (see 7.14).

All melodies have musical questions and answers. In simple songs, the answers are usually parallel. Some examples are *Hey, Betty Martin, Jingle Bells, Lavender's Blue, Home on the Range,* and *Go In and Out the Windows.* Well-known songs with **contrasting answers** are *This Old Man* (see 7.15), *Hickory Dickory Dock,* and *Swing Low, Sweet Chariot.* As the class sings these familiar songs, guide them to become aware of musical questions and answers.

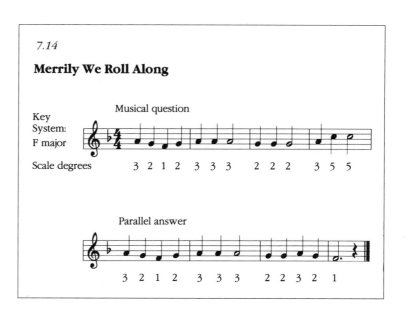

7.14

Merrily We Roll Along

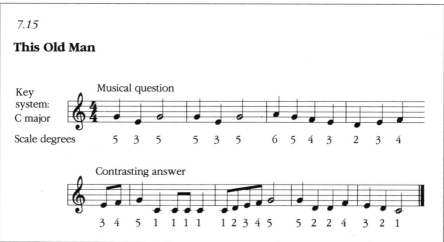

7.15

This Old Man

Melodies are created within a **tonal key system** (see *key system* in Glossary). That key system includes a **scale** and its **primary chords** (see Glossary). A scale is built from a formula of **whole steps** and **half steps** between tones, or pitches (see 7.16), and the formula is always consistent, no matter which tone a scale begins with.

A scale can be constructed beginning on any of the 12 different black or white keys on the keyboard. There is a consistent scale formula for all **major scales** and a consistent scale formula specific to each of the three forms of **minor scale:** natural, harmonic, or melodic (see *major scale* and *minor scale* in Glossary). Every scale has a **home tone,** or **resting tone,** where the melody ends. Most of our simple songs are derived from the major scale, although some are derived from the minor scale. The major and minor scales each have eight tones, and each is built from a specific formula, using whole and half steps, as shown in Insert 7.17.

The scale, as a group of tones that "hang around" together, is the skeletal framework inside every melody. Scales are the "CEO's" of music. The eight-tone scale underlies the organization of musical sounds that we have known for centuries in the Western World.

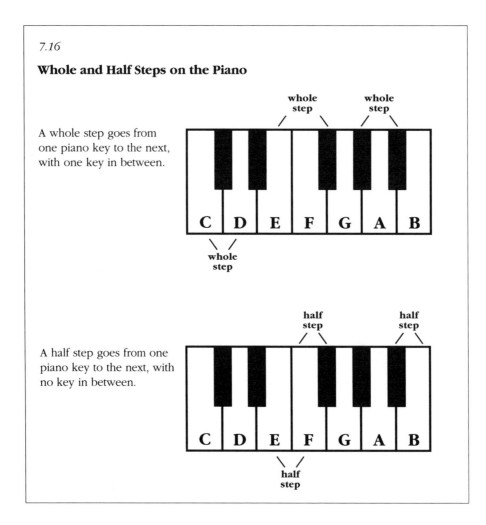

7.16

Whole and Half Steps on the Piano

A whole step goes from one piano key to the next, with one key in between.

whole step   whole step

C D E F G A B

whole step

A half step goes from one piano key to the next, with no key in between.

half step   half step

C D E F G A B

half step

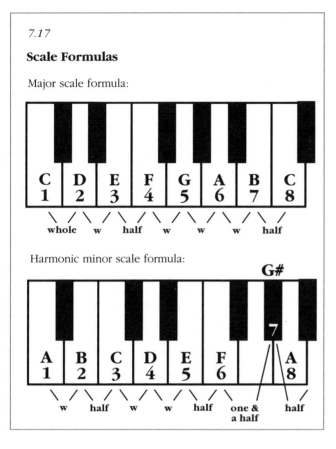

7.17

Scale Formulas

Major scale formula:

Harmonic minor scale formula:

Creating simple melodies is easy and fun; words may or may not be added. When music is at the core of the active learning environment, learners can successfully create simple melodies, because it is simply another exercise in problem solving in a tonal dimension.

> **Creating simple melodies on instruments.** As we have said before, pitched instruments such as the xylophone or keyboard provide a concrete set of tones to work with when creating simple melodies. This differs from creating melodies vocally, where, to the child, the tones are abstract. The concrete experience of using the instrument is necessary for the melodic information to become cognitive for the child. The basic background relating to **key systems** that was explained under the previous accent is necessary for this accent also. The following key systems work best for beginners:

The C-major scale with C as the resting tone

Notes: (C, D, E, F, G, A, B, C′)
Scale degrees: (1, 2, 3, 4, 5, 6, 7, 8)
Primary chords: I   C-major (C, E, G)
IV F-major (F, A, C)
V   G-major (G, B, D)

The D-major scale with D as the resting tone

Notes: (D, E, F#, G, A, B, C#, D′)
Scale degrees: (1, 2, 3,   4, 5, 6, 7,   8)
Primary chords: I   D-major (D, F#, A)
IV G-major (G, B, D)
V   A-major (A, C#, E)

A beginning strategy is to suggest that children use removable labels to identify the names of the notes on a keyboard or xylophone for the range of one **octave** (see Glossary) of a scale (tones are usually labeled on a xylophone). The resting tone (scale degree 1) can be highlighted. Creating a melody on an instrument takes time, patience, thought, and concentration. One must remember what tones and rhythms have been played and in what order. The results are well worth all the effort and become a memorable intrinsic reward. This task also creates a need to understand notation—so the melody can be written down to read and play another day. *Reading music* and *writing music* are music key experiences yet to come.

As a catalyst, Insert 7.18 provides some very simple melodic questions to be played on an instrument. You may complete them with any answer you compose—parallel or contrasting. The resting tone is supplied. Once you experience ease in doing this, you will want to initiate this concept in your classroom.

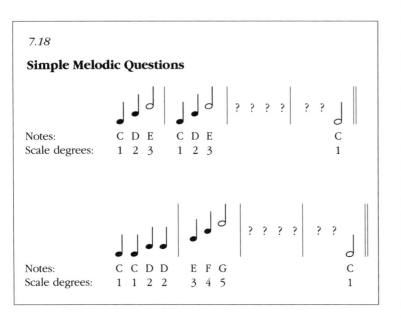

7.18

Simple Melodic Questions

Notes:	C D E	C D E		C
Scale degrees:	1 2 3	1 2 3		1

Notes:	C C D D	E F G		C
Scale degrees:	1 1 2 2	3 4 5		1

> **Improvising a variation on a melody, vocally and instrumentally.** A variation is created when you take what you know (a familiar song) and change it just a little bit. It may be that you change only one tone, or two, or three. Certainly, one would not change the last tone, because then the melody would not have closure. A variation involves decorating the main theme in some delightful way without losing its essence. Two possible variations on familiar melodies are shown in Insert 7.19.

Variations demonstrate that a child knows the song well and that he or she can change it slightly to bring renewed interest to the song. Children may create spontaneously, and this indicates the holistic way children act on a musical idea. Creating vocal variations for a favorite song fits in nicely as a musical problem-solving activity on a school trip. There is *never* a place where music does not fit into the educational scene.

> **Creating an instrumental piece with two or more sections (AB).** In normal conversation, a spoken question is often followed by an answer, and when the answer consists of one simple statement, the question and answer constitute a short conversation. Similarly, a musical question and answer constitute a simple musical section. But a musical question and answer may need elaboration, just as a written paragraph is needed to clarify a paragraph's opening, or topic, sentence. This elaboration, or musical narrative, constitutes the development of the musical section and is an extension of some melodic or rhythmic fragment already stated in the question/answer. Helpful listening examples for this are *Zemer Atik* (RM4) and *The Entertainer* (RM8).

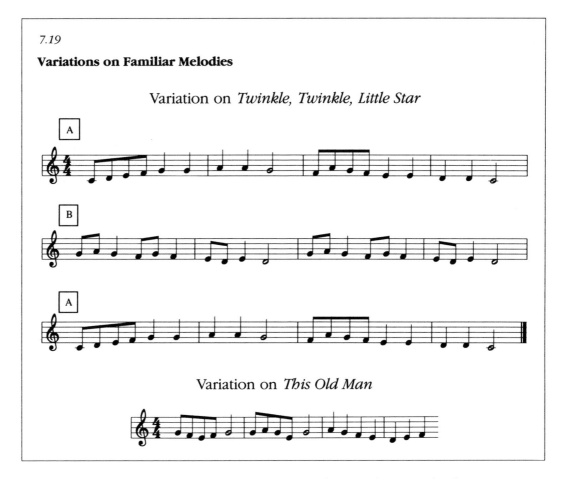

7.19

Variations on Familiar Melodies

Variation on *Twinkle, Twinkle, Little Star*

Variation on *This Old Man*

The A section of a piece contains the question/answer plus some development and may or may not return to the original question/answer as a way of finishing the section. The B section usually contains another question/answer plus development. It complements the A section (or else it would be a separate piece). A third (C) section could follow for longer compositions. Experiences in this accent do not need to be elaborate. Students may work together, with one creating the A section and the other, the B section. Students who study an instrument privately may be able to lead this activity.

The discipline involved in carrying out experiences under this category of **creating and performing music** helps all students become aware of the conceptual relationship of music to spoken language. Because of this relationship, children become better listeners, clearer thinkers, and more musical beings. Always strive for *simplicity,* in order to clarify concepts.

> **Creating an original song with words.** When creating an original song, which comes first—the words or the melody? Children first work with an *idea*—be it language-oriented or melody-oriented. They will naturally work in their strongest creative mode. It really does not matter which one they work with first, as long as they pursue the task until their goal is reached. As a child completes one component, another is begun, and work continues until the two components synchronize and the child decides it represents his or her best work.

Songs can be created by the whole class, by small groups, or by individuals. The choice of topics is wide open. The experience of creating a song with words can pull together important concepts from math, language arts, social studies, science, or health. One class wrote songs for the county's historical pageant during the nation's bicentennial celebration and received local acclaim. Another class wrote *commercials for music,* which became quite a hit. Why not write *commercials for learning?*

When children have created a song, they may want to record it in order to remember it. The tape recorder is valuable for this. Some students will become interested in using music notation to write out their songs. When a foundation has been laid for this through guiding children to use their own symbolization for music over a period of time, they will be ready to begin to use the traditional system of notation.

⌒ Reading Music

When children have experienced many good musical experiences throughout grades K–2, by third grade, they are usually inquisitive about musical notation. A rich background of singing and listening experiences, combined with experiences playing simple instruments, will have built the necessary musical vocabulary. This is similar to the way children build a speaking vocabulary before they learn to write and read. When these basic experiences have been extended to include various ways to "write" rhythm or melody maps, reading naturally follows. Most 7- and 8-year-old children are interested in rules, including the rules about specific symbols representing pitch and rhythm. Some children may be studying piano or guitar and may bring this enthusiasm into the classroom. Understanding how to read songs they know gives learners a sense of power. Now, all those "black blobs" on the lines and spaces have real meaning! They are learning to *read* the **universal musical language** with understanding based on that all-important kinesthetic base.

Preliminary reading of music has already begun if children have written music with their own notational systems. These notational systems may have employed **icons,** which are various types of manipulatives or written symbols chosen by the children to represent their musical ideas, including simple rhythm patterns or melody fragments. In reading one another's rhythm or melody maps, the children begin to understand how to code and decode music, and they become more proficient and interested in this process. To read music, one must *see* the rhythmic pattern and melodic contour, *understand* what it represents, and then *produce* the representation with one's voice or instrument. Many prior experiences in singing, moving, listening, and playing instruments form the essential foundation for reading music accurately. Many organizational and processing abilities are used in reading music notation. Children's efforts at reading the music symbol system affect their reading comprehension across the curriculum.

> **Reading one's own symbol system (icons) for rhythm *or* pitch.**
Encouraging young learners to use their own icons to create and write songs is similar to encouraging children's early writing attempts in the whole-language approach to reading and writing. Some children will write with manipulatives,

A small group reads a student's yarn representation of a long *and* short *pattern before attempting to represent the pattern through learner SAY & DO.*

others with rhythm symbols; some will be able to draw only melodic shape, while others will be able to represent both rhythm and melody in their own way and then share it with others.

Reading **rhythm "maps"** has many advantages (see Glossary; see also the accent "Showing a way to represent long/short sounds, high/low pitches, or repeated sounds [rhythm and/or melody maps]" on p. 168). When learners have a basic kinesthetic understanding of *beat* and *division of beat,* they will be able to show that understanding through their own symbol systems (see 7.20). As they explain their own notation, children are displaying *ownership* of the rhythmic concepts involved.

The children may have been playing various instrumental four-beat rhythm accompaniments to songs during grades 2 and 3. Writing and reading what they have already experienced is a natural follow-up. Again, manipulative icons for representing the relationships between the half note, quarter note, and eighth notes (see 7.21) help students to realize that there are many ways to represent rhythmic sets of four microbeats (see 7.22), as well as many rhythmic solutions to discover.

Using a system of reading that includes *consistent rhythm syllables* is helpful for the learner. Music educator Dr. Edwin Gordon in *Learning Sequences in Music*[2] has developed such a system that builds on children's understanding of beat, division of beat, and duration of beat. This system was explained

7.20

Representing Short–Short–Long Sounds

Children's representations leading to traditional music notation:

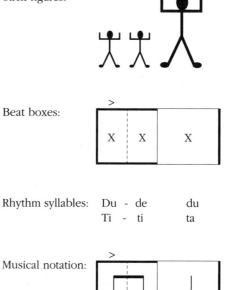

Movement: Hop, hop, jump

Drinking straws:

Stick figures:

Beat boxes:

Rhythm syllables: Du - de   du
                    Ti - ti   ta

Musical notation:

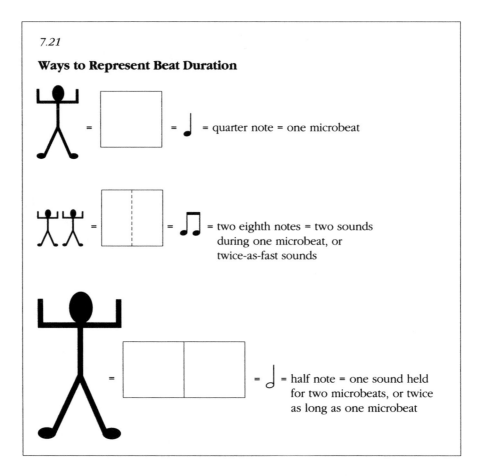

7.21

Ways to Represent Beat Duration

= = ♩ = quarter note = one microbeat

= = ♫ = two eighth notes = two sounds during one microbeat, or twice-as-fast sounds

= = 𝅗𝅥 = half note = one sound held for two microbeats, or twice as long as one microbeat

in connection with the key experience *expressing rhythm,* in Chapter 6.

Children will naturally progress to reading longer rhythm patterns of 8, 12, or 16 beats in this system. Doing so lengthens their attending skills. Try using Gordan's syllables to read Bob's rhythm pattern, followed by Dave's, Steven's, and Brian's (see 7.23). Gradually, as children's skill, interest, and confidence in reading rhythms grow, other patterns can be added.

Melody maps have their beginnings in movement, as children's hands shape the contour of simple two-and three-note melodies in the air. In transferring this from manipulative icons to written icons, some children may produce maps that look like a series of dashes representing higher, lower, and repeated tones; others may draw a continuous line that goes up and down to represent higher, lower, or repeated tones. A melody map of *Star Light, Star Bright,* for example, may look like either illustration in Insert 7.24.

The important thing is that the individual be able to read and sing his or her own melodic representation accurately. This requires tonal memory, personal organization, and the understanding of what one has written and sung.

Each student can exchange rhythm or melody maps with a partner, to see whether they can accurately read one another's maps. When students regularly have experiences such as this (usually in the third-grade classroom), they will soon gain ownership of the melodic and rhythmic concepts involved.

Different Rhythmic Sets of Four Microbeats

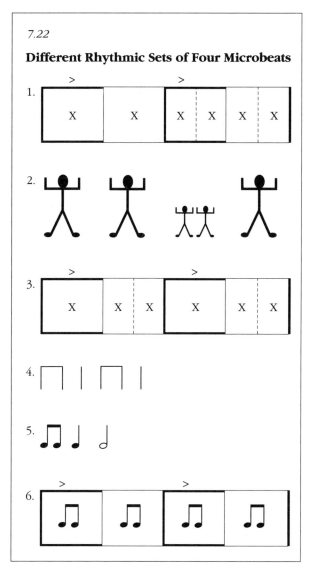

Different Four-Beat Rhythm Patterns

Bob's:

Dave's:

Steven's:

Brian's:

> Reading melody or rhythm maps created by oneself or others. As their interest, experience, and curiosity grow, children will be anxious to create and read longer rhythm or mel-ody maps. These may be created individually or by small groups of students during music time. At first, when children are not using **staff lines** or **spaces,** the maps should contain no more than four different pitches. After groups have created their maps, everyone can have a chance to develop skills by reading and performing maps prepared by others.

Interpreting melody or rhythm maps can hold much the same intrigue as decoding secret messages. Eight- and nine-year-olds seem to take great delight in solving mysteries, and this natural ability can be used to refine discrimination of rhythmic and tonal

Melody Maps

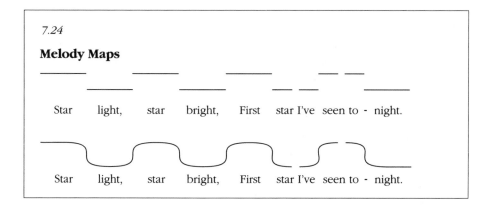

relationships. Before the year is over, third-graders will initiate opportunities to read melody *and* rhythm maps combined.

When the **tone games** explained in Chapter 3 have been played consistently, children are used to relating various pitches to certain body locations. (See "The Body Scale," Chapter 3.) The body scale children have been using can be represented by a single drawing of a stick figure, as shown in Insert 7.25. Children find this graphic helpful in reading music, as well as lots of fun to decode. It often helps children to feel personally connected to pitch relationships and thus more able to sing tunefully.

> **Reading short rhythmic and melodic phrases (conventional notation) and short songs.** The preceding accents provide readiness activities for reading traditional staff notation. A logical time to initiate regular **staff lines** and **spaces** is after children are comfortable with the body scale. The body scale creates for children a kinesthetic-cognitive link to pitch. The lines and spaces provide a consistent, visual frame of reference for those pitches. Each line and space has a definite name and pitch, which are now needed for playing and singing melodies.

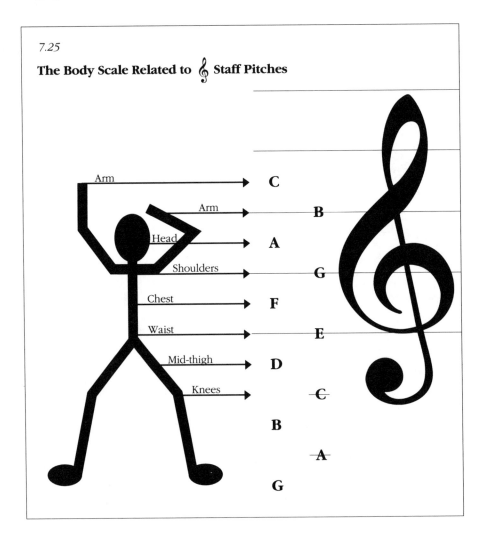

7.25

The Body Scale Related to 𝄞 Staff Pitches

While some children listen, others SING & SHAPE the two-pitch patterns created by their classmates. They will soon learn to read short phrases of familiar songs.

Guide children to read and sing short phrases of familiar songs (see 7.26) that have simple rhythms and downward direction (such as the phrase "rolling home" in *This Old Man*) or that step down and up in a simple way (such as the opening phrase in *Mary Had a Little Lamb*) or that use the same pitch repeated several times in a row (as in the opening phrase of *Farmer in the Dell*).

Reading and understanding the notation for short songs and singing them become a delightful challenge!

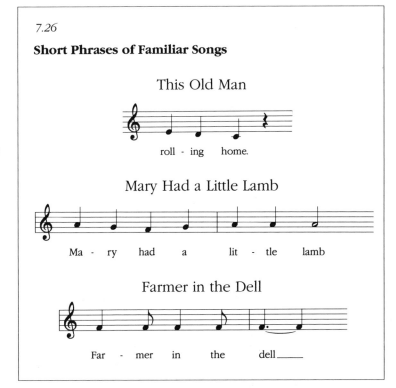

An adaptation of the **simplify** strategy from the Teaching Model for a New Song follows:

Guide children to:
1. Chant the rhythm of the song using Dr. Gordon's rhythm syllables (see pp. 117–118).
2. Read the text in the rhythm of the musical notation.
3. Sing pitches in the song's rhythm on a neutral syllable, to focus on the pitch relationships and the rhythm.
4. Sing the song at least three times, observing music and text. The eye, ear, and voice have to work together to develop this skill. Try reading and singing any of the songs in Chapter 8 with your class.

Understanding how to read and learn a new song are logical musical experiences in the classroom. According to a Chinese proverb, "The journey of a thousand miles begins with a single step." With music education, when single steps are taken in sequence, with many and varied experiences initiated for every child to feel secure, children will discover that music opens doors to the same important thinking skills that they need and apply in other areas of the curriculum. Implementing the music key experiences strengthens and synthesizes the tonal, visual, kinesthetic, creative, and cognitive capabilities of each individual.

> **Reading conventional notation for simple songs.** When learners realize the power and information involved in reading music, they will be motivated to continue. Reading music becomes a treasure hunt as each step in the reading progression gives more clues for discovering the song's secrets. Reading and singing simple, short songs well encourages children to try new songs to see how they sound. Children can begin reading and singing the following songs from Chapter 8, and they can continue reading and singing other music as their interest and skills develop:

Engine, Engine, Number Nine (p. 309)
I Like to Sing (p. 214)
Rainbows (p. 242)
Wise Old Owl (p. 245)
Traffic Signals (p. 312)
Lullaby (p. 190)
We Keep the Beat Together (p. 198)
Numbers Are Special (p. 231)

"The greater the skill, the greater the thrill" is a saying that certainly applies to reading and singing music. It requires coordination of timing, thought, inner hearing, ear, eye, and voice—one of the highest concentration levels possible in the elementary classroom. The discipline of reading and singing appropriate songs synthesizes many essential music concepts for the individual.

Students also need to continue singing many songs learned by rote. This acquaints them with our world's rich musical heritage, building the foundation for well-rounded musicianship. Children's singing skills and repertoire developed through imitating and improvising are generally two years ahead of their ability to read and sing the musical notation of simple songs. Students need experience singing simple rhythms and rhythm variations before being expected to sing more difficult rhythms. Actual experience is the strongest prerequisite to cognitive understanding.

Music's multiple media provide opportunities to connect all the vital components of both affective and cognitive learning. Challenge yourself to discover this reality.

Writing Music

When the music key experiences have occurred consistently throughout the High/Scope K–3 Curriculum, writing music becomes a skill that children will naturally want to acquire. A desire to save their musical ideas to read and use another day motivates children to learn to write music. In learning to write music, children apply both math skills and language abilities. Music notation need not be considered a foreign language. Throughout the K–3 years, all learners can be guided to write music using their own symbol systems. Eventually they will want to acquire the traditional notation skills appropriate to their age and cognitive level.

The classroom teacher and music educator will find that music-writing skills evolve naturally, in a logical fashion. First children *hear and sing the musical ideas* (high and low pitches, shorter and longer tones, rhythm patterns, etc.); then children *use movement to represent the ideas;* next they *express the concepts using their own system of symbols;* this is followed by *using traditional notation;* and finally children *read and check what has been written* (see 7.27).

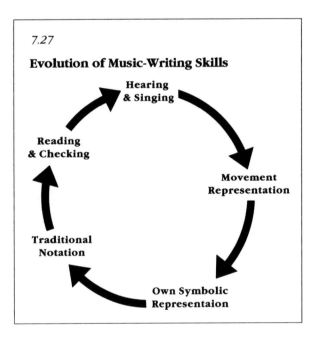

7.27

Evolution of Music-Writing Skills

Hearing & Singing

Movement Representation

Own Symbolic Representaion

Traditional Notation

Reading & Checking

Putting sound and experience before symbol leads to understanding and use. Icons are an important part of the learner's natural progression in writing music. The manipulatives used to represent musical ideas might be as simple as blocks or popsicle sticks. These icons can provide the child with experiences in representing pitch or duration before the traditional music symbols are introduced. Writing music is not an abstract exercise that can be enjoyed only by the musically elite. Small music-writing tasks can occur naturally for children as a representation game. Using their *own* symbols, children can discover how to represent a rhythm or part of a melody. Just as children learn to print before attempting cursive writing, so can they try out their own musical symbols (iconic representation) before using traditional notation. (See page 158, "Reading one's own symbol system (icons) for rhythm *or* pitch.") Simple rhythm patterns or pitch relationships can be written and understood in this manner throughout grades 2 and 3, thus making the traditional symbols meaningful when the learner is ready to use and understand them.

What experiences in kindergarten and grade 1 enable a child to write music? Beginning experiences include "writing" with the body. Movement is the most natural and the strongest tool for representing all of the following:

For elementary school children, tonal and movement experiences come before writing and reading music. This child "writes" with her body to show a high musical pitch.

- Steady beat
- Fast and slow tempo
- High and low pitches
- Loud and soft pitches
- Long and short pitches
- Same and different pitches
- Pitches that step up, down, or repeat
- Pitches that skip over other pitches and go up and down
- Same and different pitch patterns

We tap into a powerful impetus for learning when we guide children to use movement to explore these musical concepts—the foundation stones for musical literacy. Movement, like music, is a child's natural language and is often a spontaneous reaction to singing.

Manipulative icons provide children with concrete experiences for personalizing and representing their music and movement activities. Here are some suggestions for such icons:

1. Steady beats—blocks or popsicle sticks or buttons
2. Resting beats—cotton balls or uncooked rigatoni
3. Fast/slow tempo—classroom manipulatives chosen by learners
4. Pitches that rise, descend, or repeat—a 6-foot piece of yarn; different sizes of raindrops for a song about rain, etc.

The list could go on and on. Many teachers may already be familiar with ways to use manipulatives to provide key experiences in representation, classification, and seriation. Likewise, natural extensions of the use of manipulatives, along with your ideas, can help children solidify musical concepts. With iconic representation, a teacher can guide students to represent simple rhythms or melodic shapes left to right, as well as high and low, higher and lower, long and short, loud and soft (see 7.28).

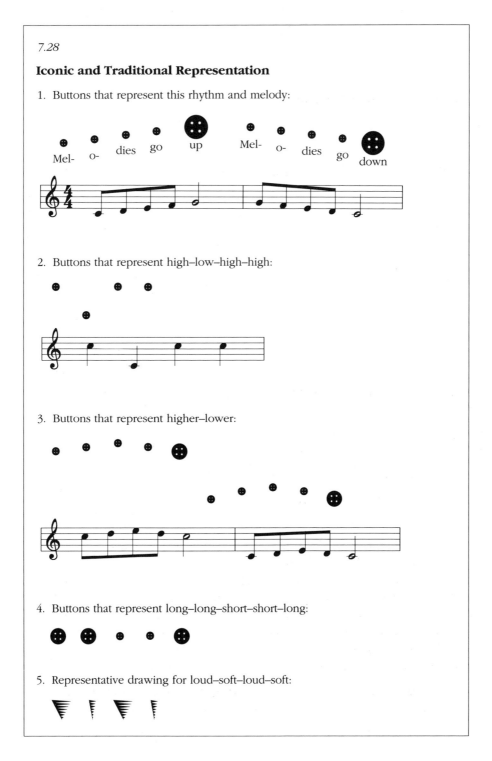

7.28

Iconic and Traditional Representation

1. Buttons that represent this rhythm and melody:

2. Buttons that represent high–low–high–high:

3. Buttons that represent higher–lower:

4. Buttons that represent long–long–short–short–long:

5. Representative drawing for loud–soft–loud–soft:

Each use of various types of child-invented icons, as each child shows his or her own way of representing what is heard, brings learners one step nearer to employing traditional notation. Icons, such as stars, may represent the contour or shape of the melody with or without musical staff lines (see the first example in 7.29). Line notation may also be used to show contour, and in this case, duration of pitches is indicated by line length (see the second example in 7.29). Icons may also represent simple rhythms (see 7.30).

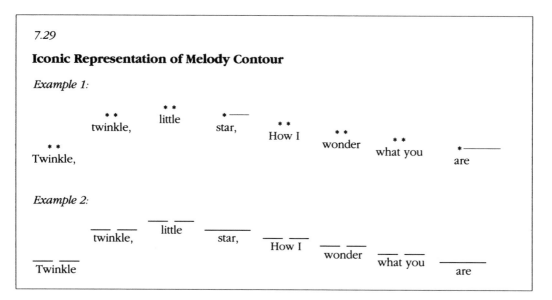

7.29

Iconic Representation of Melody Contour

Example 1:

Example 2:

7.30

Iconic Representation of Simple Rhythms

Children in second and third grades are interested in codes and rules and will have noticed that there is a traditional way that music is written. As they gradually work from invented icons to the traditional symbol system, their musical thinking skills connect with their kinesthetic, visual, aural, and cognitive processes. Starting from a kinesthetic (feeling) base, division of beat *and* duration of beat now need specific rules to link *feeling* beat, rhythm, and pitch to *seeing* notation, and then singing, playing or hearing what the notes represent (see 7.31). Pitches have names, just as friends have names. Writing and reading music go hand in hand. One writes and then reads to check for correct representation. If the classroom teacher keeps the above learning progression clearly in mind, children's musical discrimination will be well on its way to becoming a useful musical tool.

> **Showing a way to represent long/short sounds, high/low pitches, or repeated sounds (rhythm and/or melody maps).** Movement becomes the

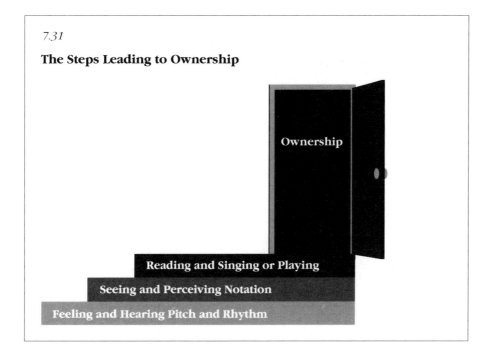

7.31

The Steps Leading to Ownership

Ownership

Reading and Singing or Playing

Seeing and Perceiving Notation

Feeling and Hearing Pitch and Rhythm

teacher's guide to assessing whether students understand and can represent the concepts in this accent. Movement exploration can enable each student to determine how best to represent each concept. For example, long and short sounds may be represented in nonlocomotor movement (moving hands far apart for *long,* moving hands close together for *short)* or locomotor movement (taking one giant step for long, taking one tiny step for *short).*

Once children have engaged in movement exploration to clarify long and short sounds, they may be interested in developing **rhythm maps** (for example, using long and short strips of posterboard) that work well for reinforcement. Insert 7.32 shows two examples, a duple-meter and a triple-meter rhythm, represented with beat boxes and also with long and short strips of posterboard.

Working in groups, children may initiate the design of long-short patterns with posterboard strips for other groups to decode on a rotational basis (see the first two examples in Insert 7.33). Each group rotates to perform the next group's long-short pattern, until all patterns have been performed.

A student volunteer can pose a long-short movement "problem," and each child can illustrate the answer with posterboard strips. Two instruments can be chosen, one to represent *long* and the other to represent *short* sounds. When children are ready for a challenge, more-extended patterns of long-short can be created and performed.

From this basic concept of long-short, refinements that will need clarification are *longer-shorter* sounds. The last two examples in Insert 7.33 illustrate beginning relationships in understanding longer-shorter. Movement gives meaning to this concept.

Using a selected list of songs the class knows well, a game called "Name That Song Rhythm" can be played. Children try to identify one another's

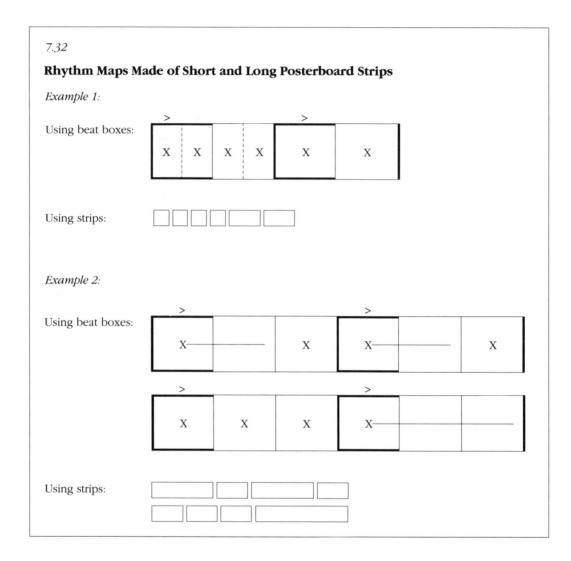

7.32

Rhythm Maps Made of Short and Long Posterboard Strips

Example 1:

Using beat boxes:

Using strips:

Example 2:

Using beat boxes:

Using strips:

songs through movement cues, instrument cues, icons, or rhythm maps (some examples are given in Insert 7.34). Children's kinesthetic and visual reading readiness for musical notation will be greatly enhanced by activities such as the ones described here. (For further information on guiding children to learn to read and understand rhythmic notation, see the section entitled "Expressing Rhythm" in Chapter 6.)

The learning process children engage in to understand high-low pitches parallels that followed to understand long-short patterns. Again, children's movement explorations can help them grasp the basic concepts that are involved. When children use their voices to make high and low sounds, and when they sing songs that reinforce these concepts (such as the middle part of the song *Traffic Signals,* Chapter 8, p. 312), they naturally add corresponding movements to show their understanding. Children can also play low and high pitches on instruments and then identify them through movement. Some of the children can present high-low "problems" through movement, and the other

7.33

Rhythm Patterns Representing Eight Beats With Various Sizes of Paper Rectangles

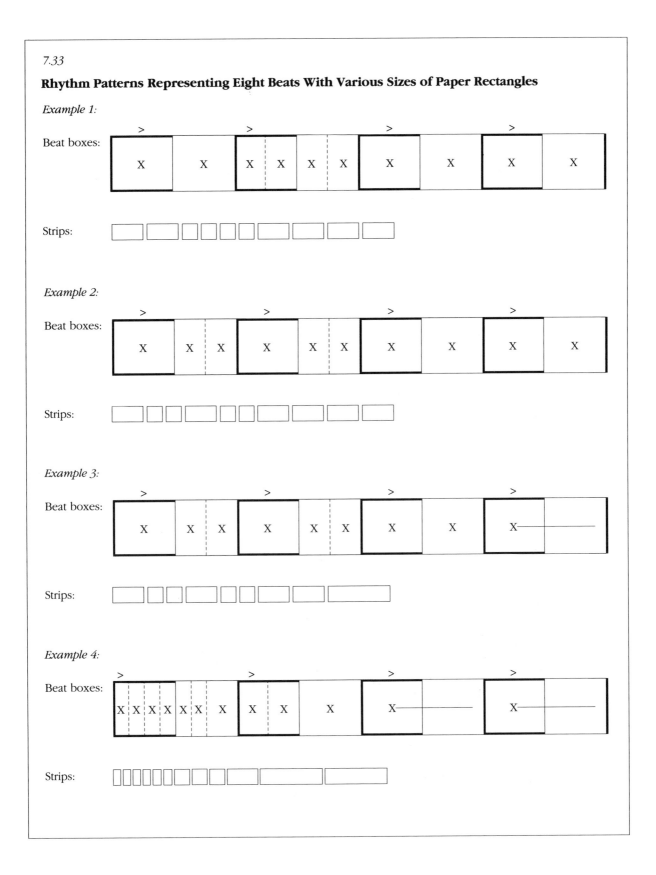

7.34

Name That Song Rhythm

Rhythm map:

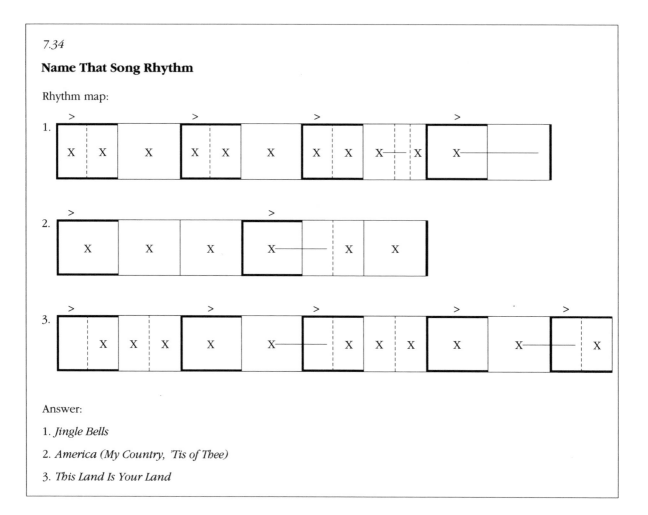

Answer:

1. *Jingle Bells*

2. *America (My Country, 'Tis of Thee)*

3. *This Land Is Your Land*

children can then make iconic representations of the movements (using paper arrows, or a plain piece of paper and buttons, as shown below in Insert 7.35).

Groups can use icons to design high-low problems for other groups to represent through movement. Individual students can use movement to show high-low patterns that classmates, in turn, play on a pitched instrument (see 7.36). Once high-low pitches are understood, children will recognize repeated pitches. Later high*er*-low*er* pitches will be recognized in songs and recordings. Experiences with these pitch relationships, whether child- or teacher-initiated, refine children's aural discrimination. This refinement then carries over to children's iconic representation of the higher-lower pitches, to their corresponding representation through movement, and to better, in-tune

7.35

High–Low Movements Represented by Icons

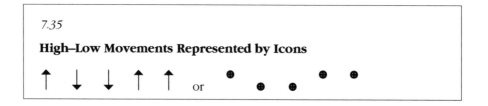

Representing High-Low Through Movement

Kindergarten: Karen wants the small group to sing what she has just shown with her total body movement: high, low, high. They move and sing one high pitch, one low pitch, one high pitch. Then Laura volunteers her movement idea—low, high, high, low—and the group sings and moves. The children are not all matching one another's high or low pitches, but they are demonstrating their individual understanding of the concepts being demonstrated through movement.

Grade 1: Connie wants to work in the music area on high-low pitches, so on the xylophone she plays high C, low C, high C. Then, as Connie sings, she puts her hands high, then touches her knees, then puts her hands high again. She makes several patterns using these two specific tones, and then plays C-D-E-F-G-A-B-C'. Later, on the playground, she sings these eight tones as she climbs up the ladder to the slide.

Name That Tune

With the body scale:
1. Waist-thigh-knee-thigh-waist-waist-waist _____ (*Mary Had a Little Lamb*)
2. Shoulders-waist-shoulders, shoulders-waist-shoulders (*This Old Man*)

With icons:

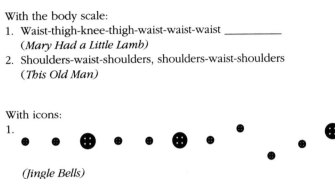

1. (*Jingle Bells*)

2. (*Happy Birthday*)

singing. The "Name That Tune" game truly engages children's *inner hearing* (beginning in second grade), when the body scale is used to "play the melody" or when icons are used to represent part of a melody (see 7.37). Students will then begin to understand that musical notation expresses pitch *and* rhythm and is logical to read.

Using movement to work with all the musical concepts helps to activate children's kinesthetic-aural-cognitive link, as has been stated before. Movement *is* the base for education in the early grades, when the goal is for each child to be able to *personally construct* his or her knowledge.

> **Showing a way to represent part of a melody.** When each of the concepts involved in the previous key experience has been explored and is understood by students, those concepts can be applied to songs being sung in the classroom. Making **melody maps** is a useful activity in this regard. For example, the teacher might ask questions like these:

- How can we represent the last three pitches of *America (My Country, 'Tis of Thee)*? (Students sing and shape this and then work with manipulatives, as shown in the first example in Insert 7.38.)

- Can you shape the melody for the middle section of *Twinkle, Twinkle, Little Star?* (Students sing and shape, then represent with their manipulatives, as shown in the second example in Insert 7.38.)

• Who can represent the first four pitches of *Are You Sleeping?*
(Students sing and shape, then represent with their manipulatives,
as shown in the third example in Insert 7.38.)

Some children will represent only the melodic shape, while others will
be able to represent melody and rhythm by how they arrange the icons on their

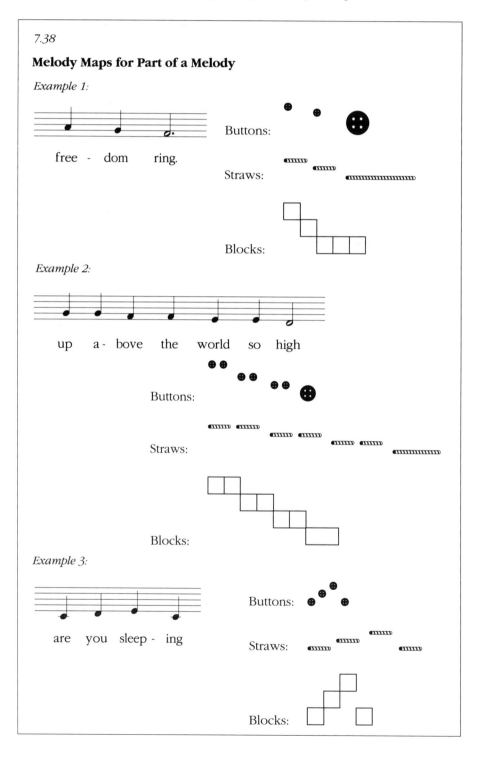

7.38

Melody Maps for Part of a Melody

Example 1:

free - dom ring.

Buttons:

Straws:

Blocks:

Example 2:

up a - bove the world so high

Buttons:

Straws:

Blocks:

Example 3:

are you sleep - ing

Buttons:

Straws:

Blocks:

melody maps. Movement representation as a child sings provides immediate assessment. Iconic representation of a melody or rhythm after it has been *expressed through movement* is important to experience, because it provides an essential link to the attending needed. Again, children's iconic representation provides observable outcomes for assessing each child's level of ownership of pitch and rhythm. Remember, with young children, since manipulative icons are the more concrete means of representation, they should be used before pencil-and-paper representation.

Manipulatives play an important role in High/Scope's active learning approach, and their use as icons in representing musical relationships is especially important. Representation with *first manipulative* and *then written icons* builds the bridge from what children *hear and relate through movement* to what they *read and understand cognitively.*

> **Writing music using one's own symbol system (icons).** This accent may involve using regular classroom manipulatives or a student-chosen symbol system. It extends the musical thinking addressed earlier to enable children to represent a musical phrase, a simple song that the child knows well, or an original song. Various seasonal shapes for students to manipulate can provide special incentives: ghosts for a Halloween melody, bells or snowflakes for a December tune, or butterflies for a spring melody. Children can initiate their ideas about the use of shapes during art or plan-do-review and then share their work with the class.

Writing music using a personal symbol system *empowers each child to express his or her own musical thinking*—which is something that young learners especially understand and appreciate. Furthermore, young learners *enjoy* reading the iconic representations that their peers have constructed, so writing and interpreting student-chosen symbol systems extends the music reading skills, inner-hearing skills, and thinking skills of all involved.

> **Using conventional notation to represent a phrase or short song.** Because children need many preparatory experiences through movement, singing, listening, playing instruments, and working with manipulatives, conventional music notation should not be introduced before third grade. Until there is a *need to know* about musical notation, there is no need to introduce it. When the proper preparatory experiences have provided children with the comfort and confidence that are prerequisites to reading "real music," it is time to introduce the special, universal notational system.

In keeping with the High/Scope active learning approach, traditional music notation can be presented in a way that enables children to relate it to prior knowledge. The teacher might begin by introducing the **quarter note,** which represents one microbeat of sound, and the **quarter rest,** which represents one microbeat of silence (see 7.39). Then, guide students to represent the last three pitches of *This Old Man* (three quarter-notes followed by a rest, as shown in Insert 7.40), asking "How can we represent the melody's contour, or shape, as well as the durational relationships?"

Children can walk and sing *Star Light, Star Bright* and feel the quarter-note pulses or beats. They will notice that in the song phrase "star I've seen to-," the melody tones move faster, and this leads to introducing the two-eighth-note

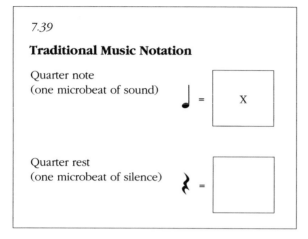

7.39

Traditional Music Notation

Quarter note
(one microbeat of sound) ♩ = | X |

Quarter rest
(one microbeat of silence) 𝄽 = | |

7.40

Short Phrases of Familiar Songs

This Old Man

roll - ing   home.

rhythm (see 7.41). Two eighth notes represent the normal *division* of a quarter-note beat. Children's understanding of this should be felt through singing, moving, reading box notation, and representing with icons *before* they are introduced to the actual notation.

Rhythm patterns occur in all songs. Often, the rhythm pattern of a song will be the component children like best. Read rhythm patterns with a neutral

Children can read rhythms they have created for one another using beat-box notation strips. The four-box strips these children are using provide a concrete way to represent microbeat, macrobeat, and simple divisions of beat.

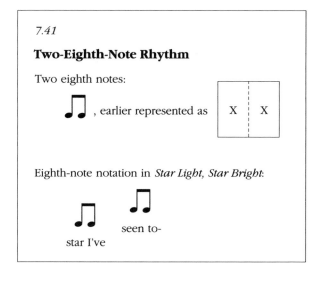

7.41

Two-Eighth-Note Rhythm

Two eighth notes:

♫ , earlier represented as

X	X

Eighth-note notation in *Star Light, Star Bright*:

seen to-

star I've

syllable in grades 1 and 2, to concentrate on the *feeling* that rhythm brings to the underlying beat (see Insert 7.42). Focusing on rhythm spoken against moving one's body to the steady beat is a valuable attending ability for children to develop. Create rhythm patterns as an extension of reading. Extract melodic rhythm patterns enjoyed in familiar songs in grades 2 and 3, when a rhythm reading *system* is in place.

Duration of beat can be approached in the same sequential manner—through movement and singing first. Until children are about age 12, their kinesthetic mode seems to be very strong, and educators who have worked with students and music notation have noticed a remarkable difference in how children sing and play rhythms when movement to the steady beat has

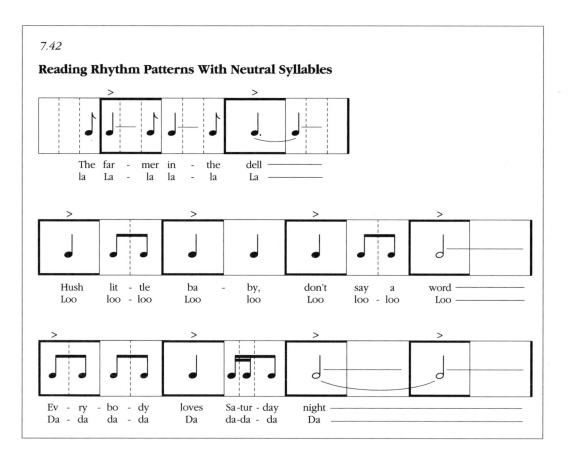

7.42

Reading Rhythm Patterns With Neutral Syllables

The far - mer in - the dell —————
la La - la la - la La —————

Hush lit - tle ba - by, don't say a word —————
Loo loo - loo Loo loo Loo loo - loo Loo —————

Ev - ry - bo - dy loves Sa-tur - day night —————
Da - da da - da Da da-da - da Da —————

7.43

Pitches Held for Two-, Three-, and Four-beat Duration

The **half note** represents the duration of two quarter notes or their rhythmic equivalent:

or various combinations of these

The **dotted half note** represents the duration of three quarter notes or their rhythmic equivalent:

or various combinations of these

The **whole note** represents the duration of four quarter notes or their rhythmic equivalent:

○ = ♩ ♩ ♩ ♩

or various combinations of these

been used as the basis for their understanding. Some melody pitches are held for two-, three-, or four-beat duration (see 7.43). These concepts may be understood by children in grades 2 and 3.

By third grade, students will be able to conduct in a pattern of two (see 7.44). When children conduct with both hands while singing a song such as *It's a Small World* or rounds such as *Are You Sleeping?* and *Row, Row, Row Your Boat,* the conducting successfully strengthens their basic timing. Third-grade children may also show competence in walking quarter, half, and whole notes while they conduct in patterns of two. Toward the latter half of grade 3, students have even conducted in the pattern of three (see 7.45) with success while singing *America.*

The musical staff and pitch identification can be introduced gradually in grade 3, when students have experienced many tone games in the context of other music key experiences. When the teacher relates ascending pitches of the musical staff to a xylophone turned vertically, learners can understand the logic used in placement of notes (see 7.46).

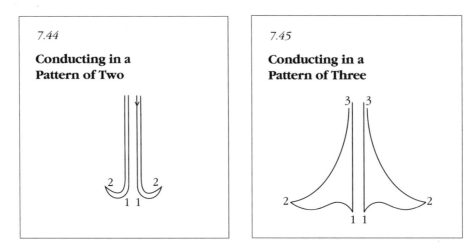

7.44

Conducting in a Pattern of Two

7.45

Conducting in a Pattern of Three

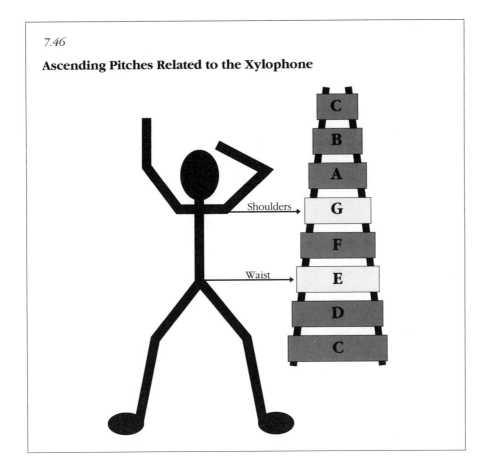

7.46

Ascending Pitches Related to the Xylophone

A basic understanding of line and space notes should precede the actual naming of each line and space. Begin where the G-pitch "lives" (2nd line) and where the E-pitch "lives" (1st line). Sing many songs that use these two pitches, such as *Rain, Rain, Go Away; One, Two, Tie My Shoe;* and *Engine, Engine, Number Nine.* Also sing nursery rhymes using these two pitches. (See "Two-Tone, Three-Tone Triumphs" in Chapter 8, p. 307.)

We suggest that pitches on the staff be introduced in the same order as the tone game pitches. The second line note (G) and first line note (E) should be introduced first, so children can read *Rain, Rain, Go Away* and other songs using these two pitches. Then introduce the A-pitch (second space), and sing, read, and write *Dr. Foster* and *Sally Go 'Round the Sun.* Then introduce the middle-C and D pitches by singing, reading, and writing *Merrily We Roll Along, Hot Cross Buns,* or *Red Gold Brown.* Then, introduce the higher-C pitch (third space), the F pitch (first space), and the B pitch (third line). Now, all of the eight-tone scale pitches in the key of C-major have been introduced (see 7.47). While not all songs are comfortable to sing in C-major, this key gives children a *beginning* base for learning to play melodies on their own. Using conventional notation for a phrase, and later for a short song, has built-in motivation for most students. They find it very exciting to write real music and can find many reasons to use this skill, once they have been guided and supported in it by a caring classroom teacher. Writing music in relevant ways is important for learners in grade 2 or 3. Teachers who support and guide children in acquiring music-writing skills will find their efforts well rewarded, because children are constructing understandings and relationships that build a solid musical foundation for life.

7.47

Order in Which Pitches Should Be Introduced

Progress from simple, two-tone songs to those using progressively more tones.

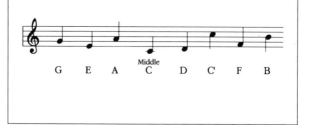

G   E   A   Middle C   D   C'   F   B

Summary

In the child-centered approach to developing musical intelligence, teachers recognize that this process of enhancing conceptual learning through movement and music is worthy of implementation because music's many components are applicable to *all areas* of the curriculum. When children are guided to explore, use, create, and perform through the music key experiences, they will also be integrating, through the "primary learning center," the language, math, science, and movement key experiences.

When teachers ask children how they figured out how to play a known melody, create a new song, or choreograph a dance, they are engaging children's thinking and problem-solving abilities. When children figure out how to represent a rhythm or a melody shape through icons, they are on the way to understanding music notation. Teachers and children share responsibility for learning. Without the guidance of the teacher in introducing the music key experiences, the child may never have opportunity to bring the "whole of learning" together in age-appropriate ways.

There *is* a place for child-initiated *and* teacher-initiated learning. There *is* a place for practice. (Repetition is the child's security blanket.) There *is* a place for seeing, listening, doing, thinking, and creating by *everyone* in the developmentally appropriate classroom. All of this will be evident in the activities of Chapter 8, which provide many catalysts for bringing together the whole of learning through music.

ENDNOTES

[1]T. Armstrong, quoting H. Gardner, in *Awakening Your Child's Natural Genius* (Los Angeles: Jeremy Tarcher, Inc., 1991), p. 145.

[2]E. Gordon, *Learning Sequences in Music* (Chicago: GIA Publishing, 1984).

Chapter 8

Active Learning Involving the K–3 Music Key Experiences

The creative arts provide us with a unique and vital perspective about our world. As performers or supporters of music, dance, art, or theater, with each experience we have the possibility of being inspired and seeing the world through a different lens.

John Sculley
Former Chairman and Chief Executive Officer
Apple Computer, Inc.

T he active learning opportunities presented here are based on the **K–3 music key experiences** introduced in Chapter 4 and listed on the following three pages (see 8.1). Thorough explanations for each broad category of these essential experiences may be found in Chapter 5, "Exploring Music"; Chapter 6, "Using the Elements of Music"; and Chapter 7, "Creating and Performing Music."

Each activity in this chapter includes specific opportunities for guiding and facilitating learners in achieving ownership of the concepts involved in the **music key experiences**. For ease of use, the activities are numbered, and a grade-level interval for each activity is suggested. (See Appendix E for the activities listed alphabetically.) Many extensions can follow from each activity. Only when learners are engaged and facilitated and allowed to reflect on the concepts involved in an activity will they experience the "aha's" of learning. The three components of Phyllis S. Weikart's Teaching Model—**separate, simplify, and facilitate**—are the strategies to use in presenting each activity. The following guidelines will also be helpful.

1. Experiences should be teacher- or child-initiated instead of teacher-directed.
2. An interactive environment is essential and will provide children with a safe and comfortable climate for learning.
3. Teachers are partners in the students' learning. Shared responsibility for learning is assumed.
4. One does not need formal music training to be successful with this area of the curriculum; a healthy curiosity and a willingness to learn with students are important.
5. Music may enhance children's learning in other subject areas and also may provide an effective transition from one subject to another.

Clearly, music experiences do not need to be—indeed, should not be—restricted to a music time.

6. Children's music education should be conducted in an atmosphere of cooperation, not competition.

7. Initiate many and varied active learning experiences, so children may understand the various music concepts that are presented. Remember that children develop at their own pace and must be engaged to *reflect on each concept* in their own way in order for understanding and ownership to develop.

8. The abstract concepts in music become understandable when movement is used as the base for music experiences.

9. Music and movement provide memorable, relevant learning experiences. Never underestimate their combined potential!

10. When music and movement active learning experiences are created and shared, learning will be joyful. Music and movement become the sweet M & M's of learning.

8.1

I. Exploring Music *(Chapter 5)*

A. *Moving to music*
> 1. Responding to different types of music
> 2. Using nonlocomotor and locomotor movements with music
> 3. Using coordination skills in performing action songs
> 4. Illustrating expressive and dynamic qualities of a musical selection
> 5. Moving to phrases of a musical selection

B. *Exploring and identifying sounds*
> 1. Making sounds with voices and instruments (musical and otherwise)
> 2. Working with percussion and melodic instrument sounds
> 3. Exploring sounds to fit with specific songs
> 4. Exploring lower/higher and same/different sounds

C. *Exploring instruments*
> 1. Trying out ways to play instruments
> 2. Discovering ways to play percussion, harmonic, and melodic instruments
> 3. Discovering pitch range and labeling the sound quality of instruments
> 4. Playing melodic phrases and known songs

D. *Exploring the singing voice*
> 1. Making pitched sounds
> 2. Exploring the singing and speaking voice
> 3. Exploring the broad range of the singing voice
> 4. Initiating singing alone and singing in tune with others

E. *Listening to and describing music*
> 1. Recognizing music versus sound
> 2. Talking about voices and instruments heard or feelings expressed in the music
> 3. Identifying previously heard or sung musical selections
> 4. Discussing the type or style of the music

II. Using the Elements of Music *(Chapter 6)*

A. *Feeling and expressing steady beat*
> 1. Moving to one's own steady beat
> 2. Matching someone else's steady beat

Continued

> 3. Matching the steady beat of recorded music, songs, rhymes
> 4. Performing single nonlocomotor movements to the steady beat
> 5. Performing single locomotor movements to the steady beat
> 6. Playing instruments in steady beat
> 7. Combining nonlocomotor and locomotor movement to the steady beat

B. *Identifying tone color*
> 1. Distinguishing different persons' singing and speaking voices
> 2. Hearing the differences in voices and percussion instruments
> 3. Distinguishing the different instrument sounds
> 4. Matching an instrument's sound with its picture
> 5. Identifying voices and instruments heard in a recording
> 6. Identifying special characteristics of tone color within the music

C. *Developing melody*
> 1. Identifying higher and lower pitches
> 2. Identifying the direction of the melody (upward/downward)
> 3. Matching intervals and repeated pitches
> 4. Imitating three- and four-note melody patterns
> 5. Distinguishing *same* and *different* in short melody patterns
> 6. Responding to the shape of the melody
> 7. Identifying and singing phrases in the melody
> 8. Recognizing patterns and sequences in melodies
> 9. Singing and shaping phrases and songs

D. *Labeling form*
> 1. Identifying the beginning and end of a song or rhyme
> 2. Identifying the verse and chorus of a song
> 3. Identifying same and different phrases
> 4. Identifying and responding to the different sections of recorded music
> 5. Labeling and using AB, ABA, and ABC forms
> 6. Labeling and using rondo form and simple theme and variations form

E. *Recognizing the expressive qualities of tempo and dynamics*
> 1. Identifying *slow* and *fast* through movement and vocabulary
> 2. Identifying *loud* and *soft* through movement and vocabulary
> 3. Identifying *slow, medium,* and *fast* through movement and vocabulary
> 4. Identifying *loud, medium,* and *soft* through movement and vocabulary
> 5. Identifying *getting faster* and *getting slower*
> 6. Identifying *getting louder* and *getting softer*
> 7. Selecting suitable dynamics and tempo for a song or instrumental piece

F. *Feeling and identifying meter*
> 1. Identifying and moving with macrobeats and microbeats
> 2. Identifying same and different meter
> 3. Identifying and moving to duple meter
> 4. Identifying and moving to triple meter
> 5. Differentiating between duple and triple meter

G. *Expressing rhythm*
> 1. Listening for longer and shorter sounds
> 2. Moving to sounds of longer and shorter duration
> 3. Moving to rhythm patterns
> 4. Distinguishing same and different rhythm patterns
> 5. Recognizing and playing even and uneven rhythm patterns
> 6. Reading, writing, and performing rhythm patterns
> 7. Recognizing and using note and rest values (quarter, two-eighth, half, dotted half, and whole)

H. *Adding harmony*
> 1. Recognizing the difference between unison singing and singing accompanied by instrument(s)
> 2. Using chords to create harmony

Continued

> 3. Singing call-response and echo songs
> 4. Adding melodic chants
> 5. Singing rounds
> 6. Finding and using ways to add harmony to a song or instrumental selection

III. Creating and Performing Music (Chapter 7)

O—x A. *Responding to various types of music*
> 1. Showing through movement the differences heard in music
> 2. Responding to *same/different* in songs children sing
> 3. Responding to *same/different* in instrumental music
> 4. Responding to different moods of a musical selection
> 5. Responding to a repertoire of different types of music

O—x B. *Playing instruments alone and in groups*
> 1. Playing an instrument alone or in a group, using steady beat
> 2. Playing an instrument in steady beat while others sing
> 3. Playing an instrument in steady beat while singing alone
> 4. Playing an instrument in a rhythm pattern
> 5. Playing instruments together using rhythm patterns
> 6. Creating and planning instrument parts for a song or ensemble

O—x C. *Singing alone and in groups*
> 1. Singing simple songs alone and with others
> 2. Singing a short solo phrase during a call-response song or a single verse when the class sings chorus
> 3. Singing songs of increasing length and difficulty with others
> 4. Singing a solo with musical competence and confidence

O—x D. *Sharing music by performing*
> 1. Creating and singing a new verse to a known song
> 2. Creating and sharing an instrumental piece on percussion or melodic instruments
> 3. Playing a musical instrument while the group sings
> 4. Sharing songs created by students
> 5. Sharing an instrumental ensemble created by students

O—x E. *Moving creatively and choreographing movement sequences and dances*
> 1. Moving creatively alone or with a group
> 2. Creating movements and variations for a specific musical selection
> 3. Creating and using different movements for AB music
> 4. Creating patterns and moving creatively
> 5. Planning and using different movement and dance sequences for a specific song or recording

O—x F. *Creating and improvising songs and instrumental music*
> 1. Choosing instruments to play and accompany
> 2. Creating simple melodies vocally
> 3. Creating simple melodies on instruments
> 4. Improvising a variation on a melody, vocally and/or instrumentally
> 5. Creating an instrumental piece with two or more sections (AB)
> 6. Creating an original song with words

O—x G. *Reading music*
> 1. Reading one's own symbol system (icons) for rhythm *or* pitch
> 2. Reading melody or rhythm maps created by oneself or others
> 3. Reading short rhythmic and melodic phrases (conventional notation) and short songs
> 4. Reading conventional notation for simple songs

O—x H. *Writing music*
> 1. Showing a way to represent long/short sounds, high/low pitches, or repeated sounds (rhythm and/or melody maps)
> 2. Showing a way to represent part of a melody
> 3. Writing music using one's own symbol system (icons)
> 4. Using conventional notation to represent a phrase or short song

1 Make Time for Music!

Grades: K–3

Key Experiences:

All key experiences, all accents

Children sing about the reason for music in the K–3 curriculum.

Materials:

Make Time for Music . . . Movement

Elizabeth B. Carlton

Activity to experience:

Kindergarten singers can learn to sing the A section (both verses) well as they keep the macrobeat.

Grade 1 singers can add the B section to their repertoire while keeping steady beat and developing healthy attitudes about music's many uses.

Grade 2 singers can add the C section to their repertoire, lead two- or four-beat movement sequences, and "take the song for a walk."

Grade 3 singers can sing the song with ownership and be able to sing it in a two-part round, and eventually, a three-part round, as they display observable and excellent musicianship.

The Nutcracker Suite

Grades K–3

Key Experiences:
    O–ㄱ **I. A. Moving to music**
               > 1. Responding to different types of music

    O–ㄱ **III. A. Responding to various types of music**
               > 4. Responding to different moods of a musical selection

K–1 students listen and explore movements to the dances in the *Nutcracker Suite*. Grades 2–3 listen and decide how they will move during the selections and why.

Materials:
Record, tape, or compact disc player
Nutcracker Suite, P. I. Tschaikovsky: *Chinese Dance, Dance of the Sugar Plum Fairy, Arabian Dance*
A variety of objects: scarves, activity wands, ribbons, etc.

Activity to experience:
Students get into a small ball-shape and explore movement as they listen to the *Chinese Dance.*

Guide students through a second listening/moving experience with the *Chinese Dance,* with suggestions such as these:

> Have one arm come out to explore. What kind of movement can you do with just one arm? With the other leg? Find a way to move your whole body to the sound of the bassoon.

> Students explore movements suggested by the imagery in the title while listening to the *Dance of the Sugar Plum Fairy.*

> Students decide what to do on the *fermatas* (held tones) in the *Dance of the Sugar Plum Fairy.* Then they resume moving to the music.

> Students listen to the *Arabian Dance,* and when ready, they explore movement suggested by the title.

Facilitation and Reflection:
What movements did the *Chinese Dance* suggest?

What images came to mind while you were moving and listening to *Dance of the Sugar Plum Fairy?*

How do objects change your ability to express what you hear in the *Arabian Dance?*

How was your response to *Arabian Dance* different from your responses to the other two dances?

How are the three selections the same? Different?

What moods were created in the three pieces?

Extensions:

Discuss the various locations and characteristics of the countries that these selections represent.

Students select movements and work in small groups of three to five to create a dance for one of these selections. They share their dances with the entire class.

Identify specific instruments or types of instruments.

| 3 | # My Choice

Grades 1–2

Key Experience:
⦿⌐ I. A. Moving to music
> 1. Responding to different types of music

Children respond to different styles of music and explain why they chose particular movements to represent what they heard.

Materials:
Record, tape, or compact disc player
Hole in the Wall (RM4)
Bekendorfer Quadrille (RM4)

Activity to experience:
Children listen to *Hole in the Wall* and move to the music when ready.

Volunteers share ways they moved and then describe feelings or thoughts they had about the music.

Children explore ways to move to *Bekendorfer Quadrille* after listening to part of the music; volunteers share movements, thoughts, or feelings about the music.

Discuss these two selections. Compare and contrast them as to same/different instruments heard, mood, tempo, feelings they inspired.

Facilitation and Reflection:
What movements did you create for *Hole in the Wall?* For *Bekendorfer Quadrille?*

How did the music for each selection make you feel?

How are the two selections different?

Extensions:
Play other contrasting selections, such as *Southwind* (RM1), and *Armenian Miserlou* (RM9). Guide children to discover that music has many different styles, each of which can evoke a particular movement/feeling response.

4 | *Lullaby*

Grades K–2

Key Experiences:

○┑ **I. A. Moving to music**
>1. Responding to different types of music

○┑ **I. D. Exploring the singing voice**
>4. Initiating singing alone and singing in tune with others

○┑ **II. A. Feeling and expressing steady beat**
>3. Matching the steady beat of songs
>4. Performing single nonlocomotor movements to the steady beat

○┑ **II. C. Developing melody**
>7. Identifying and singing phrases in the melody

Children listen and rock while the teacher sings. Children later sing this lullaby while rocking a favorite stuffed toy or while rocking with classmates.

Materials:
Lullaby on next page

Activity to experience:
Children listen to this quiet lullaby while they feel and rock the macrobeat. They explore other nonlocomotor movements that fit.

Children learn to sing the song. They may begin to rock when they feel comfortable singing and rocking.

Children may choose to rock alone, with a partner, or with a small group. They may also choose to sing this lullaby while comforting a friend or while rocking a favorite stuffed toy.

Facilitation and Reflection:
What kind of song is a lullaby?

How does a lullaby make you feel?

What movements seem natural for a lullaby?

What movements do not seem to fit a lullaby? Why?

What parts (sections) of this lullaby are the same?

What part (section) of this lullaby is different?

Extensions:

Children may wish to create a different melody for the B section. They may add their own words or choose to use a neutral syllable for their melody.

Create a special quiet time by singing this lullaby together, and follow this by playing a quiet classical or folk recording.

Learn other lullabies, such as *Brahms' Lullaby; All Night, All Day; Hush-a-Bye, Don't You Cry.*

Learn lullabies from other countries (find recordings in the public library).

Discuss how several lullabies are the same and how they are different.

Lullaby

Elizabeth Carlton

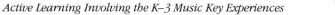

Lul - la - by, sing lul - la - by. Sun is in the West____

Lul - la - by, sing lul - la - by. Close your eyes and rest.____

Lul - la - bies are "I love you's." So you'll al - ways know.____

Though you tra - vel far and wide, I will love you so.____

Lul - la - by, sing lul - la - by. Sun is in the West.____

Lul - la - by, sing lul - la - by. Close your eyes and rest.____

5 | Movement Maps, Level 1

Grades K–1

Key Experience:

O┐   **I. A.   Moving to music**

> 2. Using nonlocomotor and locomotor movements with music

Children refine nonlocomotor or locomotor movements to music as they interpret movement maps showing different pathways.

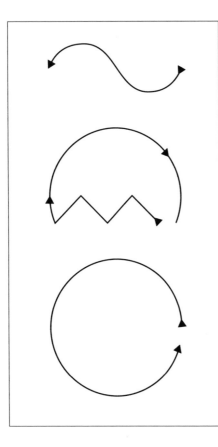

Materials:
Record, tape, or compact disc player
Plješkavac Kolo (RM3) or any
        familiar AB music (explained
        on p. 106 of Chapter 6)
Prepared simple movement maps
        (explained on p. 66 of Chapter
        5), such as these to the left

Activity to experience:
Children listen to the music and explore how they would like to move.

Children look at the movement map to figure out the pathway it illustrates.

Children choose whether they will use nonlocomotor or locomotor movement to this music. While seated, they trace maps in the air with nonlocomotor movement while using a chosen body part to lead the movement.

Children move to the music, following the pathway indicated by the map.

Facilitation and Reflection:
Describe the way you chose to move to the music.

What does this movement map tell us about our moving direction?

How could you follow this map another way and still make this shape?

Extensions:
Children work in small groups to design new movement maps and to interpret new maps, using this music or other music, such as *Djurdjevka Kolo* (RM2) or *Limbo Rock* (RM2).

6 Movement Maps, Level 2

Grades 2–3

Key Experience:

I. A. Moving to music

> 2. Using nonlocomotor and locomotor movements with music

In groups of six to ten, learners refine nonlocomotor and locomotor movements to music as they decode maps for movement.

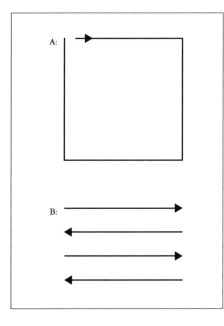

Materials:

Tape or compact disc player
Hora Medura (RM3)
Prepared movement maps, visual
(drawings like those to the
left) or written (verbal)

Activity to experience:

Students explore movement while listening to the music.

Students look at a visual or written movement map, listen to the music, and determine the movement they will use. While seated, they can trace the movement map in the air while using a chosen body part to lead the movement.

Students identify the A and B sections of the music (See Chapter 6, p. 106, for an explanation of AB music).

Students clarify which pathway they will use for each section of the music.

Facilitation and Reflection:

How did you move to this music?

During the A and B sections, what will be our movement pathways?

What types of movement would be good to use for this tempo?

Should we use the same or different movement for the A and B sections?

What strategies can you use to keep the beat steady while you move in this shape?

Extensions:

Students can also write out verbal movement maps for musical selections such as *Gaelic Waltz* (RM1). For example, they might write instructions like these:

> Form a single circle. Using macrobeat, swing arms back and forth over head eight times; bend, then straighten arms in front of you four times; walk in toward center four steps, then walk (backward) out four steps; repeat this last walking sequence.

Creating movement maps such as this creates a link between music and language proficiency.) **Learn to use language-to-dance vocabulary. Folk dance = movement maps!**

Music-Movement-Language

Grades 2–3

Key Experience:

⊶ **I. A. Moving to music**

> 2. Using nonlocomotor and locomotor movements with music

> 5. Moving to phrases of a musical selection

Students discover what a musical phrase is, comparing it to a sentence in language.

Materials:

Record, tape, or compact disc player

At Va'ani (CD1)

Activity to experience:

After facilitating a discussion about sentences, the teacher explains that a musical phrase is much like a sentence, with a beginning, a point of emphasis, and a closure.

Individual students move a body part while speaking a sentence. Students volunteer to share with others how they do this.

Students listen to *At Va'ani* and individually explore ways to feel and demonstrate the phrase.

While the music is played again, students close their eyes and repeat the previous activity while the teacher observes whether they have a beginning understanding of the concept.

All discuss the difference between a musical *phrase* and a musical *selection*.

Facilitation and Reflection:

What happens to our voices when we express a statement? A question?

What happens in a musical phrase?

What motions did you use for the phrases? What other motions could you use?

Extensions:

Listen to other selections, such as *Al Gemali* (CD4) or *Leor Chiyuchech* (RM8).

Ask questions as before, with students making decisions on movements to represent phrases.

Discover the musical form of *At Va'ani* (AB), *Leor Chiyuchech* (AB), or *Gaelic Waltz* (A). (See Chapter 6, p. 106 for an explanation of musical form.)
If phrases are related to sentences, is *form* related to paragraphs? To math formulas?

8 Feel That Phrase

Grades 2–3

Key Experiences:

O—r **I. A. Moving to music**
> 2. Using nonlocomotor and locomotor movements with music
> 5. Moving to phrases of a musical selection

O—r **II. A. Feeling and expressing steady beat**
> 3. Matching the steady beat of recorded music
> 7. Combining nonlocomotor and locomotor movement to the steady beat

O—r **III. E. Moving creatively and choreographing movement sequences and dances**
> 2. Creating and using different movements for AB music
> 4. Creating patterns and moving creatively

Movement with an exercise focus gives students many opportunities to feel phrase length.

Materials:
Chairs
Record, tape, or compact disc player
Bechatzar Harabbi (RM6)

Activity to experience:
Each student is seated in a chair, with sufficient space around to reach with arms and legs in all directions.

Moving to the microbeat of *Bechatzar Harabbi,* students explore movements of arms alone or legs alone or combinations of arms and legs.

Students volunteer to share the movements they explored, and the class copies.

Students listen to the selection without movement and try to identify the places in the music where it would be logical to change the movement, thus responding to phrases and sections of the music.

Students try out their explored movements to the music and try to change the movement at the ends of phrases and sections of the music.

Students volunteer to lead small groups of class members.

Facilitation and Reflection:
What types of movement worked well with the music?

What helped you to identify the places to change the movement?

How many beats were in the pattern before you changed the movement?

Extensions:

Try different musical selections, such as *Cherkessiya* (RM2), *Soldier's Joy* (RM2), or *Machar* (RM5).

Small groups prepare an exercise routine and share it with the class.

We Keep the Beat Together

Grades K–2

Key Experiences:

☗ **I. A. Moving to music**
>3. Using coordination skills in performing action songs

☗ **II. A. Feeling and expressing steady beat**
>3. Matching the steady beat of songs
>4. Performing single nonlocomotor movements to the steady beat

☗ **II. G. Expressing rhythm**
>1. Listening for longer and shorter sounds

☗ **III. C. Singing alone and in groups**
>1. Singing simple songs alone and with others

Children sing and keep the macrobeat, which the teacher anchors four times before the song begins and between each repetition. Children echo the leader's verbal directions and motions, which accumulate with each repetition.

Materials:
We Keep the Beat Together on next page

Activity to experience:
Children echo "in beat" each verbal direction while adding the motion designated. Each repetition of the song adds one more direction to this musical game.

Children learn the song.

Facilitation and Reflection:
Discover which of the song's four phrases are the same and which are different.

What makes this song fun to sing?

What other vocal sounds or syllables could we use for the rhythm pattern?

Extensions:
Small groups of second-graders can create other movement sequences to share with the class.

Find other well-known melodies that lend themselves to adaptations such as the above. Create other action songs that make you smile.

We Keep the Beat Together

(Go In and Out the Window)

Adapted by Phyllis S. Weikart

We keep the beat to - geth - er. We keep the beat to -
geth - er. We keep the beat to - geth - er. And
then we stop and e - cho. "Arms out" (echo__) "Thumbs up" (e -
cho) Ooh Ooh Ooh Ooh Ooh Ooh Ooh Ooh Ooh (echo)

(Move hips to beat while chanting above syllable)

With each repetition, add one more direction after "Arms out" and "Thumbs up": (2) Knees bent, (3) Toes in, (4) Seat out, (5) Head down, (6) Tongue out. Change the rhythm syllable "Ooh" to "Hee" or "Ah" or some other syllable, for added fun.

10 | Table Setting March

Grades 1–2

Key Experiences:

  ⊙┐ **I. A. Moving to music**

        > 2. Using nonlocomotor and locomotor movements with music

  ⊙┐ **I. D. Exploring the singing voice**

        > 4. Initiating singing alone and singing in tune with others

  ⊙┐ **II. A. Feeling and expressing steady beat**

        > 3. Matching the steady beat of songs

        > 5. Performing single locomotor movements to the steady beat

        > 7. Combining nonlocomotor and locomotor movement to the steady beat

  ⊙┐ **III. C. Developing melody**

        > 9. Singing and shaping phrases and songs

  ⊙┐ **III. C. Singing alone and in groups**

        > 1. Singing simple songs alone and with others

Children sing as they use nonlocomotor and locomotor movements to march and set the table.

Materials:

Table Setting March on next page

Activity to experience:

Children listen to the song and keep the steady microbeat with their feet while seated. They discover that the first section of this song is called a chorus and can be used for bringing the various items to the table.

Children learn the song and sing it as they set the table.

Facilitation and Reflection:

Who can sing and shape each phrase? (There are two long phrases in the chorus and four short phrases in each verse.)

Which phrases are alike? Which are different?

What could we do during the chorus? (March to the cabinet, collect the items we need to set the table, and march to the table.)

Why is the steady beat easy to find and keep in this song?

Extensions:

Create verses that extend to cleanup, washing, or snack times or to special party set-ups.

Adapt the song to fit a family of five or six by singing phrase 3 of the verse again and adding words that fit each verse.

Table Setting March

Elizabeth B. Carlton

March, march, march, march. Set the ta - ble nice and neat.

March, march, march, march. Neat is such a treat!

1. First we set the plates. One for you and one for me.
2. Forks go on the left. Then the knives go on the right.
3. Nap - kins next to forks. Glass - es next to knife and spoon.

One for_____ and one for_____. Set the ta - ble for four.
Then the spoons go next to knives. Set the ta - ble for four.
This looks great! We're rea-dy for food! Let's have din - ner for four!

Geometric March

11

Grades 2–3

Key Experience:

⊶ **I. A. Moving to music**

> 5. Moving to phrases of a musical selection

Students walk to music forward and backward, changing directions with each phrase. Can be used in individual small spaces, even beside a desk.

Materials:

Record, tape, or compact disc player
Saüerlaender Quadrille #5 (CD5)

Activity to experience:

Students listen to the music and recall experiences relating phrases and sentences. (Phrases are like musical sentences.)

Step in place to the music, turning ¼ turn to the right with each new phrase.

The students decide which directions to move to create a geometric shape or a mathematical symbol such as this plus (+) sign (illustrated at right):

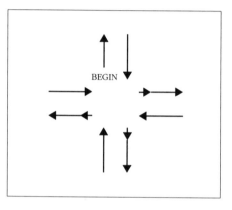

Walk forward four beats, then backward four beats.
Turn ¼ turn, walk forward four beats and backward four beats.
Continue this pattern two more times.
Repeat the shape over and over as the music is played.

Facilitation and Reflection:

How does your movement show the phrases of the music?

How else can you show the phrases?

Why do you think *all* music is constructed in phrases?

What other shapes or symbols could you design and perform to this music?

Extensions:

Students create other symbols or geometric shapes (such as the square, rectangle, or octagon) to phrases. They then share their ideas.

Create other designs to fit phrases of the music.

Use other music, such as *California Strut* (RM4) or *Bekendorfer Quadrille* (RM4).

Picture This!

Grades K–1

Key Experience:

O─┐ I. B. Exploring and identifying sounds
> 1. Making sounds with voices and instruments (musical and otherwise)

Exploring and creating sounds to represent a picture through voices and instruments

Materials:

Variety of unpitched instruments
Variety of nature pictures (animals, scenery, etc.)

Activity to experience:

Share with children a nature picture, such as a picture of mountains. (Pictures of other environments—a city street scene, a carnival scene, an ocean scene, can be used for this same experience.)

Children explore vocal sounds that they might hear in this environment.

Children explore movement to match their sounds.

Children explore unpitched instruments for appropriate sounds to contribute to the sound picture.

Children explore movement to various instrument sounds.

Children select vocal and instrumental sounds to be used to create their sound picture and then choose a conductor and perform this sound picture.

Facilitation and Reflection:

What do you see in this picture?

What are some sounds that you might hear in this scene?

Why did you choose that sound?

What kind of movements did you use for your sound?

What movements did you choose for the instrument sound?

Extensions:

Children may work in small groups to create sound pictures from a variety of prints.

Children may design their own environment pictures and create sound pictures for their art work or pass pictures to other groups to interpret.

Move That Sound

Grades K–1

Key Experience:

    ⊶ **I. B. Exploring and identifying sounds**

              > 2. Working with percussion and melodic instrument sounds

Children explore movement to each of three instruments and share their movement ideas.

Materials:

Wood block
Triangle
Maracas

Activity to experience:

Each child listens and explores movements to the sound of the woodblock, triangle, and maracas.

Children share their favorite ways to move to each particular instrument.

Children share with one another why they moved in specific ways.

The three instruments are placed in three different areas of the room, and the children go to the instrument they would like to represent through movement. Then the group of children who chose a particular instrument selects one student to play that instrument while the rest move to the sound of the instrument.

Each group performs for the rest of the class.

Facilitation and Reflection:

How did you move differently for each instrument?

Which way did you like to move best? Why?

How did each group move differently to their sound?

What are some other ways to move to this instrument's sound?

Extensions:

Draw that instrument. Write a description of each instrument's *sound*, and also describe the movement.

Make a graph showing the size of each instrument group, showing the number of students in each group.

Copy each groups' movement.

The class plans and performs movement/sound pieces. (Example: Play the triangle two times; the group moves two times for that sound. Play the wood block four times; they move four times for that sound. Play the maracas two times; they move two times for that sound.)

Add other instruments, such as finger cymbals, guiro, drum, to make the game and aural discrimination more challenging.

As children are ready (usually in grade 1), challenge them to first listen to the whole sound piece (triangle two times, woodblock four times, maracas two times) and *then* move to what they heard.

"Whale of a Tail"

14

Grades 2–3

Key Experiences:

I. B. Exploring and identifying sounds

>3. Exploring sounds to fit with specific songs

III. F. Creating and improvising songs and instrumental music

>2. Creating simple melodies vocally

Students explore and select vocal or instrumental sounds to accompany a song they have created.

Materials:

Variety of percussion instruments

Activity to experience:

Students create a rhyme about their study of a particular subject, such as whales (example below), and then create a melody:

> *A whale of a tale or tail of a whale.*
> *The largest is blue, and the smallest is asusu.*
> *Humpbacks, killer whales, mammals one and all.*
> *They can spout sea water or sing you a song.*
>
> Grade 2 students
> Neal Dow Elementary, Chico, CA.

Students explore ways to move as if they were sea creatures, and then they sing the song, accompanied by their movements.

Students explore accompanying vocal sounds for sea creatures.

Students match their movements to their vocal sounds.

Students explore and select instrument sounds to represent sea creatures.

Students decide on the form of their piece, such as ABA (A is the song or rhyme, B is movement or instruments, A is the song or rhyme).

Facilitation and Reflection:

How are you moving to your sound?

Why did you choose that vocal sound for your sea creature? How did you decide on the instrument?

Extensions:

Students in grade 3 develop beat-rhythm relationships:

> They speak the rhythm of a word phrase such as "whale of a tale" as they pat the macrobeat.

Half the class keeps the beat while the other half plays a rhythm body-percussion.

They transfer body-percussion parts to percussion instruments and use as introduction and fade-out to rhyme.

They create other verses for sea creatures.

15 | What Kinds of Sounds Can You Make?

Grades K–1

Key Experience:

    ⊶ **I. B. Exploring and identifying sounds**

        >4. Exploring lower/higher and same/different sounds

Children explore the same/different vocal and body sounds they can make.

Materials:

None

Activity to experience:

Children explore the wide range of same/different vocal and body sounds (clapping, stamping, shuffling, snapping fingers).

Children volunteer to share vocal or body sound, which other students then copy.

Children create movements to match the same/different sounds and share.

Facilitation and Reflection:

Describe the movements you chose for same/different sounds.

How did the movements match your sounds?

What made the sounds different?

Extensions:

Students work with the concept of making their sound and their movement *opposite*. They discuss same/different, sharing ideas.

Use sounds around the room, such as a chair moving across the floor, a ruler hitting a table.

Use sounds found in nature, transportation, factories, etc.

Working as partners, one child creates a sound while the partner creates movement to go with it; then they switch roles.

16 | How Do These Work?

Grades 2–3

Key Experience:

⊙━ **I. C. Exploring instruments**

> 2. Discovering ways to play percussion, harmonic, and melodic instruments

Students work with percussion instruments to create short instrument pieces.

Materials:

Variety of percussion instruments

Activity to experience:

In groups of four to six, students play their instruments together on the beat.

Students create rhythms, which all try out.

Students play rhythms and play beat, to create an ensemble.

Students volunteer to share their instrument pieces.

Facilitation and Reflection:

How can you vary the sound of your instrument? (Loud, soft? Fast, slow?)

Classify the instruments according to those that are better for beat and those interesting for rhythm.

Extensions:

Students create movements as they hear instruments being played.

Students select songs to sing while woods (metals, skins) play.

17 Peter and the Wolf

Grades K–3

Key Experiences:

○┓ **III. A. Responding to various types of music**
>4. Responding to different moods of a musical selection

○┓ **II. B. Identifying tone color**
>5. Identifying voices and instruments heard in a recording

○┓ **I. C. Exploring instruments**
>3. Discovering pitch range and labeling the sound quality of instruments

Students respond to the different moods created in this classic Russian folk tale.

Materials:
Record, tape, or compact disc player
Good-quality recording of *Peter and the Wolf* by Prokofiev

Activity to experience:
Students listen to this musical tale and create movements they feel represent specific characters. (Kindergartners might plan movements only for Peter, Grandfather, and the wolf.)

Students share various movements they have created and tell why each would be good to use.

In small groups, students decide which character they wish to represent. Each group plans and acts out the story as they listen.

In repeated listening sessions, learners begin to identify the specific instruments for the main characters in the tale and describe specific qualities of these instruments.

Facilitation and Reflection:
What ways do you think Peter might move in this story? Grandfather? The wolf? Why?

How does this music make you feel?

What creates the specific mood for each character?

Which character is your favorite? Why?

How does the use of a specific musical instrument help create the personality of Peter? Of *each* character?

Extensions:

Sketch the main characters in this story, and capture their personalities by coloring your sketch.

Identify the instrument used for *each* character, and match that instrument to its picture.

Listen to other musical selections that tell a story:

> *The Sorcerer's Apprentice*, by Dukas
>
> *Children's Corner Suite*, written by Debussy for his daughter's fifth birthday
>
> *Hansel and Gretel*, by Humperdinck.

18

"Sing or Speak" I

Grades K–3

Key Experience:
> **I.D. Exploring the singing voice**
>> 2. Exploring the singing and speaking voice

Learners discover the differences between singing and speaking; they explore the singing voice with random pitches.

Materials:

A "Sing or Speak" gameboard made from a manila file folder with a spinner arrow attached. One gameboard is needed for each small group of six to eight students.

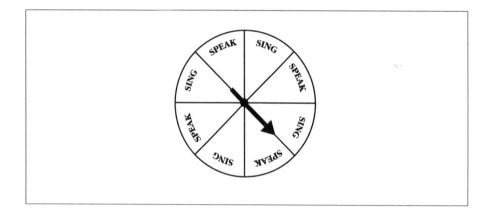

Activity to experience:

Students each explore various ways to move and *speak* their names and choose a way to share this with the others.

Individual students volunteer to share, as the class copies.

Students each explore various ways to move and *sing* their names, and they choose a way to share this with others.

Individual students volunteer to share, as the class copies.

Students discuss the differences they noticed between singing and speaking.

In groups of six to eight, students share their ways of *moving and speaking* their names; others copy. Then they share their ways of *moving and singing* their names; others copy.

Each group has the "Sing or Speak" gameboard. A student spins the arrow to determine by its position whether the group will sing or speak. That student also chooses a category, and each student in the group responds to the category with an *answer* and a *movement*, which the group copies. When each person has shared, a new student who has a category in mind spins the arrow, and the game continues.

Facilitation and Reflection:

What do you notice about how you speak your name? About how you sing?

What do you have to think about before you speak? Before you sing?

Is there anything else you can observe about the differences in singing and speaking?

Extensions:

Extend this experience to companion words (teddy bear, peanut butter); adjectives to describe a concrete object (*beach* ball, *tabby* cat); an adjective plus a noun; proper nouns; common nouns; lines of poetry or songs; sentences; addition or subtraction problems; an entire story.

When the stopped arrow points to "sing", sing all dialogue in the classroom for a determined time segment.

19

I Like to Sing (High-Low)

Grades K–2

Key Experiences:

I. D. Exploring the singing voice
>3. Exploring the broad range of the singing voice

II. C. Developing melody
>1. Identifying higher and lower pitches
>2. Identifying the direction of the melody
>3. Imitating 3- and 4-note melody patterns
>5. Distinguishing same and different in short melody patterns
>6. Responding to the shape of the melody

Children use nonlocomotor movement to identify high and low pitches in the song. Later, they learn to sing the song.

Materials:

I Like to Sing
(High-Low)

Elizabeth B. Carlton

1. I like to sing!_____ I like to sing!_____ Sing up high!
2. I like to sing my name! I like to sing my name! Jon - a - than

Sing down low! Sing and sing and sing!
Jon - a - than! Jon - a - than's my name!

Third verse can be added: I like to sing your name . . . (Any name can be filled in).

Activity to experience:
Children explore various nonlocomotor ways to represent high and low and then add vocal sounds to reinforce their movements.

Some children volunteer to share their motion and sound for the class to imitate.

Children listen to the song, and as the teacher sings, they create their own motion to represent "sing up high" and "sing down low."

Children join the teacher/leader in singing *and* representing these two concepts.

Children learn to sing all of the song.

Facilitation and Reflection:

What sound did you choose for **high**? Why?

What were you thinking of when you made your **low** sound?

How were the sounds you made for **high** and **low** different?

How did these sounds *feel* different?

How were your movements for **high** and **low** different?

How can you represent **high** with your whole body? How can you represent **low**?

Find a way to represent **high** and **low** with your head. With one leg. Choose another part of your body to represent **high** and **low** (and so on).

Which phrases of the song are exactly alike?

Which phrases of the song are opposites?

Extensions:

A volunteer shares a movement idea for **high**, and the class copies the movement and adds their **high** sound.

A volunteer sings one **high** or **low** sound, and the class responds by copying the sound and representing that sound through movement.

Play a **high** or **low** sound on the xylophone, which children identify through movement response.

Sing verse three when a new student is welcomed to the classroom. ("I like to sing your name . . .")

Encourage individual children to find other ways to sing their names, such as singing the name in a way that the class can imitate, as shown below:

Ka - tie,   Zach - a - ry,   E - liz - a - beth.

20

Who Can?

Grades 1–2

Key Experiences:

○┐ **III. C. Singing alone and in groups**
> 2. Singing a short solo phrase during a call-response song or a single verse when the class sings chorus

○┐ **III. D. Sharing music by performing**
> 2. Creating and singing a new verse to a known song

○┐ **I. D. Exploring the singing voice**
> 4. Initiating singing alone and singing in tune with others

Individual volunteers each sing a short solo phrase response during a call-response song, either as caller or responder.

Materials:

Who Can? on next page

Activity to experience:

Explore various types of locomotor movement that can be performed to one's own steady beat and to the steady beat of others.

The whole class learns a song as the teacher uses the Teaching Model strategies (Appendix A). The class keeps steady macrobeat or microbeat while singing.

Individual volunteers become comfortable "responding" by singing as a soloist or by acting as the leader of the steady beat movement, using the various choices of verses possible with this song.

Facilitation and Reflection:

Share your favorite steady beat locomotor movement with two other people. Why is this your favorite?

Who will share a movement with the class and sing the solo response?

How can you describe the soloist's voice and movements?

What mysterious thing always happens in a call-response song?

Extensions:

The song also can be used in small groups, so everyone can have a turn as soloist responder while the teacher observes each child's comfort with moving to the steady beat.

Use other extensions of this idea, as listed on the next page:

- Musical concepts: "Who can sing with two, a *duet?*" "Who can sing with three, a *trio?*" etc..

- Math facts: "2 times 7, 2 times 7, 2 times 7's always 14," etc.

- Seasonal fun: "Who did eat Thanksgiving turkey? Who did make the pum, pum, pumpkin . . . pie?"

Who Can?
(Who Did Swallow Old Jonah?)

Adapted by Elizabeth B. Carlton

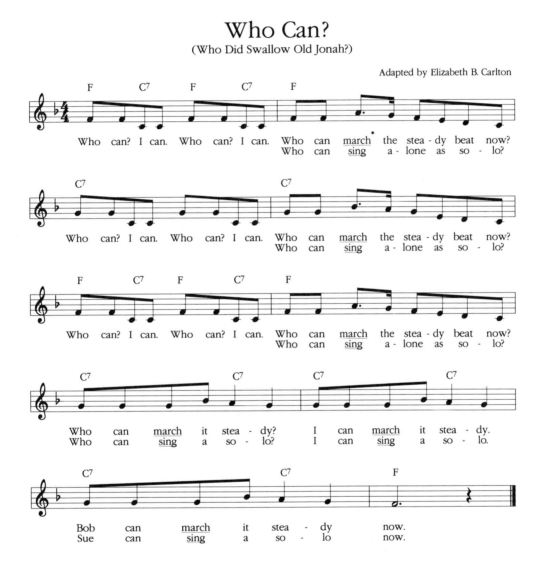

* Substitute <u>skip</u>, <u>hop</u>, <u>skate</u>, etc., for <u>march</u> and <u>sing</u>.

21 "Name That Tune"

Grades 1-3

Key Experience:

O─┐ **I. E. Listening and describing music**

> 3. Identifying previously heard or sung musical selections

Students name melodies previously heard or sung after hearing a designated number of notes in the beginning phrase.

Materials:

None

Activity to experience:

Students build a song bank of melodies they have sung or listened to as a class. As the year progresses, they add additional familiar songs or melodies.

To play the musical recall game "Name That Tune," a leader uses a neutral syllable (bom) and the correct rhythm to sing the first four notes of a song in the song bank. Class members try to identify the song. If no one can identify the song in four notes, the leader sings the first five notes. If no one can identify the song in five notes, the leader may opt to sing six notes (or even seven or eight notes) or to go to another song. The object of the game is to name the tune correctly in as few notes as possible.

In the beginning, the game can be made easier by giving more notes in the clue. As students' ears and minds become focused more sharply on tonal recall, the clues should be shorter.

The student who guesses the song in the first game gives the musical clues for the next game. The class may choose to play this game as two teams. Be flexible, and keep it challenging and interesting for all.

Facilitation and Reflection:

In how many notes can you name this tune?

What other clues would be helpful?

Extensions:

Individual students research interesting facts about any song in the class song bank and share their findings with the others. Then, their "Name That Tune" can include singing clues *and* spoken clues!

22 Where in the World Are We?

Grades 2–3

Key Experience:
⊶ **I. E. Listening and describing music**
>4. Discussing the type or style of the music

Students listen and move to two musical selections from different countries. They discuss the similarities and differences of music and instruments. (A discussion of culture, customs, climate, geography, etc., may be elicited.)

Materials:
Record, tape, or compact disc player
Africa: *Bele Kawe* (RM3), Mexico: *La Raspa* (RM3)

Activity to experience:
Students each find their own space and then listen to a short excerpt from *Bele Kawe* and identify the instruments.

Students move as the music from *Bele Kawe* makes them want to move. (This can be done individually, with a partner, in groups of three, etc.)

Students discuss with a partner what they hear in the music, how it makes them feel, and how they moved.

Students follow the same sequences for *La Raspa*.

Students discuss the similarities and differences in the two selections.

Facilitation and Reflection:
What instruments did you hear in *Bele Kawe?*

How did you move to the instruments you identified?

What instruments do you hear in *La Raspa?*

Which instruments did you move to in *La Raspa?* How did you move?

How are the two pieces the same? How are they different?

Do you have a preference for one of the selections? Why do you like it?

From listening to this music, what could you say about Africa? About Mexico?

Extensions:
Try other pairs of musical selections and discover relevant concepts about the countries represented, such as these:

Russia: *Troika* (RM2) and Israel: *Cherkessiya* (RM2)
Hungary: *Körtanc* (RM3) and Yugoslavia: *Plješkavac Kolo* (RM3)
Romania: *Hora Pe Gheata* (RM4) and Philippines: *Apat-Apat* (RM4)

23 | Magic Bubble

Grades K–1

Key Experience:
O⊐ **II. A. Feeling and expressing steady beat**
> 1. Moving to one's own steady beat

Children identify their own steady beat while enclosed in an imaginary bubble.

Materials:
None

Activity to experience:
Each child imagines being in his or her own "magic bubble." In this bubble, the child can hear only the teacher's voice, and the teacher can hear the child's voice.

Each child chooses to sit or stand inside the private bubble.

Each child thinks about and then finds a steady beat and shows that beat by rocking or by a steady hand or foot movement.

Children each find their beat again and say "beat" each time they move.

Children stop and rest; then they find their beat again as you observe their responses.

The teacher says: "Remember how your own steady beat feels and how you showed me that steady beat, so you can find it another day."

After carefully "removing" their magic bubbles, children volunteer individually to share with others how they kept their steady beat.

Facilitation and Reflection:
What does *steady beat* mean?

What objects or sounds in our world have a steady sound or steady moving part that we can hear or feel?

Students make steady beat *sounds*, accompanied by motions.

Who will share a steady movement with the word *beat*?

Extensions:
Children pat the steady beat on a stuffed animal or other object.

Children pat their own steady beats on one another.

"Rhyme Three Ways"

Grades K–1

Key Experience:

∘⌐ **II. A. Feeling and expressing steady beat**

> 2. Matching someone else's steady beat

Children show the beat of a rhyme in three ways—patting, stepping, and walking.

Materials:

"Hot Cross Buns" and other short rhymes

Activity to experience:

Children pat a macrobeat, choosing where to pat.

The teacher anchors the macrobeat shown by a student, speaking the **anchor word** four times (for example, "chin, chin, chin, chin"), and all move to the beat while saying the rhyme.

Children step to the microbeat in place.

To anchor the microbeat shown, one child speaks the anchor word eight times (for example, "step, step, step, step"), and then all say the rhyme.

One child leads a walking tempo, which the teacher anchors eight times, and other children walk the beat in a circle and recite the same rhyme a third time.

Facilitation and Reflection:

How are the macrobeat and the microbeat different?

When were each used?

What other movements can we use to play "Rhyme Three Ways"?

What other rhymes can we use? Could we also use a song in place of a rhyme?

Extensions:

Children choose other favorite rhymes and identify the macrobeats and microbeats.

Decide on three other movements to use with "Rhyme Three Ways," such as tapping desks lightly, walking tiptoe, or galloping.

25 | "Pizza Pie"

Grades 1–2

Key Experience:
 ☌ **II. A. Feeling and expressing steady beat**
  > 2. Matching someone else's steady beat

Children walk the beat and echo the leader's word-phrases.

Materials:
None

Activity to experience:
Children walk about the space to their own steady beat.

One child volunteers to lead the class. The teacher anchors that child's tempo with the anchor word "walk," spoken eight times.

Children echo each phrase two times after the teacher speaks each phrase twice:

> **Piz**za **pie** *(pizza pie)*
> **First** the **crust,** *(first the crust)*
> **Then** the **sauce,** *(then the sauce)*
> **Add** some **sau**sage, *(add some sausage)*
> **Pep**peroni **too** *(pepperoni too)*
> **Cheese** and **mush**rooms, *(cheese and mushrooms)*
> **I** love **piz**za, *(I LOVE pizza)*
> **Yum–, yum–** *(Yum–, Yum!)*

Note: These are some examples. After the teacher initiates two or three ideas, this experience should be turned over to the group for their ideas.

Facilitation and Reflection:
What strategies can we use to speak and keep someone else's beat?

What phrases can we create about this category?

Extensions:
Children develop word phrases for other categories, such as vegetable soup, banana splits, cars, sports, adjective-noun combinations, common or proper nouns, and seasonal word phrases. A leader sings the phrase, and the group echoes the melody pattern.

Extend the phrases into sentences about pizza or any chosen category.

In small groups, the leader demonstrates two-movement sequences to be echoed and spoken by the others. This is extended to three-movement and four-movement sequences to be echoed with learner SAY & DO.

Sherwood

Grade K

Key Experience:
    O▅ **II. A. Feeling and expressing steady beat**
         >2. Matching someone else's steady beat

Children use a name game with a stuffed animal to help match beat.

Materials:
Stuffed animal
Mary Had a Little Lamb tune

Activity to experience:
Children find a way to keep a steady macrobeat with both hands while seated.

A volunteer leads the beat with the stuffed animal while the class follows visually.

The teacher speaks the volunteer's name four times as the anchor word to synchronize the motions, and all sing this song to the tune of *Mary Had a Little Lamb*.

> *Sherwood wants to <u>know</u> your name,*
> *<u>Know</u> your name, <u>know</u> your name.*
> *Sherwood wants to <u>know</u> your name.*
> *Would <u>some</u>one like to <u>share</u>?*

A new volunteer holds the animal and sets the macrobeat somewhere else. The teacher uses this name as the anchor word, and the game continues.

Facilitation and Reflection:
Recall the ways that various class members chose to keep the macrobeat. What new ways can you think of to keep steady macrobeat while you are seated?

What helps us keep someone else's beat?

Extensions:
Each child can bring a favorite stuffed animal, and lead the game with this special friend.

Each older child can "adopt" a kindergarten child, and together, the two children can strengthen their timing abilities with similar songs or rhymes.

Create new verses to the *Sherwood* song. What else would Sherwood like to know?

Anchoring the Beat

Grades K–1

Key Experience:

    ⌐ **II. A. Feeling and expressing steady beat**

            >3. Matching the steady beat of recorded music, songs, rhymes

Children synchronize their beat movements to the anchor word and keep that beat while listening to, and later speaking, the rhyme.

Materials:

Rhyme (macrobeat underlined):

> I _have_ a little _shadow_
> That _likes_ to move with _me_.
> It's _very,_ very _good_ at that,
> _Watch_ and you will _see_.
>
>   E. Carlton

Activity to experience:

Working with partners, children copy each other's steady beat and bring it into a learner SAY & DO with the word "beat."

Children volunteer to be the leader for the class, showing their beat-keeping movement, and all copy, using learner SAY & DO. (This beat should be in approximately the same tempo as a macrobeat.)

The teacher demonstrates a rocking movement that all copy, and then layers on the anchor word "beat" four times, to bring all children to group synchronization. When the teacher begins to speak the rhyme, he/she no longer demonstrates the movement. The children feel the beat and listen to the rhyme.

Child volunteers also can be leaders for the movement, and the teacher can speak the anchor word four times to the student's movement tempo before beginning the rhyme.

Children learn the rhyme by repetition, so they move, speak, and feel the beat.

Facilitation and Reflection:

What helped you to follow the leader's beat?

What helped you to keep the beat when the rhyme was spoken?

If the teacher spoke the rhyme without the anchor word, how would you know when to move the beat?

Extensions:

Work in partners to speak the rhyme and keep the beat in many ways.

Use other rhymes, such as nursery rhymes.

Perform locomotor movements (such as stepping) in place. At the end of the poem, perform a locomotor movement (gallop, hop, skip) in general space.

Use the previous suggestion as a partner activity. One person leads; the other copies as the "shadow." Reverse roles.

28

I Think I Can

Grades K–2

Key Experiences:

III. C. Singing alone and in groups
> 3. Singing songs of increasing length and difficulty with others
> 4. Singing a solo with musical competence and confidence

II. A. Feeling and expressing steady beat
> 3. Matching the steady beat of songs

Children are provided with opportunities to develop responsibility and increased self esteem when they sing songs that reinforce positive values related to their environment or related to their favorite stories.

Materials:
I Think I Can on next page.

Activity to experience:
Children listen and rock or pat the macrobeat as the teacher sings. (Decide whether one, two, or all verses are appropriate for the children to hear at this time.)

Children learn to sing the song as the teacher presents it, using the Teaching Model found in Appendix A.

Verses two, three, and four may be added when the teacher feels the class is ready for an extension or when the children display a desire to read or sing the other verses.

Facilitation and Reflection:
How do you feel about yourself when you try to do your best?

How do you feel about others when they try to do their best?

Where in the shape of the melody is the suggestion to keep trying? (In the short repeated melody patterns)

Why is this song a good one to sing when you are about to give up or when someone says "I can't"?

Extensions:
Encourage the children to create other verses related to this topic and to share them with the class.

Find and memorize short poems related to doing one's best, such as these:

One, two, whatever you do,
Start it right, and carry it through.

Good, better, best,
Never let it rest,
Until your good is better,
And your better, best!

I Think I Can

Elizabeth B. Carlton

1. "Ooh_____ Ooh___ Oooh ___" said the en - gine that
2. "Work hard! Work hard! Work hard!" said the lit - tle red

could. "I think I can, I think I can. I
ant. "Just do your best on ev - ery day. Your

know I can hold on now and do it. I will give this
best will come out in ev - ery way, so show me how you'll

my ve - ry best. I can do this, watch me try."
do your___ best. Just___ go for it to - day."

Verse 3
    "Bzzz! Bzzz! Bzzz!" buzzed the bumblebee.
    "Whoever thought that I could fly,
    But I made them change their expectations,
    If I can fly, then you can try,
    Be the best that you can be!"

Verse 4
    "I'll try! I'll try! I'll try, and I'll tell you why.
    If an engine can, and an ant knows how,
    And a bumblebee can fly so freely
    I'll give this my very best,
    I can do this, watch me try!"

29 Beat-Keepers One and All

Grades K–3

Key Experience:
O–ʀ II. A. Feeling and expressing steady beat
> >4. Performing single nonlocomotor movements to the steady beat
> >5. Performing single locomotor movement to the steady beat

Students use nonlocomotor and locomotor movement to keep the steady beat (macrobeat or microbeat).

Materials:
Record, tape, or compact disc player
Hineh Ma Tov (RM4) (one of the few selections that uses a vocal)

Activity to experience:
Students explore nonlocomotor arm movements or locomotor movements in personal space, and several volunteers share with the class.

Students listen to *Hineh Ma Tov* and try out their movement ideas to the music.

Five volunteers lead the class during the sections of the music. (There are five sections in the form ABACA.) Student leaders face the class in the order in which they will lead, so the class reads left to right.

Enjoy the beat-keeping efforts and the music.

Facilitation and Reflection:
What beat-keeping movements did you like to do with this music?

Describe how you used your body for your movements in beat (two sides together, one side alone, alternating, etc.).

How was the experience following the five leaders like reading? (The motions were copied from left to right.)

What other parts of the body could be used to lead the movement?

Extensions:
Working as partners, one student makes a statue shape, and the other student pats the beat on the statue in different places.

The class works in groups of three, and each student chooses to be the A, B, or C section. This reinforces rondo form, ABACA (Grade 3).

Use other musical forms, such as *Bekendorfer Quadrille* (RM4) in ABCD form, or *Jamaican Holiday* (RM5) in a form of AB,ABC,ABC,A.

The Earth Is Our Mother

Grades 1-3

Key Experiences:

II. A. Feeling and expressing steady beat

> 4. Performing single nonlocomotor movements to the steady beat

III. B. Playing instruments alone and in groups

> 3. Playing an instrument in steady beat while singing alone

III. E. Moving creatively and choreographing movement sequences and dances

> 4. Creating patterns and moving creatively

Students use steady beat nonlocomotor movement to a Native-American song.

Materials:

For the key experience *playing instruments alone and in groups* (III B), a hand drum or tom-tom

The Earth Is Our Mother

Native-American

Activity to experience:

Students decide where to keep a steady nonlocomotor macrobeat, and they find the steady beat while the teacher sings.

The teacher synchronizes the students' motions with the anchor word "beat" spoken four times and then teaches the words by echo phrases. Teach the melody, using a neutral syllable; combine text and melody, using the echo-phrase strategy, while students keep beat.

Students create simple hand patterns for the song as they sit in a circle and sing. For example, a student may pat his/her own knees, pat the knees of the classmate on the left, pat his/her own knees, and then pat the knees of the classmate on the right.

Decide whether the hand pattern will be used as an introduction that will continue throughout the song or whether hand percussion instruments will be added. If so, what shall the instruments play?

Facilitation and Reflection:

How did your movement match the mood of this song?

What hand patterns fit the mood and include all of us in taking care of Earth?

How shall we incorporate our hand pattern, song, and percussion instrument(s) for the best performance?

Extensions:

Students may choose to create a speech section that incorporates ways to take care of Earth. Decide whether several will each speak individually or all together. This might become the B section, and the song might be the A section. The hand pattern created might be the introduction that continues throughout and then closes with a fade-out. Now you have a true class composition: Introduction, A, B, A, fade-out.

Create a movement section (C) for which two or three students perform. Add this to the above composition as the class chooses the order.

31 | *Numbers Are Special*

Grades 2–3

Key Experiences:

II C. Developing melody

>9. Singing and shaping phrases and songs

II. A. Feeling and expressing steady beat

>4. Performing single nonlocomotor movements to the steady beat

Students sing and shape the phrases and discuss how they are alike and different. As students work with number key experiences, this song can reinforce their abilities to count by fives, twos, threes, etc. Students can also reinforce beat coordination as they sing and use movement sequences they have created.

Materials:

Numbers Are Special

Elizabeth B. Carlton

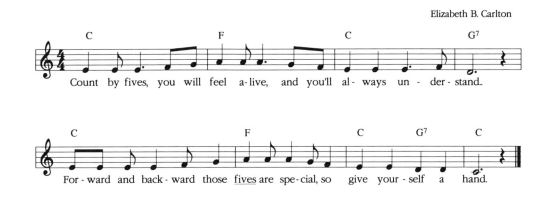

For subsequent verses, change words accordingly:
Count by <u>twos</u>, you don't need more clues . . .
Count by <u>threes</u>, hey, it's such a breeze . . .
Count by <u>fours</u>, open thinking doors . . .

Activity to experience:
Students explore ways to create movement sequences of two, such as "knees, shoulders," or "clap, snap."

Volunteers share an idea for a movement sequence *visually;* the class copies, adding learner SAY & DO when ready. (A volunteer might share an idea for a movement sequence *verbally,* and the class members join in with movement and SAY & DO when comfortable.)

Class members decide to use the sequence "knees, shoulders." The leader synchronizes the tempo for this sequence in macrobeat with the anchor words "knees, shoulders." When all are together, the teacher sings the song.

Students learn the song, and then count by fives up to 50, and then backward, down to 0.

Each verse can be accompanied by a different movement sequence if the class desires.

Facilitation and Reflection:
Why are these phrases interesting to sing and shape?

What do you notice about the shape of this melody?

What do you notice about the rhythm we sing?

Why would it be helpful to know how to count by fives (or twos or threes) forward and backward?

Extensions:
Substitute two nonpitched percussion instruments for the movement sequence.

Create additional verses as students develop interest in counting in other sets.

Create another song that develops interest in counting forward and backward by groups of five, two, three, etc.

32 Instruments to the Beat

Grades 2–3

Key Experience:
⚬┐ **II. A. Feeling and expressing steady beat**
> 6. Playing instruments in steady beat

Students accompany a song with a few unpitched percussion instruments played on the beat.

Materials:
The song *It's a Small World*
Unpitched percussion instruments, such as tambourine, finger cymbals, and
wood block

Activity to experience:
While students sing the song, they think about what percussion instruments
would be good choices for accompaniment.

Students, in small groups, discuss the instruments to use and when each might
play. The tambourine might play on the macrobeat, the wood block might play
on the microbeat, and the finger cymbals might play on every other macrobeat.

Players volunteer, one from each group, and the song and instruments have a
trial run. Then see if any changes are needed.

Sing and play again while all keep the beat. Then use other volunteers from
each group to play.

Facilitation and Reflection:
What instruments would be good accompaniment for this song? Why?

How did you decide when the instruments should play during the song? How
should we begin?

How can we keep the song and instruments together?

Extensions:
Use other types of songs and choose complementary instruments.

Work in small groups, each with a different song and choice of instruments.
Perform for each other.

33 | Integrating! Exhilarating!

Grades 2–3

Key Experience:

O-π **II. A. Feeling and expressing steady beat**

>7. Combining nonlocomotor and locomotor movement to the steady beat

Students combine upper- and lower-body movement sequences (integrated movement) to perform to music.

Materials:

Record, tape, or compact disc player
California Strut (RM4)

Activity to experience:

Students explore integrated movements (nonlocomotor movement joined with locomotor movement), using learner SAY & DO with the language for the foot movement.

Several volunteers share their creations and the labels they have chosen while the class copies and uses learner SAY & DO.

Students listen to the music and select integrated movements that fit well. They also determine where changes of pattern should occur in the music

All perform their selected integrated movements to the music. Then several volunteers lead the class.

Facilitation and Reflection:

What are some strategies for successfully combining upper- and lower-body movements?

Think about how the movement of your upper body is integrated with the movement of your lower body. (When the knee is raised, the arms bend in front of the body.) Discuss with a partner.

What integrated movements fit well to the music?

Where else are integrated movements used in music? In sports?

Extensions:

Use other musical selections, such as *Irish Washerwoman* (RM3) or *O'Keefe/ Kerry Slide* (RM1).

Review a folk dance that uses integrated movement, such as *Bannielou Lambaol* (RM8) or *Kendime* (RM5).

Make a list of integrated movements and explain when they are used in sports, music, chores at home, or activities in the classroom.

"Sing or Speak" II

Grades K–2

Key Experience:
O–¬ II. B. Identifying tone color
> 1. Distinguishing different persons' singing and speaking
> voices

Identifying classmates' singing and speaking voices by their unique tone color.

Materials:
Proverb: *One, two, whatever you do,*
             Start it right, and carry it through.

Song: *America (My Country, 'Tis of Thee)*, first phrase only

Activity to experience:
Children learn the proverb and song phrase well, so any student can recite the proverb or sing the song phrase alone.

Children volunteer to "sing or speak" alone, since all will be playing this game throughout the week or month, or intermittently throughout the year.

Children develop the game: All students have their eyes closed, and one child goes around the group and taps someone on the shoulder. The person who is tapped sings the phrase or recites the proverb, and all try to guess, from the tone color or enunciation, who sang or spoke. Continue as long as interest lasts and time is available.

Facilitation and Reflection:
What did you notice about the singer's/speaker's tone color?

Were there any other clues that helped you to identify the singer/speaker?

Extensions:
Disguise voices in some way and play the game. The class can add additional rules or challenges.

35 | Voices and Instruments

Grades 1–2

Key Experience:

⊶ II. B. Identifying tone color

> 5. Identifying voices and instruments heard in a recording

Children identify the vocal and instrumental sections of *Zemer Atik*. They identify the sections through locomotor and nonlocomotor movement.

Materials:

Record, tape, or compact disc player
Zemer Atik (RM4)

Activity to experience:

Children listen to the music in order to identify the main instruments and type of voice heard.

Children discuss the vocal part of the music (the language, melody, male voice, etc.).

Children explore nonlocomotor and locomotor movements for the vocal and instrumental parts.

Children share their movements, which others imitate.

Children decide if they like the locomotor movement with the instrumental part or if they prefer to do their nonlocomotor movement with the instrumental part and move to the music as each thinks best.

Facilitation and Reflection:

What instruments do you hear?

Describe the instrument you hear.

How did you move to the vocal part?

How was your movement different for the instrumental part?

Extensions:

Learn the dance as it appears in Phyllis S. Weikart's *Teaching Movement & Dance*.

Oomp Pa Tuba

Grades 2–3

Key Experience:

       II. B. Identifying tone color

              >3. Distinguishing the different instrument sounds

Students create two movements: one to identify the trumpet and one to identify the tuba in *Sunflower Slow Drag*.

Materials:

Record, tape, or compact disc player
Sun Flower Slow Drag (RM9)

Activity to experience:

Students listen for the trumpet and tuba.

Students explore locomotor movements for the trumpet section.

Students try their movement to the music.

Students explore nonlocomotor movements for the tuba.

Students identify the trumpet and tuba in this selection by showing their locomotor movement for the trumpet and their nonlocomotor movement for the tuba.

Facilitation and Reflection:

How are the instrument sounds different?

Which is your favorite? Why?

Describe your movement to the trumpet's sound. Why did you choose this movement?

Describe your movement to the tuba's sound. How does it represent the sound?

Extensions:

Listen to other recordings featuring trumpet and tuba. Excellent selections are the marches of John Philip Sousa.

37 | "One for the Money"

Grades K–1

Key Experience:

◓‿ **II. B. Identifying tone color**

> 3. Distinguishing the different instrument sounds

Children listen to several instruments, explore movement to each, and decide on a different movement for each instrument. They discover that each instrument has a characteristic tone color.

Materials:
Several different instruments, such as drum, finger cymbals, wood block, and
tambourine

Activity to experience:
Children listen to the instruments being played, one at a time. They next explore movement with each instrument and share their movements. Then they decide as a group how to move with each instrument.

Children chant the following rhyme, patting the macrobeat (underlined):

> _One_ for the money,
> _Two_ for the show,
> _Three_ to get ready,
> And _four_ to go.

As the rhyme is chanted, the leader plays an instrument behind a screen. Children move as they have decided earlier, according to the instrument being played.

Children verbally identify the instrument.

Children continue with other rhythm instruments, as well as pitched instruments (autoharp, recorder, guitar, etc.).

Facilitation and Reflection:
Think of some ways to describe the various sounds that you have heard.

How are the sounds the same? Different?

Which instruments have short sounds? Long sounds? ·

Extensions:
Categorize the instruments: wood, metal, ringers, shakers, clickers, scratchers.

Keep adding information to the chart as new instruments are introduced.

Make a graph of the length of the sounds, from shortest to longest.

When working with the recorder, the autoharp, and other pitched instruments, make a chart or graph of sounds, lowest to highest.

38

"Match and Move"

Grades K–1

Key Experience:
      O⌐ II. B Identifying tone color
              > 4. Matching an instrument's sound with its picture

Children show their understanding by moving when they hear the sound of the instrument. Children match the sound with the picture of an unpitched instrument.

Materials:
Hand drum, bells, and wood block (or other unpitched instruments)
Pictures of the instruments on cards

Activity to experience:
Children explore moving to the sound as the teacher makes sounds with the hand drum, bells, and wood block, one instrument at a time. They stop moving when each instrument stops.

Individual children play the instruments while the others move to the sound.

The teacher holds up the various instrument cards, and the children move to represent each instrument's sound.

Children explore ways to play instruments.

While each type of instrument is played behind a screen, the class moves to that sound.

The teacher passes out instruments so each pair of children has one of the three types explored. When the teacher holds up a card, one child in each pair having that instrument plays while the other moves to the sound.

Facilitation and Reflection:
How did you move to the sound of the drum? Bells? Wood block?

How did your movement change when you heard the next instrument? Why?

How did you know when to move? When to stop?

How did the picture help you remember the sound of the instrument?

Extensions:
Children choose an instrument, a player, and a representative way to walk to recess, lunch, etc. Continue this idea on other days, so they show ownership of identifying instrument sounds and representative movements.

Write the name of each instrument on a card. When that card is displayed, children move and play that instrument.

Add more instruments, so the discrimination tasks become more refined.

The class designs a weekly instrument "Match and Move" game for moving from one subject to another or to recess.

Vocal Pathways

Grades 1–2

Key Experience:
⚬┱ II. C. Developing melody
>> 1. Identifying higher and lower pitches

Children explore with their voices and identify higher and lower sounds.

Materials:
For each student, a 3-foot piece of yarn

Activity to experience:
Each child finds his/her own space and thinks about ways to represent higher and lower sounds.

Each child places his/her piece of yarn in any pathway and uses representative whole-body movement for that pathway while singing its higher-lower shape. The child then moves and sings it in reverse order. He or she stands at either end and moves and sings it low to high, or high to low.

Children share their vocal pathways with one another.

Children try other student's yarn pathways.

Facilitation and Reflection:
How does your voice represent your pathway?

How did you decide which pitch to begin on?

How did your pathway represent higher-lower?

Extensions:
Small groups combine their pathways. They share the combined composition with the class.

Combine the small-group pathways into one large-group pathway.

Accompany pathways with instruments, such as the drum (played on the lower pitch representations) and triangles (on the higher pitch representations).

Rainbows

Grades 1-3

Key Experiences:
    ○┑ **II. C. Developing melody**
            > 1. Identifying higher and lower pitches
            > 2. Identifying the direction of the melody
            > 6. Responding to the shape of the melody
            > 9. Singing and shaping phrases and songs

    ○┑ **II. H. Adding harmony**
            > 5. Singing rounds

Students sing this song in unison and later as a two- or three-part round. They explore and share nonlocomotor or locomotor movements that enhance interpretative singing.

Materials:
Rainbows on next page.

Activity to experience:
Students learn to sing this round in unison while patting the macrobeat.

Students create locomotor or nonlocomotor movement ideas for each section of the song and then share them.

Grade 2 and grade 3 students sing this as a two-part or a three-part round, accompanied by their movement ideas.

Facilitation and Reflection:
Describe the melodic shape of the first section of this round. (The shape moves upward by steps from scale degrees 1 to 8, and then downward by steps from scale degrees 8 to 1.)

What did you notice about the shape of the second section? (It often has three repeated pitches before the melody changes.)

What is interesting about the shape of the last section of this song? (It moves downward by steps, then upward, and sometimes has a repeated pitch that sneaks in.)

When we sing this as a two-part round, when will the other group begin singing? (When the first group begins to sing the second section.)

When we sing this as a three-part round, when will the third group begin singing? (When the second group begins to sing the second section.)

What strategies can we use to keep the round "in beat" together? (Rocking or swaying the macrobeat, singing as a team, singing and using our movement ideas to stay together.)

Rainbows

Elizabeth B. Carlton

What challenges are presented to us when we sing in rounds? (Responsibility for singing our team's part well, listening, concentrating.)

Extensions:

Students may wish to discover how to play this song on a keyboard or xylophone and then share their performances.

Create a performance plan such as this:

      A = All students sing in unison.

B = One or several students play the melody through.

C = Sing *Rainbows* as a three-part round.

Create other performance plans that incorporate all the ideas and creative skills class members have contributed.

Wise Old Owl

Grades K–1

Key Experience:

 **II. C. Developing melody**
>2. Identifying the direction of the melody
(upward/downward)

**Children identify the upward and downward direction of the melody.
They may also demonstrate knowledge of the body scale (Chapter 3).**

Materials:

Wise Old Owl

Text - Author Unknown
Music - Elizabeth B. Carlton

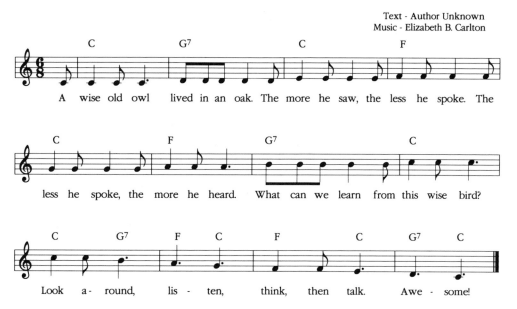

Activity to experience:
Teach the song, using the Teaching Model found in Appendix A.

Students shape each melodic phrase as they sing it. They discover that the
phrases (except for the last two) have a similar shape: The last two phrases
move downward by scale steps of the major scale.

Facilitation and Reflection:
How would you describe this melody?

How did you identify the direction of this melody?

Is there anything unusual about this melody?

Extensions:
Sing other scale songs such as the one below and *Kitty Cat, I Hear a Mouse* on the next page.

I Have a Little Puppy

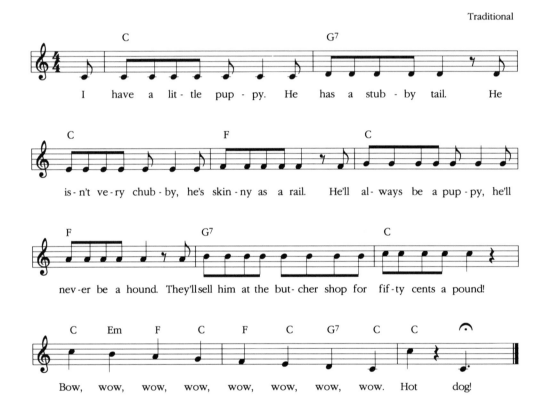

Traditional

In small groups, make up scale songs about math facts, class trips, or rhyming words, and sing them for the class.

Learn to sing *Do, A Deer*, from Rodgers and Hammerstein's "The Sound of Music," or *Rainbows* from Activity 40 in this chapter.

Kitty Cat, I Hear a Mouse

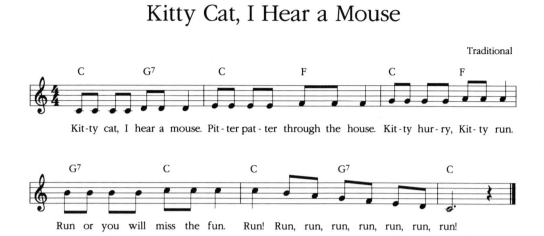

Traditional

Kit-ty cat, I hear a mouse. Pit-ter pat-ter through the house. Kit-ty hur-ry, Kit-ty run.

Run or you will miss the fun. Run! Run, run, run, run, run, run, run!

42 | *Gloomy Boomy Day*

Grades K–1

Key Experiences:

    ○━ II. C. Developing melody

         >2. Identifying the direction of the melody (upward/downward)

    ○━ III. A. Responding to various types of music

         >2. Responding to *same/different* in songs children sing

Children identify the upward and downward direction of the melody, noticing it uses a different scale (minor) from *Wise Old Owl* (major).

Materials:
Keyboard
Gloomy Boomy Day on next page

Activity to experience:
Play the song through one time, so children notice that this is a different scale (minor), which creates the mood of the song.

Teach the song, using the Teaching Model strategies found in Appendix A.

Children shape each melodic phrase as they sing it. They discover that each phrase except the last one has the same shape, although for one phrase, the pitches are farther apart. The minor scale (phrase 5) moves downward and ends with a spoken disappointment.

Facilitation and Reflection:
What can you tell me about this melody?

Compare this minor-scale song to the *Wise Old Owl* major-scale song. What can you say about these two scale songs?

Extensions:
Create other minor-scale songs for rainy days, Halloween, sad events, or thoughtful texts.

Gloomy Boomy Day

Elizabeth B. Carlton

The rain is pour-ing down out-side, the wind is fierce and cold. The lights are out, the thun-der roars, but we are brave and bold. The light-'ning flash-es bright-ly a-cross the storm-y bay. I'm at the beach and sing-ing "It's a gloom-y, boom-y day. Ooh_____ Storms! And we're on va-ca-tion!"

Frogs and Toads

Grades K–1

Key Experience:

⌛ **II. C. Developing melody**

> 3. Matching intervals and repeated pitches

Children use their ability to sing the G→E pitched interval (scale degrees 5→3) by creating a class song about a science theme.

Materials:

Frog Song

First-grade Class
Neal Dow Elementary
Chico, California

Frogs and toads are am - phi - bi - ans. Frogs are smooth and

toads are rough. They catch their meals with a stick - y tongue. They

hop and jump and leap for fun!

Activity to experience:

Children warm up by singing the G→E pitch interval (scale degrees 5→3).

Children echo sing these two pitches, using the body scale and being led by various children acting as class leaders.

Children sing a variety of intervals, moving only when they sing the pitch interval G→E.

All review facts about frogs and toads and then decide on four lines that they would like to use for the words in their song.

Children create a melody using the G→E pitches (such as the *Frog Song*, which was created by first-grade students at Neal Dow Elementary School, Chico, California).

Children sing their song and then explore appropriate frog or toad movements for the introduction, as the G pitch is played as a macrobeat eight times.

Children put it all together. (Perhaps they could perform it for another class.)

Facilitation and Reflection:

What do we know about frogs and toads?

How are the movements for the frog and toad the same? Different?

What kind of movement did you choose to do for the introduction? Why?

What do you notice about the two pitches? (One is higher than the other. Sounds like a doorbell. Sounds like mother calling me for supper.)

Are there other songs that we sing using these two pitches? *(One Two, Tie My Shoe; Star Light, Star Bright; Rain, Rain, Go Away)*

Where Have I Heard This?

Grades K–1

Key Experience:
    II. C. Developing melody
             >3. Matching intervals and repeated pitches

Children identify and explore the most used interval in singing: scale degrees 5→3 (G→E).

Materials:
None

Activity to experience:
Children listen to the scale degrees 5→3 (G→E) interval played on keyboard or recorder.

Children explore singing this G→E interval and then add movement.

Children volunteer to show and sing the 5→3 interval.

Lead movements for the G→E pitched interval on the body scale (shoulders [5], waist [3]).

Children sing *Rain, Rain Go, Away* with body scale movements.

Use these two pitches to sing any directions and responses to the class during the next hour.

Facilitation and Reflection:
As you were exploring the G and E pitches with your voice, how did you choose to move for the first pitch? For the second pitch?

When you repeat these two pitches over and over, does it make you think of any familiar song? (*One, Two, Tie My Shoe*; *Jack Be Nimble*; or *Star Light, Star Bright*)

Extensions:
Sing other nursery rhymes using these two pitches.

Use the 5→3 interval to sing directions or sing questions and answers for plan-do-review.

45 | SING & SHAPE Some More

Grades K–1

Key Experience:
    II. C. Developing melody
        >4. Imitating three- and four-note melody patterns

Children create and imitate three- and four-note melody patterns, using learner SING & SHAPE.

Materials:
None

Activity to experience:
Children work in groups of four to six, planning and singing for one another pitch patterns of three or four different tones, like these:

      1. 5, 3, 5, ___
      2. 5, 3, 3, ___
      3. 5, 3, 5, 6;
      4. 5, 6, 5, 3

Beginning on scale degree 5 provides a consistent pitch for initial experiences. This pitch can be marked with a star on the instrument, as an easy visual reference for beginners.

Children respond to one another's singing with SING & SHAPE, using the body scale to represent each pattern.

Give groups a chance to share with the class.

Facilitation:
What did you notice about the melody patterns? (asked in small groups)

Extensions:
Partners work together to strengthen aural discrimination. One can sing the two-, three-, or four-note pattern while the other SINGS & SHAPES it. This safety net of working one-on-one strengthens interval relationships and singing in various keys for all children.

One child can play on the melody bells a three- or four-note pattern, which the group can SING & SHAPE.

Melody Detectives

Grades 1-3

Key Experience:

⚷ **II. C. Developing melody**

> 5. Distinguishing same and different in short melody patterns

Students develop and refine their aural discrimination skills by distinguishing same and different in short melody patterns and in phrases of a new song.

Materials:

The song below and *Traffic Signals* (in Activity 79)

Hot Cross Buns

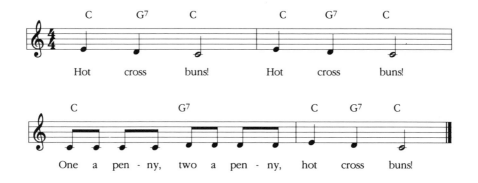

Activity to experience:

Students focus on becoming "melody detectives" by singing *Hot Cross Buns*.

They identify any short melody patterns they recognize as being the same, such as the three times they sing the phrase "Hot cross buns!"

Students identify any melody patterns that were different from the first, such as the pattern for "One a penny," and they explain how the two patterns are different.

Guide them to discover that "two a penny" has the same melody shape as "One a penny," with the exception of one thing: It starts on a different pitch.

Students sing the song again, realizing that their detective work has given them some new ownership of this song.

Sing *Traffic Signals* for the class, and teach this new song, using the Teaching Model found in Appendix A.

On another day, when the students sing this song well, they can play "melody detectives" with *Traffic Signals* or any other songs they sing well.

Facilitation and Reflection:

How did we become "melody detectives" of *Hot Cross Buns?*

How will becoming "super melody detectives" help us in all the things we learn?

What did you detect as we sang *Hot Cross Buns?* What else? What did you detect as we sang *Traffic Signals?*

Extensions:

Acknowledge individual students who detect same and different melody patterns independently, because they are exhibiting ownership of this concept. Invite their leadership in developing acute hearing for music.

After students detect same and different short patterns in songs, extend this activity to detecting same and different melody patterns used as *phrases* of a song.

Work in small groups to graph same and different melody patterns in songs students know.

47 | *Mule Ride*

Grades 2–3

Key Experience:
○┓ **II. C. Developing melody**

> 6. Responding to the shape of the melody

Students draw the melodic shape of the mule ride in the Grand Canyon Suite.

Materials:
Record, tape, or compact disc player
Mule Ride, from the *Grand Canyon Suite* (F. Grofé)
Paper
Markers or crayons

Activity to experience:
After each student finds her/his own space, they listen to the melody of *Mule Ride* from the *Grand Canyon Suite*.

Students explore movements to the selection, and volunteers share their movements.

Students form "mule trains" in groups of three to five, using a leader's movement. (Stop the music occasionally to give them time to change leaders.)

Children listen and shape the melody with their bodies.

Children draw the melodic shape of the selection as the music plays again, and then they share their drawings.

Facilitation and Reflection:
Close your eyes and listen to the shape of the melody. What do you hear?

How did you move to the music?

Describe the music and your movement with your mule train.

How did you represent the melody on paper?

When the music accelerates, what do you imagine happening to the mule train?

Extension:
Discuss instruments heard, mood, use of introduction, and musical hee-haw. This can be done for all the movements of the suite, with minor variation of groupings.

Make a list of specific things learners hear in the music. Keep the list going by having learners add to it as this selection is played throughout the year.

Fascinating Form

Grades 2–3

Key Experience:

O⌐ II. D. Labeling form

> 4. Identifying and responding to the different sections of recorded music

Students identify and move to the three sections of this piece, labeled A, B, and C.

Materials:
Record, tape, or compact disc player
Fado Blanquita (RM7)

Activity to experience:
Introduce the experience and guide students to listen and move to music in personal space when ready.

Students identify the three sections by creating three different movements.

They make any changes they need and respond to the music again.

They plan which three movements they are going to do and share with another student.

Volunteers share their movements with the class for each section while other students copy.

Facilitation and Reflection:
What can you say about the music you've just heard?

What form labels would we give the large sections of *Fado Blanquita?*

How did the sections differ from one another?

How did your movement change from one section to the other?

Which was your favorite section? Why?

Extensions:
Students work in groups of three or four and create movements for another selection in ABC form, such as *Zigeunerpolka* (RM4), *Doudlebska Polka* (RM2), or *Little Shoemaker* (RM2).

Students may share their creations with the class.

Three-Ring Circus

Grades 1–2

Key Experience:

℈ **II. D. Labeling form**

> 5. Labeling and using AB, ABA, and ABC forms

Children use recorded music and a circus theme to identify ABC form.

Materials:

Record, tape, or compact disc player

Danish Masquerade (CD4)

Streamers, hoops, etc.

Activity to experience:

Using streamers, hoops, and other circus props, children explore and create movements that circus performers or animals might use for the three sections of this music. They share ideas with the class.

Children listen to the music again and think of specific circus acts that go with each of the three sections.

Children divide into three groups, create circus acts to go with each section of the music, decide on the movement and props for each act, and try these out with the music.

Each group shares its performance.

Facilitation and Reflection:

What did you hear in this music?

How were the three sections different? Alike?

How did you know when to change acts?

What in the music led you to choose this particular circus act?

Extensions:

Play other music in ABC form, such as *Nigun* (RM1) or *Haya Ze Basadeh* (RM2), and see if the class can identify the major sections through their movement ideas.

Move That Form

Grades K–1

Key Experience:

⚬┐ II. D. Labeling form

> 5. Labeling and using AB, ABA, and ABC forms

Children use space inside and outside the hoops for nonlocomotor and locomotor movement to part A and part B of the musical selection.

Materials:

Record, tape, or compact disc player
A hoop for each student
Bannielou Lambaol (RM8)

Activity to experience:

Scatter hoops on the floor; each child is inside a hoop.

Children listen to *Bannielou Lambaol* and explore movements inside the hoop; they then share their movements.

Children explore moving around outside the hoops and share their experiences.

They listen to the music without movement, identifying the A and B sections.

Children choose a favorite way to move inside the hoop for one section and outside the hoop for the other section; they then recall the first and second ways they moved.

Play the music again, and by their movement responses, see if children know when the music changes from A to B (or B to A).

Facilitation and Reflection:

How did you move to the music inside your hoop? Outside your hoop?

What did you hear in the music?

How would you describe the form of this piece?

What movement will you choose for the A section (first part of the music)? For the B section (second part)?

Extensions:

Listen to other selections in AB form, such as *Road to the Isles* (RM5), and identify A and B sections. How is AB form used in math? In art? In physical education? In sports? In science?

51 | "ABACA"

Grade 3

Key Experience:

⚸ **II.D. Labeling form**

>6. Labeling and using rondo form and simple theme and variations form

Hearing and identifying rondo form as ABACA in Mozart's *Turkish Rondo* and other selections.

Materials:

Various percussion instruments
Record, tape, or compact disc player
Recording of Mozart's *Turkish Rondo*

Activity to experience:

Students learn to say the following rhyme while keeping macrobeat (underlined):

> *ABACA!*
> *Rondo form we say.*
> *A is the same, that is the game,*
> *ABACA!*
>
> Bev Boardman

In small groups, students create ways to move to two different unpitched percussion instruments. They decide who will play and for how long, as the rest of the group moves. Then they build the rondo form:

    A = rhyme + beat
    B = first unpitched percussion instrument and group movement
    A = rhyme + beat
    C = second unpitched percussion instrument and group movement
    A = rhyme + beat

After listening to Mozart's *Turkish Rondo*, students identify the major sections with beat-keeping cues such as this:

    A = spider pat on chest
    B = spider pat, fingers on two hands lightly touching each other
    C = spider pat on shoulders (or other choices students create)

Facilitation and Reflection:

How did you choose to move for each percussion instrument sound?

Why does that seem to fit?

How did you decide on the length of the B and C sections?

How are our rondos and Mozart's *Turkish Rondo* alike? Different?

How could you use shapes to represent a rondo form?

Extensions:

Identify other rondo forms from selections such as *Hineh Ma Tov* (RM4) or *Mexican Mixer* (RM3).

In small groups, create a "vocal and movement" rondo, with each section having 16 beats. Perform these for the class.

Create jump-rope rondos, using three different rhymes or types of jumps.

Create art rondos, using shapes, colors, and textures.

Lento and *Presto*

Grades K–1

Key Experience:
II. E. Recognizing the expressive qualities of tempo and dynamics

> 1 Identifying *slow* and *fast* through movement and vocabulary

Children express slow and fast (*lento* and *presto*) through movement and recognize and label these qualities in musical selections.

Materials:
Record, tape, or compact disc player
Hora Hassidit (RM5)

Activity to experience:
Children listen to *Hora Hassidit* to identify the slow sections (A for *lento*) and fast sections (B for *presto*). They pat the macrobeat while listening.

Students explore moving slowly and quickly and find ways to describe their movement with the slow and fast musical labels. Volunteers share their ideas.

Play *Hora Hassidit* again, so students can try to fit their movements to the music. On repetitions, they label *lento* and *presto* sections.

Facilitation and Reflection:
What do you hear in the music?

What kinds of movements did you do for *lento?* For *presto?*

Extensions:
Use the words *lento* and *presto* throughout the day.

Listen to other musical selections, such as Dvořák's *New World Symphony* (*lento*), Rimsky-Korsakov's *Flight of the Bumblebee* (*presto*), Debussy's *Jimbo's Lullaby* (*lento*) from *Children's Corner Suite*, and Anderson's *The Typewriter* (*presto*).

Forte and Piano

Grades K–3

Key Experience:

      ○¬ **II. E. Recognizing the expressive qualities of tempo and dynamics**

               > 2. Identifying *loud* and *soft* through movement and vocabulary

Students express loud (*forte*) and soft (*piano*) and identify and label these qualities in movement and in musical selections.

Materials:

Unpitched percussion instruments

Activity to experience:

Students explore loud and soft locomotor movements with their musical labels of loud (*forte*) and soft (*piano*). Volunteers share their movements for the class to copy.

Half of the class play instruments while the other half moves. A student conductor leads the instrument section to play *forte* or *piano*. The students who are moving will respond to the dynamics played. Then the groups exchange roles, so each group has a chance to move and to play.

Facilitation and Reflection:

How did you decide on what movements to use for *forte?* For *piano?*

Discuss the differences *forte* and *piano* make in music and playing instruments.

Extensions:

Use musical selections from *Carnival of the Animals* by Saint-Saëns to express these qualities: *Royal March of the Lions* to represent *forte* and *Turtles* to represent *piano.*

Use *forte* and *piano* throughout the day.

Play one instrument at a time *forte* and then *piano*, while the students move to the sound.

Trolls

Grades 1–2

Key Experience:
    ⊶ **II. E. Recognizing the expressive qualities of tempo and dynamics**

         >5. Identifying *getting faster* and *getting slower*

Children identify the increasing tempo of a musical selection.

Materials:
Record, tape, or compact disc player
In the Hall of the Mountain King, from *Peer Gynt Suite* (E. Grieg)

Activity to experience:
Peer Gynt was the hero of an old Norwegian folk tale. For several months, he lived inside the mountain with the trolls, who treated him royally. However, when the king urged him to marry his daughter and attempted to force the trolls' rules upon Peer, he decided to escape. This selection represents the trolls' pursuit of Peer through the cracks and crevices inside the eerie mountain.

After children discuss what trolls look like, how they move, and how they might fight, they explore this type of movement and share typical examples.

Children listen to the music, matching troll-like movements to the increasing tempo and intensity of the music.

Facilitation and Reflection:
What do you know about trolls? What other troll stories do you know?

How could your movement represent that of a troll? Why?

How does the music create the feeling that trolls are here?

When the music is getting faster, how do your movements show this change?

Extensions:
Create a rhyme such as the following, and gradually increase the tempo of the speech and the microbeat movement:

> <u>We</u> are <u>mov</u>ing <u>to</u> the <u>beat</u>, <u>to</u> the *beat*, <u>to</u> the *beat*,
> <u>We</u> are <u>mov</u>ing <u>to</u> the <u>beat</u>, we <u>feel</u> it <u>in</u> our <u>feet!</u> _____

Feel *accelerando* (gradual increase of tempo) in *Fjäskern* (RM2) and *Debka Le Adama* (RM9). For the A section: Walk counterclockwise to the beat during the first melody. For the B section: Plan a movement sequence to use in the B section of *Fjäskern* (RM2), (such as "toes, knees, waist, head" eight times), and feel the increase in tempo.

Categorize things that begin slowly and increase in speed.

Grouping of Beats I

Grades 2–3

Key Experience:
    ○┐ **II. F. Feeling and identifying meter**
        > 1. Identifying and moving with macrobeats and
           microbeats
        > 3. Identifying and moving to duple meter

Children work with groupings of two beats and identify duple meter.

Materials:
None

Activity to experience:
Students explore nonlocomotor and locomotor movement to the beat as they sing a familiar song, such as *Yankee Doodle.* They explore ways to move to the macrobeat (weighted beat) and to the microbeat (regular walking beat).

Students share how they moved and why. They demonstrate ways to feel that these beats are grouped in twos. Their choices might include rocking the macrobeat, patting the microbeats with alternating motions, conducting in a two-motion pattern (see Insert 6.27, p. 111), or marching.

Guide students to discuss their ideas, so they may discover that in *Yankee Doodle*, one microbeat occurs *on* the macrobeat and one occurs *between* the macrobeats; therefore the meter is duple.

Facilitation and Reflection:
What ways did you discover to move to the macrobeat? To the microbeat?

What locomotor movements work well with beats organized in sets of two? (Duple meter songs for marching, walking, strolling, etc.)

What other songs do we know that have beats grouped in twos?

Extensions:
Make a list of all the songs the class sings that have beats grouped in twos.

Listen to recordings, such as *Sneaky Snake* (RM4) and *Jambo* (RM7), to discover which selections are in duple meter.

Relate duple meter to sets of two in mathematics, recurring art patterns of tall and short, other relationships of strong/weak or loud/soft.

Create patterns with rhythm instruments for duple meter, and use them to accompany songs.

How Are Beats Grouped? II

Grades 2–3

Key Experience:

 II. F. Feeling and identifying meter
> 1. Identifying and moving with macrobeats and microbeats
> 4. Identifying and moving to triple meter

Students explore ways to express the grouping of strong and weak beats in a familiar song such as *America*.

Materials:
None

Activity to experience:
Students sing *America* (*My Country, 'Tis of Thee*) while rocking to the macrobeat. Then they sing it again and step to the microbeat.

Students explore other nonlocomotor and locomotor movement to the beat as they sing *America*. They may choose to explore moving to the macrobeat or to the microbeat.

Students share how they moved and why. Guide students to discuss their ideas and facilitate their discovery that in this song, there are three microbeats organized by the accented macrobeat; the beats in this song are grouped in threes (triple meter). When walking microbeats, the students discover that the strong beat occurs on the *alternating* foot each time.

Students demonstrate ways to feel that these beats are grouped in threes. Their choices might include rocking to the macrobeat, patting the microbeats, conducting in a three-motion pattern (see Insert 6.27, p. 111), or walking/feeling which beats are strong and which are weak.

Facilitation and Reflection:
What movement did you choose to do for the macrobeat? For the microbeat?

How did you discover how beats are grouped in threes?

Extensions:
Continue this exploration with other songs, and make a continuing list of all the songs the class sings that have beats grouped in threes.

Listen to recordings to discover which selections are in triple meter.

Create patterns with rhythm instruments for triple meter, and accompany songs in triple meter.

Create and demonstrate movement hand patterns that work in triple meter.

Relate triple meter to math sets of three, as well as to other groupings of three such as these: flowers with three petals, three leaves together on a stem (poison ivy), the three sides of a triangle, the three legs of a tripod.

57 | "Magic Eight"

Grades K–1

Key Experience:
O┐ II. G. Expressing rhythm
> 2. Moving to sounds of longer and shorter duration
> 3. Moving to rhythm patterns
> 7. Recognizing and using note and rest values (quarter, eighth, half)

Children explore movement to sounds of the wood block, guiro, and finger cymbals. They show their ability to discriminate and respond to these durations by movements determined by the class or group as the "Magic Eight" game is played.

Materials:
Wood block, played as steady walking tempo
Guiro, played twice as fast as wood block sounds
Finger cymbals, played half as fast as wood block sounds

Activity to experience:
Children explore movement that fits the characteristic sound for each instrument.

Volunteers share their movement ideas, and the class decides on a characteristic movement for each instrument.

Three volunteers are needed to play each of the three instruments; one child is the director who determines when each instrument plays. The safety net for the first game is to have the instruments seen as they are played. Afterwards, the instruments may be played behind a screen, so the focus remains on discrimination.

The student conductor chooses one instrument sound to be played for eight beats. *In beat,* the students respond with the movement for that sound. Another sound is played for eight beats, and students respond with the class-determined movement for that sound. (Note: The wood block would sound eight times for the eight beats. The guiro would sound sixteen times, because it would be playing twice for each wood block beat. The finger cymbals would sound four times, because each sound lasts for two wood block beats.)

When the children are ready for the *real* "Magic Eight" game (in late second and third grade), the conductor may combine two instrument sounds for the class to respond to, such as four beats played on the wood block and four beats played with the finger cymbals (but only two sounds, because the finger cymbal sound represents two beats for each sound). Another example is four beats played on the guiro (eight fast sounds), followed by four beats (two sounds) played on finger cymbals. This problem solving ties in beautifully with math.

Facilitation and Reflection:

What is special about the sound of the wood block? Of the guiro? Of the finger cymbals?

How can we compare the three tempos?

In how many ways can we describe each of these instrument sounds?

What movements could represent the wood block's sound? Why? Which one would be best for our class? (Determine same for guiro and finger cymbals.) Why?

Should we consider anything else before we play the "Magic Eight" game?

Extensions:

Combine all three instrument sounds into movement problems that are posed and answered through movement.

Add other instrument sounds and movements to the game as the year progresses and as students need a challenge. The triangle is good for representing the whole note (four beats), and the tambourine can shake for the half-note-dot (three beats).

Play this game in teams. The winning team conducts the next game.

Graph the relative durations of the instrument sounds for this game. Add to the graph as new sound durations are included.

The Length of the Sound

Grades K–1

Key Experience:
 II.G. Expressing rhythm
> >2. Moving to sounds of longer and shorter duration

Children identify longer and shorter sounds with movement and manipulatives (icons).

Materials:
Long and short strips of cardboard

Activity to experience:
Children explore making long and short sounds to accompany their movements.

A volunteer gives either three sounds or three movements, and the class responds with the opposite sound or movement.

Children divided into small groups make patterns with the short and long pieces of cardboard, matching the patterns with sounds and movements. They rotate to other group's locations and work out their patterns in sound and movement.

Facilitation and Reflection:
What kinds of movements did you use to represent long? Short?

What kinds of sounds did you use for long? For short? Were they all on the same pitch?

How did you represent the pattern with the cardboard strips? Are there other ways to represent the pattern?

Extensions:
Volunteers may give longer patterns of movement or sound.

Combine the patterns of two groups, and have everyone move to the combined pattern. Move the combined pattern with two sounds agreed on by the class— one sound for long and one for short.

Use other manipulatives, such as pencils and paper wads or items representative of art, math, science, etc.

Seven Jumps

Grades K–3

Key Experiences:

O⌐ II. G. Expressing rhythm
> 2. Moving to sounds of shorter and longer duration

O⌐ III. E. Moving creatively and choreographing movement sequences and dances
> 2. Creating movements and variations for a specific musical selection

Students respond to the musical selection *Seven Jumps* (RM2) by identifying the longer and shorter sounds through movement.

Materials:

Record, tape, or compact disc player
Seven Jumps (RM2)

Activity to experience:

Students copy static movements performed by the leader in the following order:

1. Arms overhead	5. Both knees on the floor
2. Hands on knees	6. Both elbows on the floor
3. Hands out to side	7. Extended push-up position
4. One knee on the floor	8. Lying on back with knees pulled in

Source: Jennifer Weikart Danko

Try out the sequence of running in place followed by one jump.

Perform to the music as follows:

A section: Run in place 12 running steps followed by one jump held four beats. Repeat.

B section: On each of the held chords, do static movements number 1 and 2 above (arms overhead on first chord; hands on knees, second chord). Return to the A section.

Second B section: Add static movement 3 above (hands out to side) after the first two static positions. *Note:* Each B section has one additional chord. Add the next static position with each repetition.

Final A: Stay on back, "bicycle" with arms and legs.

Facilitation and Reflection:

How many of the static positions can you recall in the order in which they occurred?

What does the running movement remind you of?

What does each static position remind you of?

What kinds of movements did we use for sounds of longer duration?
Shorter duration?

Extensions:

Different members of the class generate the movements to be performed with the chords. They face the class in the order they will perform, so students are reading left to right.

Groups of four create the static movements (each member of the group should create two).

60 | Same or Different Rhythm Patterns

Grades 2–3

Key Experience:
⚬━ **II. G. Expressing rhythm**
> >4. Distinguishing same and different rhythm patterns

Students respond to pairs of rhythm patterns that they echo, and then they identify the pair as "same" or "different."

Materials:
Short, prepared rhythm
     patterns such as
     these to the
     right:

Activity to experience:
The teacher or a student
initiates this experience
by asking the class, "Are
these two rhythm pat-
terns the same or differ-
ent? Please echo me."

The leader pats the mac-
robeat and chants one
of the short rhythm pat-
terns, either on a neutral
syllable or using the
Gordon rhythm syllables
(see page 41); the class
echoes. A second pat-
tern is chanted (same or
different as chosen by
the leader), echoed, and
the class responds by
identifying "same" or
"different."

A hand code may be
used, so each student
responds with individual
responsibility.

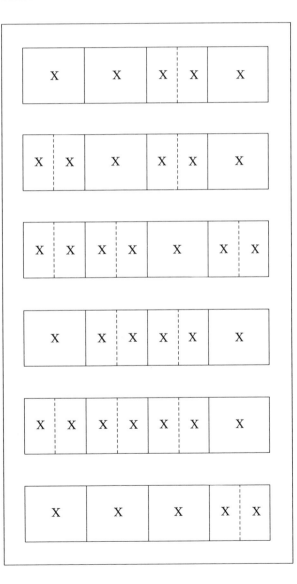

Decide what the hand signal will be for "same" and for "different," and proceed.

Facilitation and Reflection:

What are you listening for in same and different rhythm patterns?

Are differences easier to distinguish with neutral syllables or with Gordon syllables (such as "Du, du, Du-de, du")? Why?

How does this game prepare us to read and write short rhythm patterns?

How does this game fine-tune our ability to hear and feel longer and shorter sounds?

Extensions:

Play the rhythm patterns on an unpitched percussion instrument.

Extend the four-beat rhythm patterns to eight-beat patterns to echo in duple. Develop three-beat and six-beat patterns in triple.

Divide into two teams and play this game every day for a week. The two teams can alternate in providing accompaniment with unpitched percussion instruments for the closing song of the day.

Operation Rhythm

Grade 3

Key Experience:

II. G.   Expressing rhythm
> 5. Recognizing and playing even and uneven rhythm
> patterns

Students "operate" on familiar songs to determine which measures of the song have even rhythm patterns and which have uneven rhythm patterns.

Materials:

Printed copies of familiar songs, such as *This Old Man, Hot Cross Buns,* or
Mary Had a Little Lamb
Variety of unpitched rhythm instruments

Activity to experience:

In three groups, students examine the musical notation for a familiar song. Each group can use the same song, or each can examine a different familiar song.

The students look for measures in the song that contain *even* rhythms (those with four quarter notes; two half notes; quarter, rest, quarter, rest; or eight eighth notes). Then they choose a rhythm instrument to play for the various even patterns. They search for measures that contain *uneven* patterns (such as quarter, quarter, half; or quarter, quarter, two-eighths, quarter) and choose a different rhythm instrument to play for the measures containing uneven rhythms.

Students decide which student is to play each pattern found. They choose a conductor, decide what information to share with the rest of the class, rehearse, and share their performance with the class. They may even choose to put their performance into an A-B-C form: A = sing the song; B = share their "operation" by playing the percussion instruments; C = sing and play at the same time.

Facilitation and Reflection:

Which measures of this song have rhythm patterns that are even? Uneven?

What instruments shall we choose for measures with even rhythms? For measures with uneven rhythms? Why?

How shall we operate and play the even measures? With two to three players? With one player?

How shall we play the uneven measures that are alike? Different?

How does this game help us use our growing knowledge about rhythm?

Extensions:

Small groups create even and uneven rhythm patterns to play on percussion instruments. They perform these patterns for one another. Some may wish to try out their patterns while others sing a familiar song.

"Rhythm! We're Movin' On Up!"

Grades 2–3

Key Experiences:

    II. G. Expressing rhythm

            > 6. Reading, writing, and performing rhythm patterns

    III. G. Reading music

            > 3. Reading short rhythmic and melodic phrases (conventional notation) and short songs

Students use manipulatives to read, write, and perform simple rhythm patterns.

Materials:

Plastic soda straws or craft (popsicle) sticks

Uncooked rigatoni pasta

Any classroom manipulatives appropriate for representing stems of quarter
        notes or two-eighth notes, and something to represent the quarter rest

Activity to experience:

Each student has the manipulatives needed to represent the quarter note, the
quarter rest, and the two-eighth note symbols in any order given.

The students chant the following, spoken twice accompanied by thumbs up
beat-keeping movement:

        "Rhythm! __ We're movin' on up!"

The teacher or a class volunteer pats the macrobeat and speaks a four-beat
rhythm, such as "Du, du, Du-de, du," or "Du-de, du-de, Du-de, du." The class
will echo the rhythm pattern while keeping macrobeat in the body. This step is
repeated, and then students write the pattern, using the manipulatives.

Partners check each other's work.

The cheer is spoken again, and a new rhythm pattern is given,
following the same procedure.

Students are encouraged to see how many different rhythm patterns
can be developed from these three musical symbols.

Facilitation and Reflection:

How will you know if your "writing" of the rhythm just given is correct?

What skills are alike in reading language and reading music?

How is the skill associated with reading rhythms a way to move on up in our ownership of rhythm concepts?

Why do we need to be able to read and understand rhythm?

Extensions:

The rhythm problems for this game may be presented in nonlocomotor movement, such as "swing, swing, twist/twist, swing," while the class writes with manipulatives. A whole host of nonlocomotor possibilities may be developed.

Present the rhythm problems for this game in locomotor movement, such as "jump, jump, hop/hop, jump." Discover how many different problems can be presented using locomotor movement.

Use a rhythm instrument to "play" a problem for the class to write.

List repetitive rhythms heard anywhere (in cars, machines, etc.), and write these rhythms, using manipulatives.

63

"A Name, A Place, A Sound!"

Grades 2–3

Key Experiences:

II. G. Expressing rhythm
>7. Recognizing and using note and rest values (quarter, eighth, half, and whole) and their placement on the treble staff

III. G. Reading music
>4. Reading conventional notation for simple songs

Students recognize and identify the primary note and rest values used in the musical notation of familiar songs, and their name and pitch placement on the treble staff.

Materials:
Printed copies of the song *Rain, Rain, Go Away*

Activity to experience:
Students read and sing *Rain, Rain, Go Away*, discussing discoveries about the notation.

Just as each student has a name, a distinct personality, and a home address, each musical note has a musical name, a pitch name, and an identifying pitch. Students learn the following:

> *Each note has a name, a place, a sound.*
> *Each note is special. Each note must be found!"*
> E. Carlton

Students discuss the four important characteristics of each note and then discover their importance in the reading of *Rain, Rain, Go Away*.

1. Reading *music notation* from left to right is just like reading language and therefore reinforces all other reading.
2. Reading just the *rhythm* of the song gives important information (Du, du, Du-de, du), but there is *so much more* to be discovered as we read musical notation.
3. Reading just the *placement* of pitches gives us an idea of how the melody will be sung, but there is *so much more* information to be discovered!
4. Knowing and reading the *pitch names* (G, E, GG, E) gives us the exact pitches to sing and would enable us to play this melody on any tuned instrument.

Students read with ownership while they sing *Rain, Rain, Go Away*.

They volunteer to play *Rain, Rain, Go Away* on a keyboard or xylophone, using the G and E pitches.

Students chant this rhyme frequently, so they will understand how much information is encoded within musical notation.

Facilitation and Reflection:

What important things can we discover about this song as we actually read all of the information stored within musical notation?

Why is it important to know that we read music from left to right?

What does reading only the rhythm of a song tell us?

What does reading the melody shape tell us?

Why is it important and exciting to read the actual note names?

Will actual note names in the treble clef ever change from what they are in this song?

Why is learning to read music much like learning to use an international code?

Extensions:

Read other songs that use only two pitches and very simple rhythms, such as *Star Light, Star Bright* and *One, Two, Tie My Shoe.*

From nursery rhymes or poetry that the students like or create, create a song that uses only the G and E pitches.

Play these simple G-E songs on a keyboard, on a xylophone, or even on tuned Coca-Cola bottles!

Extend the reading skills to songs that include A, then C, and then D (scale degrees 6, 1, 2). Do not rush this process. Keep it exciting as students learn to use the international musical code!

Discovering Chords

64

Grades 2–3

Key Experience:

⚷ **II.H. Adding harmony**

> 2. Using chords to create harmony

Students explore pitches in order within a C-scale to discover which groups of three pitches form chords (i.e., sound good when played at the same time).

Materials:

One keyboard and one tuned autoharp

Large piece of construction paper and marker to list musical pitches that form chords

Activity to experience:

In a small group, students discover, with the teacher's guidance, that a musical chord is created when three tones that sound good together are played at the same time.

Students discover that the pitches C, D, and E do not sound good together, nor do C, E, and F. The pitches C, E, and G do sound good together, so they can be listed on the chart as a chord. This chord sounds positive, or complete. It is a *major* chord. This *quality* should be added to the chart.

Students discover that the pitches D, E, and F do not sound good together. Pitches D, F, and G might be used; pitches D, F, and A do sound good. This chord has a different sound (*minor*), and this *quality* can be written on the chart.

Continue this process of exploration, beginning on each ascending tone. Students discover that most of the time, pitches next to each other are too close to sound good when played at the same time, but that playing *every other pitch*, when one is playing three pitches together, does sound good.

At the end of this experience, the chord chart information may look like this:

Chords found	Chord quality
C-E-G	Major
D-F-A	Minor
E-G-B	Minor
F-A-C	Major
G-B-D	Major
A-C-E	Minor
B-D-F	Sounds squished (*diminished*)
C-E-G	Major

Facilitation and Reflection:

Describe the sound(s) you hear when C-D-E are played at the same time. What else can you tell me about this sound?

Describe the sounds of C-E-F played at the same time. Would these three pitches sound good as accompaniment to any of our songs?

Could we use the sounds of C-E-G to accompany our singing of *Row, Row, Row Your Boat* or of other songs we sing?

Continue the facilitation for pitches D-E-F, D-F-G, and D-F-A. Follow this process through for each ascending pitch until you arrive at C-E-G again.

Describe the sounds of a major chord and a minor chord.

How will we decide what chord(s) to use for the songs we sing?

Extensions:

Use the information discovered, and play C-E-G (the C-chord) while the class sings rounds, such as *Frères Jacques*. The F-A-C pitches (F-chord) and *Make New Friends* work well. The D-F-A pitches (d-minor chord) work well for *Indian Canoe Song*.

Find the C-major chord on a tuned autoharp, and strum the macrobeat while singing *I Bought Me a Cat* or *Traffic Signals*, or other pentatonic songs the class knows.

Encourage students to use this information to play chords on a keyboard or tuned autoharp during plan-do-review.

"Music's Muscles"

Grades 2–3

Key Experience:
⚬⊺ II. H. Adding harmony
> 2. Using chords to create harmony

Students build on the understanding of chords they developed in "Discovering Chords," using this knowledge to create harmony for familiar songs. Memorization of the chant strengthens their growing understanding of chords.

Materials:
Keyboard or tuned autoharp

Activity to experience:
Students learn and use the following poem to strengthen their understanding of chords.

> *Chords are music's <u>mu</u>scles! <u>Ve</u>ry neces<u>sary</u>!*
> *<u>Chords</u> support the <u>me</u>lodies we <u>all</u> love to <u>sing</u>!*
> *<u>Mu</u>scles in our <u>body</u> and <u>mu</u>scles in our <u>mu</u>sic,*
> *<u>Ve</u>ry neces<u>sary</u>, if we <u>sing</u> and move, "first-<u>string</u>"!*

> *The <u>I</u> (one) chord, the <u>I</u> (one) chord!*
> *<u>Built</u> on the first note <u>of</u> the scale!*
> *The <u>V</u> (five) chord, the <u>V</u> (five) chord!*
> *<u>Built</u> on the fifth note <u>of</u> the scale!*

> *<u>Chords</u> are music's <u>mu</u>scles! Very necessary!*
> *<u>Chords</u> support the <u>me</u>lodies we <u>all</u> love to <u>sing</u>!*
> *<u>Mu</u>scles in our <u>body</u> and <u>mu</u>scles in our <u>mu</u>sic,*
> *<u>Ve</u>ry neces<u>sary</u>, if we <u>sing</u> and move, "first-<u>string</u>"!*

Students play the I chord in C-major (C,E,G) on the keyboard or autoharp four times as an introduction, and the class sings songs that can be sung with this one chord as "muscle," such as *Frères Jacques*, *I Bought Me a Cat*, and *Rocky Mountain*.

Students discover that the top note of the I chord is also the bottom note of the V chord, which makes it easy to find on the keyboard. If the autoharp is used, the V chord will be called the V7 chord and will be found to the left of the I chord, to be played with the middle finger.

During plan-do-review time, a student can discover when to use the V7 chord as well as the I chord with *Hokey Pokey* or other familiar songs. When the student is ready, this sharing will be exciting, because other students will want to learn to add these two chords to familiar songs.

Facilitation and Reflection:

What do you notice when we sing a song with just our voices and no instrumental accompaniment?

What happens when we add chords?

Why are muscles necessary in our body?

How do chords add to the pleasant sounds of our singing?

Why are chords music's muscles?

Extensions:

Several students may play chords in steady beat together as the class sings.

Discover how many songs can be accompanied using just the I chord, and make a progressive list throughout the year. Do the same for songs that can be accompanied with the I and V, or V7, chord. This enables students to group songs according to the chords used, which makes another connection to classification.

Students can discover which songs are best to sing using the I chord (C-major) and which are best to sing using the I chord (G-major or F-major). Do the same for songs in d-minor and a-minor. This helps learners understand why there is always more than one key in which to sing a song and why vocal comfort is important to consider.

66

Making Music With Each Other

Grades 2–3

Key Experience:

O⊸ II. H. Adding Harmony
> 2. Using chords to create harmony
> 5. Singing rounds
> 6. Finding and using ways to add harmony to a song

Students sing in unison while playing the I chord tones (scale degrees 1, 3, 5, 8) on the macrobeat. Students learn to sing this as a two- or three-part round.

Materials:

Making Music With Each Other
(Oh, How Lovely Is the Evening)

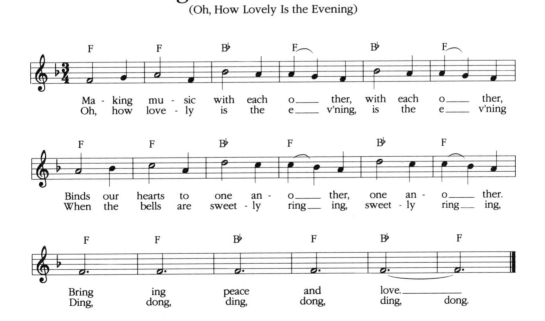

Making music with each o___ther, with each o___ther,
Oh, how love - ly is the e___v'ning, is the e___v'ning

Binds our hearts to one an - o___ther, one an - o___ther.
When the bells are sweet - ly ring___ing, sweet - ly ring___ing,

Bring ing peace and love.___
Ding, dong, ding, dong, ding, dong.

Activity to experience:

Students learn to sing this round in unison while patting the macrobeat.

Students create and share locomotor or nonlocomotor movement ideas for each section of the song. The class then chooses movement sequences to fit the song.

Student volunteers play the I chord tones F, A, C, high F (scale degrees 1,3,5,8) on the xylophone or other tuned instrument for each macrobeat while the class sings.

Students explore ways to create a repeating microbeat pattern of three tones that complements the melody (such as F, D, C) as the macrobeats are played. (In this song, one macrobeat organizes three microbeats.)

Facilitation and Reflection:

What did you notice about the melody shape of the whole song? (Phrase one is a melody pattern; phrase two is a sequence of phrase one; phrase three has a different shape, because it repeats one tone six times.)

What was interesting about the shape of the first phrase? (The last part [Bb—A, A, G, F] is repeated.)

How can you describe the shape of the second phrase? (The last part is also repeated; it is a sequence of the first phrase, because it has the same shape and begins on a higher pitch.)

How can you describe the shape of the third phrase? (It is made up of one tone repeated six times.)

When we sing this as a two-part round, when will the other group begin singing? (When the first group begins the second phrase.)

When we sing this as a three-part round, when will the third group begin singing? (When the second group begins the second phrase.)

What strategies can we use to keep the round "in beat" together? (Swaying or rocking the macrobeat, singing as a team, creating a hand jive or a choreography, etc.)

What challenges are presented to us when we sing in rounds? (Responsibility for singing our team's part well, listening, anticipating, etc.)

Extensions:

Create a performance plan, such as this:

> A = everyone sings unison while performing the movement sequences
> B = everyone sings this as a three-part round, accompanied by the movement sequences
> A = same as A above

Students may wish to discover how to play this melody on a keyboard or xylophone and then perform it for the class.

Students may learn this folk dance sequence choreographed by Phyllis S. Weikart for *Oh, How Lovely,* found in *Teaching Movement and Dance.*

Counterclockwise, walk to the macrobeat.

FWD	2	3	4	5	6
R	L	R	L	R	L

SIDE	SIDE	SIDE	SIDE	SIDE	SIDE
R	L	R	L	R	L

IN	OUT	IN	OUT	IN	OUT
R	L	R	L	R	L

67

Now It Is December

Grades 1-3

Key Experience:
    II.H. Adding harmony
        >3. Singing call-response and echo songs

Students sing an echo song and then share the sounds or phrases they hear connected with the holiday month of December.

Materials:

Now It Is December
(Charley Over the Ocean)

Now it is De-cem-ber. (Now it is De-cem-ber.)
Char-ley over the o-cean. (Char-ley over the o-cean.)

Ho-li-days are here.____ (Ho-li-days are here.)____
Char-ley over the sea.____ (Char-ley over the sea.)____

Ev-'ry one is hap-py! (Ev-'ry one is hap-py!)
Char-ley caught a black-bird. (Char-ley caught a black-bird.)

What do you hear? (What do you hear?)
Can't catch____ me! (Can't catch____ me!)

Activity to experience:

Students learn this echo song and decide how the class will sing it. There can be a class leader who "calls" a phrase that is then echoed by the class; everyone can "call" the song, with one person singing the echo; or the class may divide and choose to have half of the class "call" and half sing the echo response.

Students think of a steady macrobeat sequence that can be activated with the arms, such as "straighten, bend," or "knees, shoulders." They rehearse their movement, adding learner SAY & DO. After the students share their ideas, one sequence can be chosen for the beat-keeping movement for the game.

Students think of a characteristic sound they hear during this holiday season and replace the learner SAY & DO ("knees, shoulders") with words or a phrase that expresses their idea ("jingle bells," "carols sung," "You'd better watch out!"), accompanied with the movement sequence. As each idea is expressed, it is echoed by the class to a steady macrobeat sequence.

The song is sung again after four people share their ideas, and then the class echoes. The song and game continue until all have shared.

Facilitation and Reflection:

What special sounds do we hear during December?

What makes them special?

Where do these sounds come from?

Extensions:

Extend the aural discrimination game into other months by changing the song to *Now It's January* (February) or *It's the Month of March Now*. This can be used earlier in the year by simply changing the month (*Now It Is September*), and having the class create words appropriate to what they are studying in the classroom.

The song can be extended to other subjects; for example, children may sing, "Let's work on addition," (subtraction). The class can create the text for the rest of the song.

68

Sounds of Rounds

Grades 2–3

Key Experience:

 II.H. Adding harmony
> 5. Singing rounds

Students develop ownership and responsibility for singing in tune with steady tempo by singing rounds and by "taking the song for a walk."

Materials:

Music for learning the following rounds:

Sing, Sing, Together
Frères Jacques/Beat Is Steady
Row, Row, Row Your Boat
Make New Friends
Make Time for Music
Oh, How Lovely Is the Evening/Making Music With Each Other
Canoe Round

Activity to experience:

Students sing a familiar round, such as *Frères Jacques.*

Students "take the song for a walk," walking to the microbeat while singing.

The teacher can add to this adventure by explaining that he/she will be singing the same song as the students sing, yet something will be different. They are to determine what is different while continuing to sing and walk.

Discuss what the students heard. Volunteers (four to six students) may join the teacher in singing the "delayed" song. Try the adventure several times, using four to six other students each time until all have had the opportunity to become comfortable with this concept.

By continuing to sing various rounds, the students are creating one of the first successful adventures with vocal harmony.

Facilitation and Reflection:

Who will be singing *and* listening for the difference heard in the round?

Could all songs be sung as rounds? Why?

Describe what happens when the class sings rounds.

What things are needed by each class member in order to sing rounds well?

Extensions:

After the class is comfortable "taking the song for a walk," create hand jives or locomotor movement sequences for the rounds sung.

When ready for a challenge, the children may sing two-part rounds as three-part rounds.

Add the I chord on keyboard or autoharp, played on the macrobeats, for additional accompaniment.

Simple, repeating rhythm patterns on unpitched percussion instruments may be added to the I chord played on keyboard or autoharp.

Viva la Difference!

Grades 1-3

Key Experience:

◎➜ **III. A. Responding to various types of music**

>3. Responding to *same/different* in instrumental music

Students recognize characteristic differences between the ensemble sounds of the band and orchestra when they play the same musical selection.

Materials:

Record, tape, or compact disc player

A band *and* an orchestra recording of *Rodeo* by Aaron Copland or *Chester* by William Schuman

Activity to experience:

After listening to *Rodeo* (or *Chester*) played by an orchestra, students respond with movement in personal space to the selection.

They discuss why they chose that specific movement and what sounds they can identify as being characteristic orchestra sounds.

Students then listen to the same piece played by a band and respond with movement in personal space to this selection.

Students compare the movements they chose for each selection, discussing and identifying the characteristic band sounds heard.

Students may also compare the sounds, dynamics, and tempo of the two recordings of this same piece.

Facilitation and Reflection:

What movements did you choose for this piece when the orchestra played? When the band played?

How were your movements for the two recordings alike? Different?

What were the differences in the sounds you heard when the orchestra played? When the band played?

Which recording do you prefer for this musical selection? Why?

Extensions:

Play other musical selections that have been recorded by both band and orchestra, such as Canon in D, by Pachelbel, or Bach's Toccata and Fugue in d Minor (from *Phantom of the Opera*), by Andrew Lloyd Webber. Discuss the differences between the sounds of an orchestra and a band when each plays the same musical selection.

70

I Walk in Beauty

Grades 2–3

Key Experiences:

    III. A. Responding to various types of music
        5. Responding to a repertoire of different types of music

    III. B. Playing instruments alone and in groups
        4. Playing an instrument in a rhythm pattern

Students sing a melody set to a Native-American (Navajo) text and respond to the mood created when a drum or other percussion instrument is used for a simple rhythm accompaniment.

Materials:

I Walk in Beauty

Navajo Text
Music - Elizabeth B. Carlton

Activity to experience:

As students prepare to listen, the teacher guides their attention to the way each of the directions (before, behind, above, below, around) is tonally represented. The teacher asks them to be listening for any other interesting things that express the thoughtful mood. Then the song is sung.

Students discuss the tonal representations and also notice that the melody pattern for *I Walk in Beauty* is the same for each phrase. They may also notice that a thoughtful mood is created because a different scale system is used.

Students learn the song and create accompanying movements that enhance the text. They work until they are satisfied with their results.

Small groups explore possible accompaniments on nonpitched instruments and share ideas with the class.

The class tries out each group's ideas and chooses the most appropriate accompaniment. Then, singing, movement, and accompaniment are performed together.

Facilitation and Reflection:

How can you describe the mood created by this song?

What do you notice about the tonal representation of each phrase in the song?

How does the text suggest movement ideas?

What did you think about when you created an accompaniment?

Extensions:

Listen to authentic recordings of Native-American songs and dances, or view relevant videotapes on various tribes.

Learn other songs from Native-American sources.

From classroom or public library resources, research the following topics for various Native-American tribes and share the information you find: use of music, dance, instruments, beliefs, customs, ceremonies, respect of elders, education, myths, wisdom, nature, or any other topic of importance relative to the many significant contributions of Native-Americans.

71

Song With a Beat

Grades 2–3

Key Experience:
Oᴛ **III. B. Playing instruments alone and in groups**

> 2. Playing an instrument in steady beat while others sing

Students play instruments in steady beat while other students sing *Bale O' Cotton*.

Materials:
Variety of unpitched instruments

Bale O' Cotton

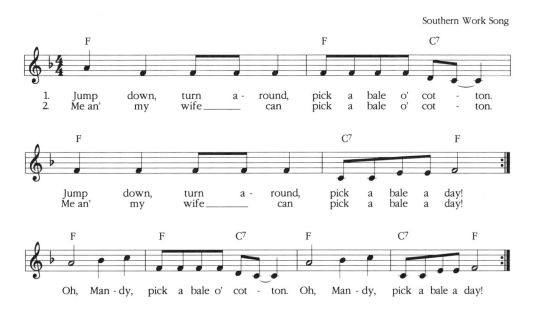

Southern Work Song

1. Jump down, turn a - round, pick a bale o' cot - ton.
2. Me an' my wife____ can pick a bale o' cot - ton.

Jump down, turn a - round, pick a bale a day!
Me an' my wife____ can pick a bale a day!

Oh, Man - dy, pick a bale o' cot - ton. Oh, Man - dy, pick a bale a day!

Activity to experience:

After learning the song *Bale O' Cotton*, students identify the chorus and verse through movement.

Students try different instrument combinations while playing in steady beat while others sing.

They select which instruments to play for the verse and which to play for the chorus.

Students may be divided into two groups: singers/movers and instrumentalists. After the students perform the piece, they switch parts.

Facilitation and Reflection:

How did you know which part was the chorus? The verse?

How did you decide to move for the chorus? The verse?

What instruments did you choose? Why?

Extensions:

Sing and play other instruments in steady beat to accompany well- known songs such as *This Land Is Your Land* or *When the Saints Go Marching In.*

72 Decorate a Song

Grades 2–3

Key Experience:
       O╍ III. B. Playing instruments alone and in groups
             >5. Playing instruments together using rhythm patterns

Students create a musical accompaniment to a song they know and sing well.

Materials:
Various rhythm instruments

Activity to experience:
In small groups, students choose a favorite song and choose instruments to accompany the song.

Students try out several accompaniment ideas suggested by individuals in the group.

Students plan an accompaniment that fits the song and try it out, making changes as necessary. They decide if instruments begin before the song and when the instruments end.

Students in each group choose a leader to start the instrumental accompaniment (conductor) and a song leader. Then each group performs for the class.

Facilitation and Reflection:
What do you need to think about in order to get started?

What ideas do you have about playing the instrument(s)?

When do instruments begin? How will you decide?

Why did you choose those instruments for the song?

How will you decide who will play? Who will sing?

Extensions:
Represent the accompaniment on paper.

Record the performances on the tape recorder and listen to them another day.

Create movement to accompany the selection.

Have a volunteer sing the verse as a solo the second time through.

Sleepy Sailor

Grades 1-3

Key Experience:

    III. D. Sharing music by performing

        > 2. Creating and singing a new verse to a known song

Students create new verses for this familiar song.

Materials:

Sleepy Sailor
(What Shall We Do With the Drunken Sailor?)

Adapted by Judy Johnson

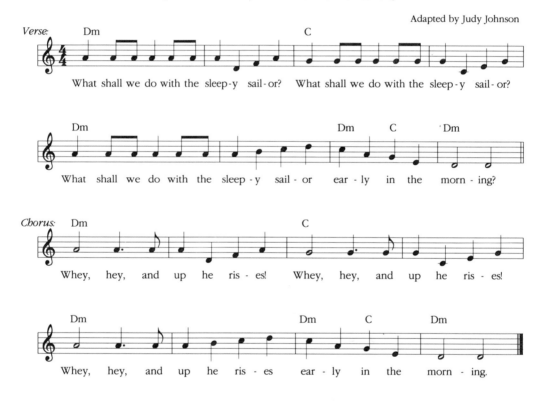

Verse:

What shall we do with the sleep-y sail-or? What shall we do with the sleep-y sail-or?

What shall we do with the sleep-y sail-or ear-ly in the morn-ing?

Chorus:

Whey, hey, and up he ris-es! Whey, hey, and up he ris-es!

Whey, hey, and up he ris-es ear-ly in the morn-ing.

Activity to experience:

Students learn the song.

They brainstorm, planning things to sing about for that sleepy sailor, and then they explore, planning a sailing movement for the chorus.

Small groups create and try out a movement for their verse as they sing.

Facilitation and Reflection:

What did you hear in the song?

What movements work with this melody?

What is happening when we sing, "Whey, hey, and up he rises"?

In what order shall we sing these verses?

Extensions:

Make up new verses to other songs the class knows well.

Sing other songs that tell a story (ballads), such as *Davy Crockett, Old Joe Clark, Johnny Appleseed,* and *Casey Jones.*

Rocky Mountain Dancing

Grades 2–3

Key Experience:

III. E. Moving creatively and choreographing movement sequences and dances

> 1. Moving creatively alone or with a group
> 2. Creating movements and variations for a specific musical selection
> 3. Creating and using different movements for AB music
> 5. Planning and using different movement and dance sequences for a specific song or recording

Students create two-part dance sequences for the song *Rocky Mountain*.

Materials:

Rocky Mountain

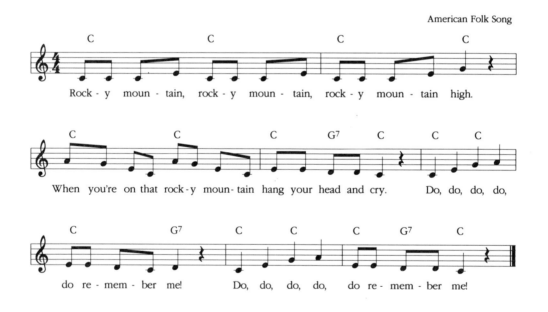

American Folk Song

Rock - y moun - tain, rock - y moun - tain, rock - y moun - tain high.

When you're on that rock - y moun - tain hang your head and cry. Do, do, do, do,

do re - mem - ber me! Do, do, do, do, do re - mem - ber me!

Activity to experience:

Students sing the song through, discussing movement sequences that would be interesting to dance to for the verse and chorus.

They explore these movement sequences for the song and decide on dance formation (circle, line, random, etc.).

Students share, try out different ideas, and decide, singing the SAY & DO dance vocabulary.

Finally, they sing the song and perform the dance.

Facilitation and Reflection:
What movement sequences would be good to use in our own dance for *Rocky Mountain?*

What labels shall we use for learner SAY & DO?

What do we know about the song's form?

What musical clues do you hear that would help us know when to change our movement sequence?

Extensions:
Small groups could create other dance sequences or other verses for this song.

Movement sequences can be choreographed for other songs.

75

I Can Sing a Melody

Grades K–2

Key Experience:

      III. F. Creating and improvising songs and instrumental music

         >2. Creating simple melodies vocally

Students attempt to create a melody by creating the last phrase of a song.

Materials:

I Can Sing a Melody

Elizabeth B. Carlton

I can sing a mel-o-dy and fin-ish it with ease.

Here is my own end-ing. I'll sing it as I please.

Activity to experience:

Students suggest favorite songs for the class to sing. As these are sung and enjoyed, the teacher guides their attention to how their favorite songs end.

Students learn to sing this "unfinished" song. (See Appendix A for help in teaching a new song, using the Teaching Model.)

The teacher guides them in this special musical adventure where only they will decide how the song should end!

In their "magic bubble," students try out their musical ideas for the ending.

When students are ready, the class listens to their musical solutions and recognizes them as "positive possibles."

Individuals may choose to sing their finished songs into the tape recorder, so they may be listened to and enjoyed another day.

Facilitation and Reflection:

How will you decide on a solution to this "unfinished" song?

How does your favorite song end?

How will you remember your solution so you can share it with us?

Extensions:

Invert the melody of the first phrase of the song *I Can Sing a Melody* to create a variation of this melody, and create endings for this variation. The teacher may then show the class what the new melody looks like.

Variations

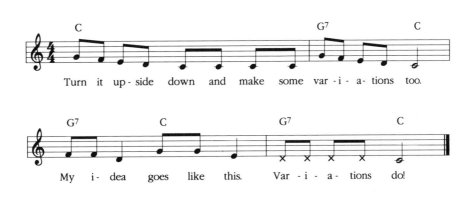

Turn it up-side down and make some var-i-a-tions too.

My i-dea goes like this. Var-i-a-tions do!

SING & SHAPE the concept song about melodies that is on the next page.

Motivate students to create a melody all their own. Words may be added to create a new song if the composer wishes.

Melodies

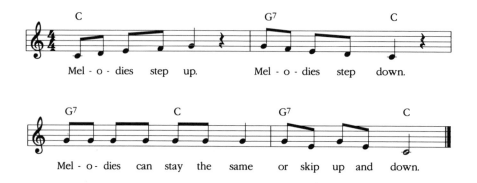

Mel - o - dies step up. Mel - o - dies step down.

Mel - o - dies can stay the same or skip up and down.

76

Melody Map

Grades 2–3

Key Experience:

O⌐ **III. G. Reading music**

> 2. Reading melody maps created by oneself or others

Students create a melody map for the class to perform.

Materials:

Classroom manipulatives

Activity to experience:

The teacher creates a melodic idea with the whole class, such as one of these:

Students sing and move to the melodic idea, representing it with their manipulatives.

Each student creates a melodic idea and then sings or moves to it.

He/she represents the melodic idea with manipulatives, sharing ideas with the class.

Working as partners, each student sings his/her "map" on a neutral syllable, then the partner's. They move to other maps and sing what has been represented.

Students may choose four melodic ideas, arranging the ideas in one large melody map for the class to sing.

Facilitation and Reflection:

How would you describe your melodic idea?

How did you decide which pitch to begin on?

If you read it another way (upside down, backwards), or if you begin on another pitch, how would it sound?

Extensions:

Working as partners, students may combine maps and sing, one after the other.

Make a group melody map using four to eight ideas that fit nicely together. (Some melodic ideas could be repeated, just as we notice in the songs we sing. All songs use repetition in some form.)

Two-Tone, Three-Tone Triumphs

Grades 2–3

Key Experience:

⚬ⲧ III. G. Reading music

> 3. Reading short rhythmic and melodic phrases (conventional notation) and short songs

Students show their ownership of basic concepts of conventional music notation by reading and singing songs of two or three different pitches.

Materials:

Simple two-tone and three-tone songs, such as these (see next two pages):
> *Morning Red and Ev'ning Gray*
> *Zany Zack Broke His Back*
> *Engine, Engine, Number Nine*

Activity to experience:

Students learn to read music notation when the following strategies are used consistently and enthusiastically:

1. Chant rhythm using a neutral syllable.
2. Read text using the rhythm of the musical notation.
3. Sing pitches in song's rhythm on a neutral syllable to focus on the pitch relationships and the rhythm.
4. Sing song at least three times, with text. The eye, ear, and voice have to work together to develop this skill.

Individuals who are motivated to read music, sing songs with correct pitch, rhythm, beat, text, and confidence.

Facilitation and Reflection:

What are the important things to think about as we learn to sing songs from the printed music notation?

How will we put all these skills together at the same time?

Are there any other strategies you use to read music notation?

Extensions:

Plan a treasure hunt through children's songbooks to see how many songs you can find that use only two notes (G and E) or three notes (G, E, and A).

Have a song-writing extravaganza! Encourage individuals to compose "two-tone triumphs" or "three-tone triumphs" in class, using nursery rhymes, silly ditties, riddles, or proverbs as text. Compile these into a class songbook, and share the songs with other classrooms, senior citizens, or relatives, or with those at home.

Morning Red and Ev'ning Gray

Morn - ing red and ev'n - ing gray,

Sends the trav' - ler on his way.

Morn - ing gray and ev'n - ing red,

Brings down rain up - on his head.

Zany Zack Broke His Back

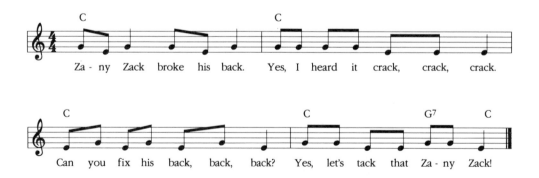

Za - ny Zack broke his back. Yes, I heard it crack, crack, crack.

Can you fix his back, back, back? Yes, let's tack that Za - ny Zack!

Engine, Engine, Number Nine

En - gine, en - gine num - ber nine, go - ing down Chi - ca - go line.

If the train jumps the track, will I get my mon - ey back?

It's Higher, It's Lower

Grades K–1

Key Experience:

⊶ **III. H. Writing music**

> 1. Showing a way to represent long/short sounds, high/low pitches, or repeated sounds (rhythm and/or melody)

Children discriminate between higher and lower sounds by creating a visual representation of the sound.

Materials:

Yarn, paper, markers, or any classroom manipulatives chosen for this representation

Activity to experience:

Students select the materials that they would like to use to represent higher/lower sounds.

Half of the class performs a pattern of higher/lower sounds conducted by one student while the rest of the class uses their movements to show if the sounds are higher or lower. Then the groups switch parts.

Children work as partners. One person performs sounds while the other person uses materials to represent the sounds. Then the partners exchange roles.

Children share their visual and vocal representations.

Facilitation and Reflection:

How did you move your body when the sound was high? When it was low?

How did you represent the sounds with your materials?

Extensions:

Grade 1: Make two, three or four sounds before "writing" them with manipulatives. Work in sets of twos, threes, fours, fives, etc., to lengthen attending.

Find ways to use this active learning experience with longer/shorter sounds.

Sing a familiar song. Choose one phrase to represent the longer/shorter or higher/lower sounds.

Traffic Signals

Grades 1-3

Key Experiences:

☛ **III. G. Reading music**
> 4. Reading conventional notation for simple songs

☛ **II. C. Developing melody**
> 2. Identifying the direction of the melody (upward/downward)
> 5. Distinguishing *same* and *different* in short melody patterns
> 6. Responding to the shape of the melody
> 7. Identifying and singing phrases in the melody

☛ **II. D. Labeling form**
> 5. Labeling and using ABA form

☛ **III. F. Creating and improvising songs and instrumental music**
> 1. Choosing instruments to play and accompany

Students sing a song that provides important information about traffic signals. They also reach levels of ownership for each of the accents above, depending on the grade level.

Materials:
Traffic Signals on next page

Activity to experience:
Students keep the macrobeat as they choose while listening to this new song and discovering important safety information.

They learn the song as the teacher employs the strategies for teaching a new song, found in Appendix A.

As they sing, grade 1 students identify the three main sections of the melody as ABA. They also identify the direction of the melody in section B and distinguish between same and different phrases of the whole song.

Later, or in grade 2, they identify the shape of the melody in the A section, distinguish between same and different phrases, and identify and sing phrases in the melody.

In grade 2 or 3, they identify the question and answer phrases, reading the conventional notation for simple songs.

Traffic Signals

Elizabeth B. Carlton

Traf - fic sig - nals, red, yel - low, green! Traf - fic sig - nals are a team!

Traf - fic sig - nals, green, yel - low, red! Help us use feet, eyes, and head.

Green on the bot - tom means go on green. Don't ex - ceed the

speed on green. Yel - low means cau - tion, some - thing's gon - na' hap - pen.

Cau - tion! Cau - tion! Please slow down. Red on top means

STOP! No ex - cus - es, STOP!

(Sing lines 1 & 2 again.)

Facilitation and Reflection:

How did you choose to keep the macrobeat?

What important information was given in the song?

How did you figure out how many sections there are in this song? What is interesting about the melody in the B section?

What do you listen for when you want to know if a phrase is the same or different? When you want to know if a phrase is a question or an answer?

What do you think about when you read the music to this song?

Extensions:
Develop a traffic signal game, using the information in the song, and an attractive visual. Each year, this game can be extended as additional information concerning traffic safety is acquired.

In small groups, students might decide how they will accompany the song with unpitched percussion instruments. They can rehearse, make any needed adjustments, and have each group share results.

80 | *Make Your Own Music*

Grades: K–3

Key Experiences:
>   All key experiences, all accents

At any and all levels, ownership, bonding, and aesthetics are activated to enable every learner to better reach his/her potential.

Materials:
Make Your Own Music on next page

Activity to experience:
Kindergarten students learn to sing the A section well while rocking or swaying to the macrobeat.

Grade 1 students add the B and final A sections to their repertoire as they develop tuneful singing.

Grade 2 students continue to display musical competence and a growing awareness of the many ways music affects every area of life.

Grade 3 singers continue to grow and display musicianship in singing, playing instruments, and moving as they creatively interpret and choreograph movement sequences that enhance the song. This may lead to the sharing of something meaningful, developed into ABACA form, theme and variations, or something yet to be determined.

Make Your Own Music

Elizabeth B. Carlton

Chapter 9

Assessment and Key Experiences Checklist

I n music learning, assessment is ongoing. Assessment can take place while children are involved in small- or large-group experiences or in individual projects. The High/Scope educational approach, which incorporates child-choice and all the other components of active learning, includes the belief that assessment is most meaningful when it occurs in "real time" and is based on observable outcomes. Thus, observation and assessment by the teacher should be part of every classroom musical experience.

Assessment based on the music key experiences enables teachers to determine each child's development of aural discrimination (essential to in-tune singing, expressive speech, identifying sounds and instruments, and using musical elements) and visual discrimination (developed through a reading system that begins with processing movement and extends to processing musical notation). This musical assessment is holistic in that it enables children to use their eyes and ears in many new ways to see and perceive with feeling. Formal testing in music is replaced by *informal supportive assessment.* Competition is replaced by *cooperation.*

The key experiences explained in Chapter 4 and listed on the checklist in this chapter (each experience is marked with a key) are developmentally sequenced to lead children to ownership and use of the elements of music. Under each key experience are listed several proficiencies, labeled as accents (>), each of which is an *observable outcome that becomes the core of the assessment.* The active learning experiences that occur throughout the K–3 music curriculum provide opportunities for children to construct knowledge of the concepts involved in each accent.

In the checklist, each accent is followed by a grade interval indicating when the accent is introduced and extended. Accents introduced in kindergarten form the base of the learning spiral and should be extended in later grades. The accents should be assessed over the interval of grades immediately following that accent. We suggest a simple scoring procedure for each accent:

1 = exposure to the concept

2 = partial competence with the concept

3 = ownership of the concept

The scores recorded in the checklist can be shared with parents during conference time. The checklist is designed as a K–3 comprehensive assessment that can remain in the child's permanent record. The teacher should note the date (e.g., 11/94) by which partial competence (2) or ownership (3) of a given concept is achieved. This record of the child's development will then be available to share with the parent. In the checklist, the two columns under each grade level can be used as the child is assessed once each semester during that grade.

I. Exploring Music

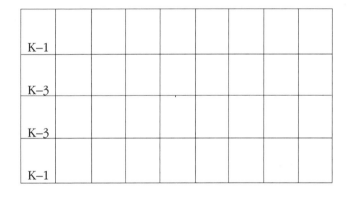 A. Moving to music

> 1. Responding to different types of music

> 2. Using nonlocomotor and locomotor movements with music

> 3. Using coordination skills in performing action songs

> 4. Illustrating expressive and dynamic qualities of a musical selection

> 5. Moving to phrases of a musical selection

	1	2	3	4	5	6	7	8
K–1								
K–1								
K–1								
2–3								
2–3								

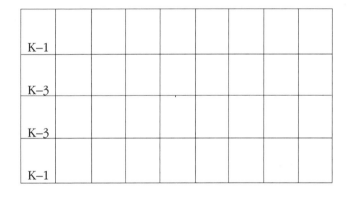 B. Exploring and identifying sounds

> 1. Making sounds with voices and instruments (musical and otherwise)

> 2. Working with percussion and melodic instrument sounds

> 3. Exploring sounds to fit with specific songs

> 4. Exploring lower/higher, same/different sounds

	1	2	3	4	5	6	7	8
K–1								
K–3								
K–3								
K–1								

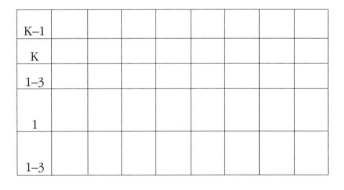 C. Exploring instruments

> 1. Trying out ways to play instruments

> 2. Discovering ways to play percussion, harmonic, and melodic instruments

> 3. Discovering pitch range and labeling the sound quality of instruments

> 4. Playing melodic phrases and known songs

	1	2	3	4	5	6	7	8
K–1								
K								
1–3								
1								
1–3								

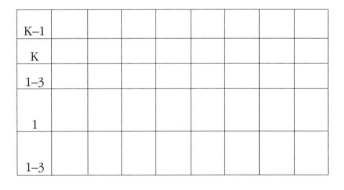 D. Exploring the singing voice

> 1. Making pitched sounds

> 2. Exploring the singing and speaking voice

> 3. Exploring the broad range of the singing voice

	1	2	3	4	5	6	7	8
K–1								
K–1								
K–3								

	Kindergarten		Grade 1		Grade 2		Grade 3	
Level	**1**	**2**	**3**	**4**	**5**	**6**	**7**	**8**

> 4. Initiating singing alone and singing in
  tune with others — **3**

O⊷ E. Listening and describing music

> 1. Recognizing music vs. sound — **K**

> 2. Talking about voices and instruments
  heard or the feelings expressed in the
  music — **1–3**

> 3. Identifying previously heard or sung
  musical selections — **1–3**

> 4. Discussing the type or style of the music — **2–3**

II. Using the Elements of Music

O⊷ A. Feeling and expressing steady beat

> 1. Moving to one's own steady beat — **K–3**

> 2. Matching someone else's steady beat — **K–3**

> 3. Matching the steady beat of recorded
  music, songs, rhymes — **1–3**

> 4. Performing single nonlocomotor
  movements to the steady beat — **K–3**

> 5. Performing single locomotor movements
  to the steady beat — **K–3**

> 6. Playing instruments in the steady beat — **1–3**

> 7. Combining nonlocomotor and locomotor
  movement to the steady beat — **2–3**

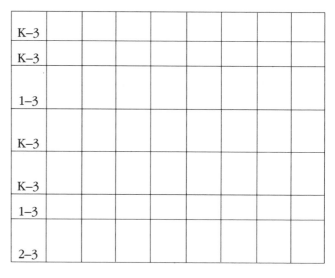

O⊷ B. Identifying tone color

> 1. Distinguishing different persons' singing
  and speaking voices — **K–1**

> 2. Hearing the differences in voices and
  percussion instruments — **K–1**

> 3. Distinguishing the different instrument
  sounds — **1–3**

> 4. Matching an instrument's sound with its
  picture — **1**

> 5. Identifying voices and instruments heard
  in a recording — **2–3**

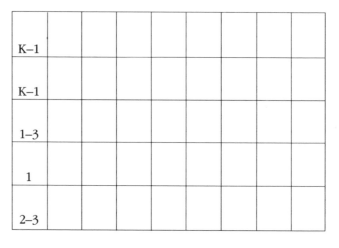

	Kindergarten		Grade 1		Grade 2		Grade 3	
Level	1	2	3	4	5	6	7	8

> 6. Identifying special characteristics of tone color within the music

	Kindergarten		Grade 1		Grade 2		Grade 3	
2–3								

C. Developing melody

> 1. Identifying higher and lower pitches

> 2. Identifying the direction of the melody (upward/downward)

> 3. Matching intervals and repeated pitches

> 4. Imitating 3- and 4-note melody patterns

> 5. Distinguishing *same* and *different* in short melody patterns

> 6. Responding to the shape of the melody

> 7. Identifying and singing phrases in the melody

> 8. Recognizing patterns and sequences in melodies

> 9. Singing and shaping phrases and songs

Level	1	2	3	4	5	6	7	8
K–1								
K–1								
K–3								
1–3								
1								
1–3								
1–3								
2–3								
2–3								

D. Labeling form

> 1. Identifying the beginning and end of a song or rhyme

> 2. Identifying the verse and chorus of a song

> 3. Identifying same and different phrases

> 4. Identifying and responding to the different sections of recorded music

> 5. Labeling and using AB, ABA, and ABC forms

> 6. Labeling and using rondo form and simple theme and variations form

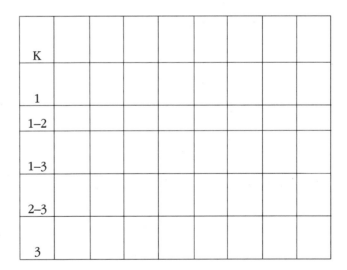

Level	1	2	3	4	5	6	7	8
K								
1								
1–2								
1–3								
2–3								
3								

E. Recognizing the expressive qualities of tempo and dynamics

> 1. Identifying *slow* and *fast* through movement and vocabulary

> 2. Identifying *loud* and *soft* through movement and vocabulary

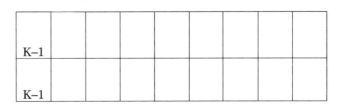

Level	1	2	3	4	5	6	7	8
K–1								
K–1								

	Kindergarten		Grade 1		Grade 2		Grade 3	
Level	1	2	3	4	5	6	7	8

> 3. Identifying *slow, medium,* and *fast* through movement and vocabulary — Level 1

> 4. Identifying *loud, medium,* and *soft* through movement and vocabulary — Level 1

> 5. Identifying *getting faster* and *getting slower* — Level 1–2

> 6. Identifying *getting louder* and *getting softer* — Level 1–2

> 7. Selecting suitable dynamics and tempo for a song or instrumental piece — Level 2–3

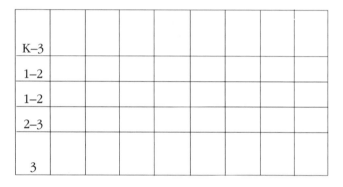

F. Feeling and identifying meter

> 1. Identifying and moving with macrobeats and microbeats — Level K–3

> 2. Identifying same and different meter — Level 1–2

> 3. Identifying and moving to duple meter — Level 1–2

> 4. Identifying and moving to triple meter — Level 2–3

> 5. Differentiating between duple and triple meter — Level 3

G. Expressing rhythm

> 1. Listening for longer and shorter sounds — Level K–1

> 2. Moving to sounds of longer and shorter duration — Level 1–3

> 3. Moving to rhythm patterns — Level 2–3

> 4. Distinguishing same and different rhythm patterns — Level 2–3

> 5. Recognizing and playing even and uneven rhythm patterns — Level 2–3

> 6. Reading, writing, and performing rhythm patterns — Level 2–3

> 7. Recognizing and using note and rest values (quarter, two-eighth, half, dotted half, and whole) — Level 2–3

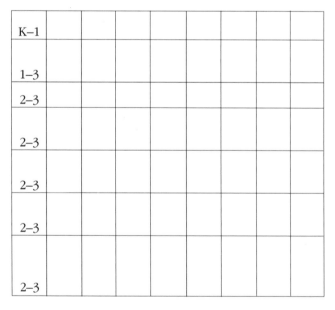

	Kindergarten		Grade 1		Grade 2		Grade 3	
Level	1	2	3	4	5	6	7	8

○┓ **H. Adding harmony**

> 1. Recognizing the difference between unison singing and singing accompanied by instrument(s)

> 2. Using chords to create harmony

> 3. Singing call-response songs and echo songs

> 4. Adding melodic chants

> 5. Singing rounds

> 6. Finding and using ways to add harmony to a song or instrumental selection

K–1								
1–3								
1–3								
3								
3								
3								

III. Creating and Performing Music

○┓ **A. Responding to various types of music**

> 1. Showing through movement the differences heard in music

> 2. Responding to *same/different* in songs children sing

> 3. Responding to *same/different* in instrumental music

> 4. Responding to different moods of a musical selection

> 5. Responding to a repertoire of different types of music

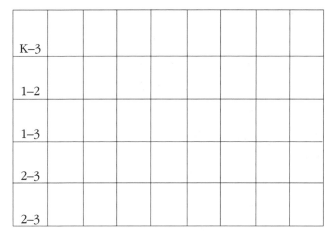

K–3								
1–2								
1–3								
2–3								
2–3								

○┓ **B. Playing instruments alone and in groups**

> 1. Playing an instrument alone or in a group, using steady beat

> 2. Playing an instrument in steady beat while others sing

> 3. Playing an instrument in steady beat while singing alone

> 4. Playing an instrument in a rhythm pattern

> 5. Playing instruments together using rhythm patterns

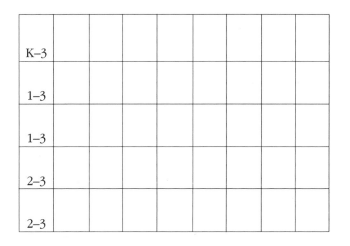

K–3								
1–3								
1–3								
2–3								
2–3								

> 6. Creating & planning instrument parts for a song or ensemble

Level	1	2	3	4	5	6	7	8
3								

C. Singing alone and in groups

> 1. Singing simple songs alone and with others

> 2. Singing a short solo phrase during a call-response song or a single verse when the class sings chorus

> 3. Singing songs of increasing length and difficulty with others

> 4. Singing a solo with musical competence and confidence

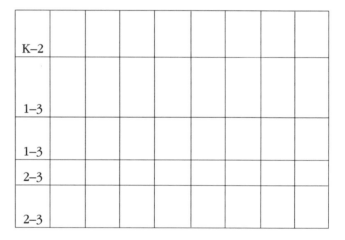

Level	1	2	3	4	5	6	7	8
K–1								
1–2								
1–2								
2–3								

D. Sharing music by performing

> 1. Creating and singing a new verse to a known song

> 2. Creating and sharing an instrumental piece on percussion or melodic instruments

> 3. Playing a musical instrument while the group sings

> 4. Sharing songs created by students

> 5. Sharing an instrumental ensemble created by students

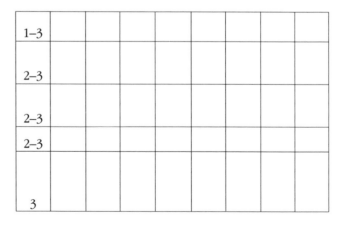

Level	1	2	3	4	5	6	7	8
K–2								
1–3								
1–3								
2–3								
2–3								

E. Moving creatively and choreographing movement sequences and dances

> 1. Moving creatively alone or with a group

> 2. Creating movements and variations for a specific musical selection

> 3. Creating and using different movements for AB music

> 4. Creating patterns and moving creatively

> 5. Planning and using different movement and dance sequences for a specific song or recording

Level	1	2	3	4	5	6	7	8
1–3								
2–3								
2–3								
2–3								
3								

	Kindergarten		Grade 1		Grade 2		Grade 3	
Level	**1**	**2**	**3**	**4**	**5**	**6**	**7**	**8**

F. Creating and improvising songs and instrumental music

> 1. Choosing instruments to play and accompany — 1–2

> 2. Creating simple melodies vocally — 1–2

> 3. Creating simple melodies on instruments — 2–3

> 4. Improvising a variation on a melody, vocally and/or instrumentally — 2–3

> 5. Creating an instrumental piece with two or more sections (AB) — 3

> 6. Creating an original song with words — 3

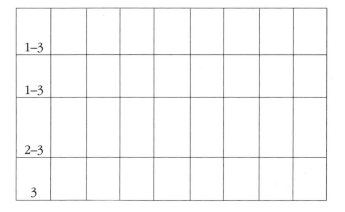

G. Reading music

> 1. Reading one's own symbol system (icons) for rhythm *or* pitch — 1–3

> 2. Reading melody or rhythm maps created by oneself or others — 1–3

> 3. Reading short rhythmic and melodic phrases (conventional notation) and short songs — 2–3

> 4. Reading conventional notation for simple songs — 3

H. Writing music

> 1. Showing a way to represent long/short sounds, high/low pitches or repeated sounds (rhythm and/or melody maps) — 1–2

> 2. Showing a way to represent part of a melody — 2–3

> 3. Writing music using one's own symbol system (icons) — 2–3

> 4. Using conventional notation to represent a phrase or short song — 3

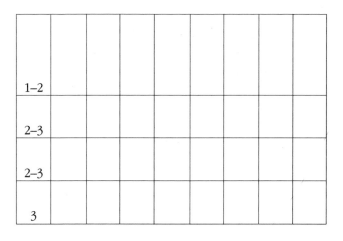

Appendixes

Appendix A

Teaching Model for a New Song

The **Teaching Model** provides the teacher with active learning strategies for teaching a song so that each learner can be successful. You may wish to prepare the class for the musical experience by relating interesting facts or stories about the song. Does it introduce or strengthen a musical concept? Does the song have value in view of the long-term significance of building musical competencies, worthy attitudes, and tuneful, expressive singing? Does the song enable students to develop integrated, cooperative, and creative learning strengths?

The **Teaching Model** makes **process** relevant in all active learning involving the **music key experiences.** When **process** is emphasized consistently, the result is students' ownership of musical concepts, leading to confidence, competence, creativity, and excitement in learning. The process employed with the **Teaching Model** activates and fine-tunes all the students' modes of learning in ways that are relevant to the young student's way of exploring, using, creating, singing, performing, and knowing. The major components of the process are as follows:

Separate

1. Prepare the students to listen and attend. (For example, for an action song, prepare children for the motor sequences visually *or* verbally before they learn the melody or text of the song, so the motor sequences can "go on automatic.")
2. Set the macrobeat for learners either visually *or* verbally, and ask them to continue keeping the beat as they listen while you sing the new song.
3. Do not keep leading the beat and singing. This would employ the "show and tell" approach. Instead, guide students in their listening by asking them to attend to something specific the second time they listen, and then observe their responses.

Simplify

1. Introduce the *melody alone,* one phrase at a time, for students to echo. Instead of singing the words, use a neutral syllable (such as "bom") for introducing the melody. Have students continue to keep the macrobeat as they echo (learner SAY & DO). Work on any difficult melodic sequences or phrases until each phrase is secure. Sometimes, difficult melodic sequences can be clarified by use of the **body scale.** (Step 1 could be introduced after Step 3, depending on the discretion of the teacher. It is important to *simplify by focusing* on learning the melody and the text *before* joining the two components.)
2. Introduce the *text alone,* one phrase at a time, for students to echo. Accompany with the macrobeat.
3. Have students speak the complete text, accompanied by the mac-

robeat. Determine whether the text is secure or whether more repetitions are needed.

4. Sing the song (melody and text) one phrase at a time, having students echo. Listen carefully for melodic and text security as they echo.

5. Sing the song together. Then, have students sing while the teacher listens. Strengthen any weak places in the song through clarification, repetition, or movement reinforcement.

Facilitate

1. Engage learners in ways that elicit their best work. Comment on the quality, the attending, and the developing musical abilities given to the task.

2. Ask facilitating questions that engage learners to participate, identify, reflect and expand on any musical concepts the song illustrates. (What did you notice about the melody? Which phrases were repeated? Which phrases were different?)

3. Ask divergent questions that enable the classroom teacher to assess the musical growth of each student.

4. Become a partner in this learning experience by encouraging student initiation. Have different students begin the song. Share the responsibility for learning.

Most of today's young singers need the **separate, simplify,** and **facilitate** strategies because their song repertoire is limited. When learning a new song, they often cannot attend and respond accurately to text *and* melody at the same time. Because language is usually the more comfortable mode for them, they focus on the text and tune out the melody. The Teaching Model's strategies allow learners to attend to how melody and text fit together and therefore enable them to succeed with confidence.

Supplementary Sources for Children's Songs

Songs occurring throughout this text have been created specifically for developing young students' knowledge and facility with musical concepts. Many other developmentally appropriate songs can be found in the sources listed below. You, as a teacher, may be aware of other valuable sources of developmentally appropriate songs. In choosing songs, please keep in mind the need for considering whether the vocal range, tempo, and complexity of words is appropriate for the children you will be singing with.

Music for Fun, Music for Learning
by Lois Birkenshaw
Magnamusic-Baton, Inc.
10370 Page Industrial Blvd.
St. Louis, MO 63132

Wee Sing Song Books
Price Stern Sloan, Inc.
11150 Olympic Blvd.
Los Angeles, CA

World Around Songs
5790 Highway 80 South
Burnsville, NC 28714

Movement Plus Rhymes, Songs, & Singing Games
by Phyllis S. Weikart
High/Scope Press
600 North River St.
Ypsilanti, MI 48198-2898

Movement in Steady Beat
by Phyllis S. Weikart
High/Scope Press

Children's Selected Listening

Instrumental Recordings

A Child's Introduction to the Orchestra, Golden Record LP–1

Adventures in Music, RCA Victor Record Series (Grades 1–6) Detailed teacher's manual

Bowmar Orchestral Library, Belwin Mills Publishing Corporation Detailed teacher's manual

Anderson, Leroy
  Syncopated Clock
  Trumpeter's Lullaby
  The Typewriter

Bach, Johann Sebastian
  Fantasia in D Minor
  Jesu, Joy of Man's Desiring
  Little Fugue in G Minor

Beethoven, Ludwig van
  Symphonies 1–9

Copland, Aaron
  Appalachian Spring
  Cat and the Mouse
  Lincoln Portrait
  Rodeo

Debussy, Claude
  Jimbo's Lullaby
  The Little Shepherd
  Golliwog's Cakewalk (The Children's Corner Suite)

Dukas, Paul
  The Sorcerer's Apprentice

Dvořák, Antonin
  New World Symphony

Gould, Morton
  American Salute

Grieg, Edvard
  In the Hall of the Mountain King (Peer Gynt Suite No. 1)

Grofé, Ferde
  Cloudburst
  Sunrise (Grand Canyon Suite)

Handel, George Frederick
  Music for Royal Fireworks
  Water Music

Haydn, Franz Joseph
  Surprise Symphony (Symphony No. 94)

Holst, Gustav
  The Planets
  Second Suite

Ives, Charles
  Variations on America

Joplin, Scott
  The Entertainer

Menotti, Gian Carlo
  Amahl and the Night Visitors

Moussorgsky, Modest
  Pictures at an Exhibition

Mozart, Wolfgang Amadeus
  Eine Kleine Nachtmusik
  Variations on Twinkle, Twinkle, Little Star

Orff, Carl
  Music for Children

Pachelbel, Johann
  Canon in D

Prokofiev, Sergei
  Peter and the Wolf

Rimsky-Korsakov, Nicolai
  Scheherazade
  Flight of the Bumblebee

Rodgers and Hammerstein
  Sound of Music

Saint-Saëns, Camille
  Carnival of the Animals

Sousa, John Philip
  Marches

Strauss, Johann
  Tales from the Vienna Woods

Tschaikovsky, Peter Ilyitch
Nutcracker Suite

Vaughn-Williams, Ralph
Fantasia on Greensleeves
Folk Song Suite

Vivaldi, Antonio
The Four Seasons

Weikart, Phyllis S.
Changing Directions 1–5
Rhythmically Moving 1–9
(High/Scope Press)

Williams, John
Close Encounters of the Third Kind
The Empire Strikes Back
Star Trek
Star Wars

Song Collections

Roger Wagner Chorale:
Folk Songs of the New World
Songs of the South

Norman Luboff Choir:
Songs of the West
Songs of the Sea

Robert Shaw Chorale:
Sea Chanties
Stephen Foster Favorites

Other

Tubby the Tuba

Music from Walt Disney movies:
Mary Poppins
Beauty and the Beast
Peter Pan
Fantasia

Glossary

accelerando (uh-chel´-uh-rahn-do) Gradually becoming faster.

accent Greater emphasis on a note, chord, or beat.

accents (>) Designated points of special emphasis under each key experience.

active learning Learning in which movement is basic to exploration of any concept and in which manipulatives, materials, learner choices, language development, and adult and peer support create a safe, interactive environment.

anchor pitch The beginning pitch of a song sung by the leader three to four times, using "Ready let's sing" or "One, two, ready, sing," so the class begins together on the same pitch.

anchor word The single word spoken by the leader four or eight times to bring the group to beat synchronization before the rhyme or song is added.

auditory Related to or experienced through hearing.

aural discrimination Identification of specific voices, songs, or instruments through hearing; processing spoken or sung directions.

autoharp An American stringed instrument that can be strummed and is often used to accompany songs.

basic timing The outcome observed when a student can independently feel, express, and keep the steady macrobeats and/or microbeats to any rhyme, song, musical selection, or live ensemble.

beat (steady beat) The consistent pulse that occurs throughout a rhyme, song, or recorded musical selection.

beat awareness The realization that music has an underlying steady pulse or beat and that this concept of beat is composed of the microbeat and the macrobeat.

beat competence Demonstrated proficiency at expressing microbeat and/or macrobeat with either hands or feet while listening, moving, singing, or playing instruments. See Insert 3.7 for goals per grade level.

body scale Designated locations on the body that enable children to make a kinesthetic-tonal link in understanding pitches of the major scale. (See Insert 3.11, p. 35.)

changing meter Changes in duple or triple meter within a musical selection.

chant Simple repeated melody fragment sung on one pitch.

chord Three or more pitches sounding simultaneously.

chorus The repetitive part of a song that occurs between the verses; also, a large group of singers.

cognitive Having to do with the process of mental learning or understanding.

concept An abstract idea fundamental to a specific body of knowledge.

contour Sequential arrangement of pitches in a musical phrase or melody.

contrasting answer The second phrase of a simple song that does not replicate the melodic pattern of the song's first phrase (the musical question) but still ends on scale degree 1.

crescendo (kre-shen´-do) Gradually becoming louder.

decrescendo (day-kre-shen´-do) Gradually becoming softer.

duple meter Meter based on groupings of two beats, or multiples of two.

dynamics The relative softness or loudness of the music; includes the shaping of the musical phrase, accents, getting louder, getting softer.

facilitate The component of the Teaching Model that deals with engaging learners in many and various ways to construct their own knowledge.

fermata A musical symbol (⌢) that is placed directly over a note, indicating that pitch should be held longer.

form The organization of a musical composition according to its sections of repetition, contrast, variation, or development.

forte (for´-tay) The Italian term for loud.

fragment A portion of a melodic phrase.

half step The interval between one musical pitch and the next adjacent pitch, ascending or descending.

harmony The texture that enhances or decorates a melody with any simultaneous combination of sounds.

icon Any manipulative or written symbol that enables a learner to represent musical concepts in a symbol system.

improvisation Invention or creation without prior preparation.

interval The distance between two musical pitches.

key experiences Essential experiences that support the development of specific observable processes or outcomes that are relevant to a learner's understanding of a particular concept.

key system The tonal organization of a musical composition based on a specific key (C Major, A minor, etc.), which designates the scale, the melodic tones, and the primary chords used for the creation of the piece (see **primary chords;** see also Chapter 7, p. 154).

kinesthetic Pertaining to the processing and awareness of body movements.

learner SAY & DO A process whereby the learner chants a word and performs accompanying movement simultaneously to create a cognitive-motor link.

locomotor movement Non-anchored movement consisting of full transfers of weight (foot patterns) in personal space or in general space.

macrobeat The weighted, organizational beat that is the first beat of any *group* of two or three beats.

major scale The arrangement of eight pitches that begins with two whole steps, establishing the *major characteristic sound, and* in which the half steps fall between scale degrees 3 and 4 and between scale degrees 7 and 8. A major scale can be constructed beginning on any note of the keyboard. (See Chapter 3, Insert 3.10; see also Chapter 7, p. 154).

melody A pattern of musical pitches within a key system. Arranging these pitches creates a specific tonal and rhythmic succession of sounds that makes each piece recognizable and expresses a musical idea.

meter The grouping of accented and unaccented beats in a pattern of two (ONE, two, ONE, two) or three (ONE, two, three, ONE, two three) or combinations of two and three, which gives internal organization, consistency, and flow to the music.

microbeat The regular walking beat; each beat of a group of two or three beats.

minor scale The arrangement of eight pitches that begins with a whole step followed by a half step, establishing the *minor characteristic sound*. The formula for the upper part of a minor scale depends on which form of minor (natural, harmonic, or melodic) is employed in the creation of the specific musical selection. (See Chapter 7, p. 154.)

nonlocomotor movement Anchored movement in personal space in which there are no full transfers of weight (foot patterns).

notation A system of writing music that indicates specific pitches and the duration of each pitch.

note A musical symbol that denotes both pitch and duration.

octave The interval between a pitch and the next higher (or lower) pitch of the same name, for example, the interval between C and C′. One octave includes eight pitches (e.g., C, D, E, F, G, A, B, C′ is one octave).

off-beat clapping Clapping that occurs on the unaccented beat (beats two and four in duple meter, or beats two and three in triple meter).

parallel answer The second phrase of a simple song that copies the melodic pattern of the first phrase (musical question) and ends on scale degree 1.

pentatonic scale A scale using scale degrees 1, 2, 3, 5, 6, and sometimes 8, of the major scale.

pentatonic song A song using scale degrees 1, 2, 3, 5, 6, and 8 of the major scale. See Insert 5.0 for an example.

phrase A musical thought that is part of a melody; often the voice or instrument "breathes" at the end of a phrase.

piano The dynamic term for *soft*.

pitch The specific lowness or highness of a musical sound, based on the frequency of the sound waves produced.

pitched instrument An instrument having capability to produce various musical pitches when it is played.

primary chords Chords built on the first (I), fourth (IV), and fifth (V) scale degrees. Primary chords are the chords most frequently used for creating traditional harmony.

rest A silent beat.

resting tone Scale degree 1 of the major, minor, or pentatonic scale.

rhythm Action of pitches or instrumental sounds within and among the beats.

rhythm map The representation of a rhythmic idea through manipulatives or written symbols. (See Chapter 7, p. 161.)

ritardando (ree-tahr-dahn′-do) Gradually slowing down at the end of a musical selection.

rondo A musical form characterized as ABACA. (See Chapter 5, Insert 5.5., p. 65)

round A song imitated at the same pitch by a second (or third) group of singers who begin at a designated time during the song.

scale An organization of pitches in ascending or descending sequence that is made according to a specific order of half steps and whole steps. This order follows a consistent formula for each type of scale—major, three forms of minor, pentatonic, etc. The scale is considered the skeletal framework of a key system. (See Chapter 7, p. 154.)

scale degrees A scale's ordered, step-wise arrangement of pitches from low to high. Each pitch is numbered, with the lowest tone numbered 1.

section A large portion of a song or musical composition.

separate A component of the Teaching Model in which the leader uses only visual demonstration, spoken directions, or hands-on guidance when presenting content.

sequence Repetition(s) of a melodic phrase, with each repetition beginning on a different pitch; also, a succession of movements.

simplify A component of the Teaching Model in which the leader breaks a task into subtasks for learner success. These subtasks are usually precursor skills.

solfège Application of sol-fa syllables (do, re, mi, fa, sol, la, ti, do) to a musical scale or melody.

spiral learning An approach in which a concept reappears at intervals with increasing sophistication and complexity. The accents for each key experience are examples of implementation of spiral learning.

staff The five horizontal lines in which "line notes" or "space notes" for musical notation are placed.

tempo The pace of the microbeat of a musical selection; musical tempos are expressed in Italian and include *lento,* very slow; *adagio* (ah-dahj´-ee-oh), slow; *moderato* (mod-uh-rah´-to), moderate; *allegro* (ah-lay´-gro), lively; *presto,* fast; *vivace* (vee-vah´-che), very fast.

tonal center Scale degree 1, of a song.

tonal memory The ability to remember a specific melody or a combination of pitches.

tone color The specific characteristic by which a particular sound, voice, or instrument can be identified.

triple meter Meter based on three beats or multiples of three.

uncommon meter Meter based on combinations of two and three beats.

unpitched percussion Instruments that only have one pitch and are often thought of as rhythm instruments.

verse A song's first section, which may have several different sets of words, all fit to the same melody.

whole step An interval between two musical pitches having exactly one musical pitch in between them (two half steps).

Appendix E

Alphabetical Index of Chapter 8 Activities

About the Authors

Elizabeth B. Carlton, Director and teacher in the Catawba College Community Music School in Salisbury, North Carolina, brings to this guide many years of music teaching in public school settings. She is currently Music Consultant for the High/Scope Foundation and serves on the Board of Advisors for the "Education Through Movement: Building the Foundation" program. She is also Assistant Professor of Music at Catawba College, where one of her favorite classes to teach is "Music Methods for Classroom Teachers." Because of her outstanding and innovative teaching strategies, the Catawba College Faculty Senate recently awarded her the Swink Prize for Outstanding Classroom Teaching. Elizabeth ("Libby") has presented for many state and national music and early childhood conferences. She also serves as organist for her church and for Catawba College.

Phyllis S. Weikart, Director of the program "Education Through Movement: Building the Foundation," is a nationally known and highly respected educator-author. She is Associate Professor Emeritus in the Division of Kinesiology, University of Michigan, and visiting Associate Professor at Hartt School of Music, as well as Movement Consultant for the High/Scope Educational Research Foundation. For years, Phyllis has conducted state and national workshops and conference sessions for music, physical education, and early childhood educators on the importance of developmentally appropriate methods for using the kinesthetic intelligence to support all learning.

This book does not represent the first collaborative effort of the two authors. As an Endorsed Trainer in the program "Education Through Movement: Building the Foundation," Elizabeth Carlton has contributed to Phyllis Weikart's books *Movement Plus Rhymes, Songs, & Singing Games* and *Round the Circle.* She has also integrated music and movement to develop a special program for 5- to 8-year-olds and a class piano program for children. The two authors co-present movement and music workshops for educators. They are presently collaborating on a series of guides to the *Rhythmically Moving* and *Changing Directions* recordings and a volume on movement to be included in High/Scope's *Foundations in Elementary Education* series.